"*Engaging Latino/a/x Theologies* is an exercise in academic-intellectual border-crossing. It is a conversation with the project of Latino/a Theology by way of six fundamental topics, drawing on voices from both past and present. The resultant border-crossing is excellent, which is both a call to and an example for us all to do likewise."

—FERNANDO SEGOVIA
Professor of New Testament and early Christianity,
Vanderbilt University Divinity School

"Sharon Heaney charts a journey from Northern Ireland to el corazón of Latin@ theologies. Her travels, guided by encounters with Latine y Latinx colleagues, students, scholars, and new friends, explores and testifies to the wealth and diversity of theological and biblical scholarship arising from nuestras comunidades for well over half a century. This volume respectfully engages key insights and sources rooted in daily lived experience and models the wisdom of doing theology en conjunto."

—CARMEN M. NANKO-FERNÁNDEZ
Professor of Hispanic theology and ministry, Catholic Theological Union

"This book is essential reading for all who wish to construct a bridge forward to spiritual healing and reconstruction. It is an excellent introduction to key Hispanic theologians who have built the field over the past four decades and who have wrestled through the central social questions facing the larger church today."

—ROBERT CHAO ROMERO
Vice chair and director of graduate studies, UCLA Chavez Department of Chicana/o and Central American Studies.

"In a time of theological selfies among Latino/a/x theologians, Sharon Heaney skillfully captures a family portrait that radiates with a vibrant diversity of unique knowledge bases. *Engaging Latino/a/x Theologies* showcases a passionate dance of en-conjunto theologizing, illustrating how individual insights weave into a rich, communal tapestry. This book serves as a poignant reminder of the wonderful cloud of Latino/a/x Christian witnesses that envelop and inspire us."

—OSCAR GARCÍA-JOHNSON
Professor of theology and Latino/a/e studies, Fuller Theological Seminary.

"Sharon Heaney deeply and honestly engages the decades of LatinoXa theologies in the USA. This book not only avails profound research, it also manifests the author's transformation by these materials. *Engaging Latino/a/x Theologies* functions as a model for theologians reflecting upon colonial realities from their particular contexts."

—NEOMI DE ANDA
Associate professor of religious studies, University of Dayton

"Sharon Heaney has produced 'a marvelous example of *teología en conjunto*. We are connected to, and with, each other. This book does what all great works of theology do: with hope, it helps us to better understand our place in the world.'"

—AMIR HUSSAIN
Professor of theological studies, Loyola Marymount University

"Intentionally theologizing with both minoritized and dominant hermeneutics is uncommon; few are willing to try and build community with the *Other*. Without appropriating *Teología en Conjunto*—and with a reflexive humility in the endeavor—Sharon Heaney engages in theologizing *latinamente*: embodying a commitment to and solidarity with Latina/o/x theologians and practitioners. This book is a welcome model of a much-needed path for teachers and students of any background to collaborate creatively and with integrity across difference."

—CARLA E. ROLAND GUZMÁN
Assistant professor of church history, The General Theological Seminary

"'This book is a sincere invitation to engage in deeper conversations with other authors, personal experiences, cultural traditions, and community practices inspired by Latino/a/X theologies. If you accept Sharon Heaney's invitation to this dialogue, you will be able to see the world, the church, our communities, and yourself with fresh and Spirit-like eyes."

—YOIMEL GONZÁLEZ HERNÁNDEZ
Dean of Latino Deacon's School, Episcopal Diocese of Washington

"Latino/a/x theology at its finest—*en conjunto*. Sharon Heaney masterfully weaves together theological engagement, reflection, conversation, story and so much more—all in one text."

—ANTHONY GUILLÉN
Missioner for Latino/Hispanic ministries, The Episcopal Church

"In her work, *Engaging Latino/a/x Theologies*, Sharon Heaney demonstrates a true collaboration that amplifies the diverse perspectives and voices of rising Latinx faith leaders. A must-read for anyone seeking to engage with theology in a way that embraces inclusivity and celebrates the vibrant diversity inherent in the Latinx theological landscape."

—NANCY FRAUSTO
Director of Latinx studies, Seminary of the Southwest

"Sharon E. Heaney's superlative book is must for anybody seeking an understanding of U.S. Latino theology. Heaney manages to adroitly unpack current US Latinae theological thought, using the contextual backdrop of the everyday, diasporic experiences of Latinos/as as they negotiate, adjust to, and alter the classical, but distressed notions of who God is."

—AL RODRIGUEZ
Consultant in Latino cross-cultural training, The Episcopal Church

Engaging Latino/a/x Theologies

Engaging Latino/a/x Theologies

A Conversation

SHARON E. HEANEY

Foreword by
ELIZABETH CONDE-FRAZIER

CASCADE Books • Eugene, Oregon

ENGAGING LATINO/A /X THEOLOGIES
A Conversation

Copyright © 2024 Sharon E. Heaney. All rights reserved. Except for brief quotations in critical publications or reviews, no part of this book may be reproduced in any manner without prior written permission from the publisher. Write: Permissions, Wipf and Stock Publishers, 199 W. 8th Ave., Suite 3, Eugene, OR 97401.

Cascade Books
An Imprint of Wipf and Stock Publishers
199 W. 8th Ave., Suite 3
Eugene, OR 97401

www.wipfandstock.com

PAPERBACK ISBN: 978-1-6667-0108-1
HARDCOVER ISBN: 978-1-6667-0109-8
EBOOK ISBN: 978-1-6667-0110-4

Cataloguing-in-Publication data:

Names: Heaney, Sharon Elizabeth, 1976- [author].

Title: Engaging Latino/a/x theologies: a conversation / by Sharon E. Heaney

Description: Eugene, OR: Cascade Books, 2024 | Includes bibliographical references and index.

Identifiers: ISBN 978-1-6667-0108-1 (paperback) | ISBN 978-1-6667-0109-8 (hardcover) | ISBN 978-1-6667-0110-4 (ebook)

Subjects: LCSH: Hispanic American theology | Theology—Methodology | Christianity and culture

Classification: BT83.575 H43 2024 (paperback) | BT83.575 (ebook)

VERSION NUMBER 022124

The Scripture quotations contained herein are from the New Revised Standard Version Bible, copyright, 1989, by the Division of Christian Education of the National Council of Churches of Christ in the U.S.A. Used by permission. All rights reserved.

To Jayne and John

Contents

Foreword by Elizabeth Conde-Frazier | ix
Acknowledgments | xiii

Introduction | xvii

1 *Teología en conjunto:* Collaborative Theologies | 1
2 *Mestizaje:* The Complexity of Histories, Stories, Cultures, and Identities | 19
3 *Lo Cotidiano:* Understanding God and Community in the Every Day | 42
4 *Santa Biblia:* Interpreting Scripture *latinamente* | 65
5 *En la Lucha:* Voices of Women in the Struggle | 91
6 *La Justicia:* The Spirit at Work in the Public Square | 116
Conclusion: Colleagues in Conversation | 146
    Altagracia Pérez-Bullard

Bibliography | 155
Name/Subject Index | 177
Scripture Index | 183

Foreword

WHEN WE READ A book, we expect to have an internal dialogue with the author about a particular subject. The author may offer other interlocutors as a part of the conversation, but the primary dialogue partner is the author and the argument that she wants to make. When this is a theological argument, one expects the stimulation of our rationality with the purpose of accumulating rational knowledge about a subject so as to impart or transmit the information. This means that it is handed down from one to another. However, the citizen of the twenty-first century looks at knowledge differently. They are seeking knowledge for inquiry, for freedom of thought and life, which invites responsibility and commitment to the construction of life together or the common good. This then is knowledge that facilitates collaboration, relationship and team building and synergy. Finally, it is knowledge for promoting a robust exchange of ideas that is inclusive as it recognizes the diversity of humanity. It is knowledge for learning and problem-solving rather than knowledge that is merely handed down.

Knowledge for learning and problem-solving is knowledge with the hope that one can reflect critically and more deeply to find meaning and purpose for one's life. This now is more in the realm of personal discernment, perhaps spiritual discernment, for seeking and aligning one's life with God's purpose in the world, the *basileia*, or for informing one's passion for engaging the world in life-giving and healing ways: justice and peace.

Latinx theology is a collaborative construction that emerges from a reflection of faith in the everyday life. As Heaney documents, it is shared "experience of social invisibility, cultural marginality, economic inequality, discrimination, and everyday struggles for a better life."[1] How does one write a book that not only defines what Latinx theology is but also models

---

1. Recinos, *Jesus in the Hispanic Community*, xii.

Foreword

it? Heaney does just this in the pages that follow. From its inception, the idea of the book was to show, not just tell, how Latinx theology takes place as a collaborative project, a *teología en conjunto*. Therefore, at the end of each chapter there is a response from one of the participants of the dialogue with her. These participants are engaged in a variety of ministries and speak from their experience with the themes discussed as committed persons of faith.

The reading creates a space for hospitality and a lively welcome is received by the reader as one is invited to serious reflection that engages and challenges us as dedicated practitioners and thinkers who wish to engage other theologians for the purpose of a more just and inclusive world. It is a space for listening intently to the complexities of stories, identities, cultures, and communities that leads to an inquiry about how we incarnate biblical teaching for faithful living. In this space, our imagination is provoked by each section and the diversity of theologians included. Interlocutors use protest, lament, hope, and faith as they journey through their experiences of injustice, and understanding of Scripture, and expressions of faith as community.

This is a book written by a master teacher who enters into Latinx theology through the worlds and writings of those who profess it, and brings us into community with them and with each other. Sharon is able to see her own world in light of Latinx theology and to sense a mutual solidarity in the midst of the struggles of her own peoples. She has learned to abstain from speaking into the words, worlds, and intentions of others but instead maintains a posture of humility that allows the voices of others to reveal who they are and who God is to them. In the conversation, God who is perichoretic community, is revealed to us in community by way of our relationships, by empowerment, repentance, forgiveness, and the reformulation of righteousness and renewed commitments enabling us for the life-giving work of justice and peace. It is the very listening, silence, dialogue, and the humility that emerges from it that prepares us for this work. This is a reading for justice-empowerment because it invites us and shapes us into paying attention to others and into an openness to the facts and messages of others with new senses. The format of this book creates a mutual accountability that provides not only a space for speaking, but an invitation to silence, especially for those who have had the use of the space for their own autonomy and dominance.

FOREWORD

Beyond this study, I would invite each reader to enter into the realities here described and discussed so that we do not insert or superimpose our own perceptions upon the subjects presented but instead we are moved to discover our personal realities through the readings—the ways in which we are implicated in injustice and invited into the communal work of justice-making.

This book is about *teología* done in community and the writing and teaching that led to it were also done in community. It is teaching a way of relating to each other and to the world that we might be formed in a communal ethic. This is a communal process for us as educators and ministers, to "pursue the moral purposes of our work and address the ongoing challenges of daily life and work" in our contexts of ministry and schools.[2]

Make no mistake, hospitality is not always warm and fuzzy. Hospitality in the face of injustice is offered so that we can be truthful with one another and therefore it is a space that can sustain the pain of what that means. Parker Palmer describes it as a space for "exposing ignorance, challenging false or partial information and mutual criticism of thought."[3] This allows for such things to get out of our way and perhaps we are able to listen for a deeper knowledge hidden away in us by lack of obedience or practice of the truth we truly know. Deeper knowledge can now emerge from its places of hiding. We can sustain each other when navigating through the scary places of radical obedience to honor each other's humanity.

The institution of the academy has formed habits for status that require that a book be written as proof of being an achieved specialist or expert, one who is a distinguished academic. One is writing to show one can rise above others, to show off one's voice and knowledge. It cannot be a communal or collaborative act for it is individually competitive in nature. Therefore, after demonstrating that one has mastered the arguments one must rise to generate solo knowledge, a new argument that goes beyond the others, that makes a unique discovery. However, the very nature of Latinx theology resists this colonizing, domineering paradigm of knowledge. It is a collaborative construction with a purpose for the common good. It is an invitation to deliberate together, to honor experience as a part of theoretical formation, to include diversity, standing side by side and not in opposition to each other. It is collaboration in the service of wisdom, faith, and faithfulness for the creation of a better reality for all.

2. Furman, "The Ethic of Community," 215–35.
3. Palmer, *To Know as We Are Known*, 74.

Foreword

Knowledge is information, but wisdom is the ability to apply that knowledge in a variety of situations. Knowledge tells us about justice but wisdom guides us into the love that is needed for seeing justice done. This can only take place *en conjunto*. These pages invite us into an *en conjunto* space and ways for the seeking of wisdom for the *basileia*. Only a wise teacher can set the table for such an occasion. Heaney does just this by providing us a book that is not about the usual academic endeavors but about the formation of a community that seeks and shares wisdom with the hope of emancipation and justice. You as the reader are invited to actively participate in that quest and sharing. Come with humility to honor one another at that table with the understanding that today's world is one of different identities, journeys, and experiences of God. It is a world of histories told from places of dominance and histories untold, made invisible in order to subject others. Faith in this context seeks righteousness, right relationships. Theology is not about propositions of belief but the witness of God with us in the everyday—*lo cotidiano*. It is not about one expert voice but the voices of many, questioning and witnessing. Theology is seeking wisdom among the particularities of each other's treasures. We do not coopt but reimagine the healing of the brokenness in ourselves and the world with a compassion that comes sensing the brokenness of the heart of God. When we learn the wisdom of compassion in one another's presence then, perhaps, doing *teología en conjunto* will reveal a glimpse of *el sueño del corazón de Dios*—the dream of God's heart.

Elizabeth Conde-Frazier

Acknowledgments

ALWAYS, OUR CHAPTERED LIVES and our personal testimonies are part of larger stories and the witness of the church across the ages. The work of scholarship is the work of community. The scholars I have learned most from are those whose work builds community. Thus, at the very outset, I wish to honor and pay tribute to the community and testimony that shaped and framed this work.

I am indebted to Elizabeth Conde-Frazier who graciously agreed to write the foreword to this book. Her wisdom, guidance, and mentorship continue to shape my life's work and I am deeply grateful. For frank, collegial, and generous conversations I owe thanks to Edwin Aponte, Robert Chao Romero, Neomi De Anda, Orlando Espín, Oscar García-Johnson, Carla Roland Gúzman, Loida I. Martell, Carmen Nanko-Fernández, and Fernando Segovia.

I give thanks to God for the Virginia Theological Seminary (VTS) community. In the work for this study, I am particularly thankful for the leadership and theologizing of Omar Rodriguez De La O, Yoimel González Hernández, Omar Cisneros, Luis Hernández Rivas, Maria Teresa Bautista-Berrios, and Daisy Colon. Your insight, witness, and example are an inspiration to me as I seek to become a more faithful teacher, scholar, and follower of the risen Christ. I am especially grateful to my colleague and friend Altagracia Pérez-Bullard. She is generous, patient, wise, and good humored. She brings joy to the journey as we navigate academy, classroom, and church. The board of VTS and the dean and president, Ian Markham, kindly granted me sabbatical time to bring this book to completion. Under the leadership of Melody Knowles, as vice president for academic affairs, I have benefitted from a series of research seminars, research grants, and ongoing conversations with her and with faculty colleagues that have resourced my desire to become a better teacher and scholar. My colleague

Acknowledgments

Mitzi Budde graciously and kindly acted as the director of academic writing for the duration of my sabbatical. Susan Sevier competently and gracefully led our team of Academic Resource Center (ARC) coaches and consultants at that time. It is a delight to work with Susan, Katie Beaver, Cynthia Bullard-Pérez, and Beth Friend in ARC. I am also grateful to Mitzi and the Bishop Payne Library team for their partnership in this project. Vincent Williams, Jim Fitch, and Kathy Graham have always been enthusiastic and patient in response to my many requests for library assistance and guidance. I am grateful to the students who join me in the classroom willing to engage, who shape and model the possibility of multicultural worship, who enact and embody the promise of a more just world, and who seek and find a deeper grace because of diversity. Thank you all.

Amir Hussain kindly took time to meet with me and share his memories of his beloved colleague, the late David Sánchez (1960–2019). His stories and remembrances honor the memory of his friend. He helped me learn more about David's scholarship, teaching, and vision. Anthony Guillén, Al Rodriguez, Estella Guillén, Leigh Preston, and Nancy Frausto have modelled collaboration, connection, and community. It has been a joy and privilege to work with them in the Episcopal Latino Ministry Competency course.

A book needs a publisher, and it has been a pleasure to work, again, with Robin Parry and the team at Wipf and Stock. Lastly, and most importantly, I am grateful to my family. There are moments in life when the goodness and the grace of God break in. The summer of 1993 when I met the young man who would become my life partner was one of those moments. I could not make this journey without my husband, Robert, whose love and laughter make each day more meaningful. Courage, vision, and integrity set him apart. He is my example. He is a faithful and gracious scholar-priest, wholly committed to critical yet constructive conversation, grounded firmly in the grace of God. Our son, Sam, is a gift to us in every way. His ability to look for the why, his imagination for what might be possible, and his compassionate discernment of what really matters, challenge me more than he will know. Godparents are family we choose for our children. Dana, Craig, and Uncle Robert have shown us what encouragement, wisdom, and care look like year after year, and I will always be thankful.

I dedicated my first book to Robert and Sam. I humbly dedicate this book to my parents, who raised Andrew and me with steadfast love. They faithfully live out the gospel of Jesus in the ordinary, unseen moments of

Acknowledgments

family and community life, not least through their care and advocacy for Nanny, Jim, and Jeanette who shared our home. For their witness and for their love, I am profoundly grateful.

Introduction

CONTEXTS AND COMMUNITIES

DESCRIBING HIMSELF AS "A citizen of the United States of Mexican ancestry," theologian David A. Sánchez knew about bounded and bordered complexities.[4] One month before his untimely death in 2019, his article "Troubled Northern Ireland: Talking Walls Open Wounds" was published. In it he explores the significance of the "partisan murals" painted on gable walls in Belfast. Sánchez recognizes how this art expresses the intricacies and enduring pains of communities living side by side amid difference in a so-called post-conflict context. He notes that in Northern Ireland "wounds are fresh on both hearts and walls." In reading this art, Sánchez is reading "neighborhoods . . . caught in the malaise of painful recollection facilitated by the rhetorical vestiges of war," and he is reading my childhood.[5]

To be born and brought up in Northern Ireland brings with it a particular kind of informal hermeneutics for reading symbols, territory, boundaries, and one another. To be born in Northern Ireland means that when someone asks me my name, they are not so much asking *who* I am. They are asking *what* I am. They are asking *where* I belong and/or *if* I belong. My name bears the story of family and community. In Northern Ireland, my very name can be the giveaway. In one moment, I might be welcomed as an insider, dismissed as an outsider, or further queried to establish in what way I might belong or not belong. The nexus of family, history, politics, and religion speak to peculiar processes of formation that continue to define place, self, other, and belonging.

To be born in Northern Ireland is to be raised in a small but fierce country of contradictions. Boundaries are drawn, legislated, and enacted. Different

4. Sánchez, *From Patmos to the Barrio*, ix.
5. Sánchez, "Troubled Northern Ireland."

churches. Different names. Different schools. Different sports. If you happen to find your way into one of the more integrated sports, the difference is unspoken but understood. Sunday morning training sessions in the swimming pool made it plain when I was growing up. Protestants were absent because they were at church. Catholics were present because they went to church the night before. I never swam a Sunday training session in my life.

My church formation means I could recite the books of the Bible by the time I was seven years old. It means I learned verses and chapters by heart, week after week, month after month. It means the stories in Scripture were told and retold as we sat on the floor, cross legged, just hoping we would be called on to add the next picture to the flannelgraph. It means Scripture was a part of life, a source of strength, encouragement, and guidance. But it also means Scripture could be narrowly understood and we often heard only one telling of truth. The version of the Bible somebody carried in their hand may have been considered more important than how they lived out the teachings in their life. In the hands of some, Scripture kept women firmly in their place and Catholics clearly outside the kingdom of God.

To be born in Northern Ireland means I was raised with Queen Elizabeth on the throne, Margaret Thatcher as prime minister of the United Kingdom, and Mary Robinson as president of Ireland. The irony did not escape me that while women were to be silent in my church, it was women who were leading in my world. We were mostly silent in the theology classroom too. We sat quietly at traditional wooden desks in the third row, on the right-hand side, by the tall windows. A couple of "girls" in a class of over forty men. I never met a woman professor in that room. I never asked a question. I only remember answering one. The Old Testament professor was re-telling the story about King David, a courageous woman, and a foolish husband. Did we know her name? The room was silent, and I did not know why. The light slowly dawned on me that none of these men knew her name. I raised my hand and said, "Abigail." I knew her name. For women in my church made sure that I did. These gracious women who led even when they were "silent." Grandmothers and mothers teaching faith at the very heart of homes and churches in traditions that question their place.

To be born in Northern Ireland in 1976 was to be born in the year of the hottest summer on record, until now. In our small, coastal town we lived quietly together as best we could. Catholics went to school up the hill by the Catholic church. Protestants went to school in the other direction. We met on Wednesday afternoons at the Girls Guides in the Church

Introduction

of Ireland parish hall. I did not learn until years later that the flourishing Guide pack around the corner in the Presbyterian church was only attended by Protestants. In her own way, then, my mother wanted me to be part of a community willing to do life together.

To be born in Northern Ireland means you experience deep disorientation when you leave the island. Your accent is loved, mocked, and cause for suspicion. It is an accent that tells the stories of history, and mixing, and movement, and migration, and the power of language. It is an accent that testifies to presence in the face of "proper English." It is an accent that testifies to resistance and struggle. Where the accent situates you though is never straightforward. "North" and "South" have meaning at home. "Irish" and "British" have a meaning at home. In Spain and Argentina, when I was asked where I was from, I found myself reaching for the word *irlandesa*. I would say *irlandesa* because I am from the island of Ireland, not from England. Making a home in Oxford, England years later, "Irish" meant something different and I was not that. In East Africa, where I would live and teach for three years, I would be "Irish" again because in a global context the island is my home. I definitely was not English in Tanzania. For Tanzania, like Ireland and Northern Ireland, has a tumultuous relationship with colonial and post-colonial histories.

To come to the United States of America brings disorientation about identity on a whole new level. I meet many US Americans who tell me they are "Irish." The histories and stories of the connection to the island have, however, faded. They often do not know where their family comes from. They cannot name a town or townland to latch onto. They assume that I can dance with my back straight and my arms by my sides, that my violin plays jigs and reels at the speed of light and that I know how to cross myself. But a Protestant child of my time would never do any of those things. When US Americans learn I am Protestant, then they talk about the "Scots-Irish." This is close, though I am not aware of any of my Ulster-Scots ancestors coming to colonial North America.

As a student in Belfast in the 1990s, my theological journey was interrupted first by Latin American poets, novelists, and artists. Later, I would discover that artistic depth was equaled by the theological depth of contextual Latin American theology. Through the literature and through the lively welcome of theologians in Latin America, I found a witness to the gospel that renewed my faith and my teaching. I was drawn to a way of doing theology and a way of being a theologian that show what it might be like to be responsive yet serious, gracious yet challenging, academic yet practical, dedicated yet provocative.

I am an outsider to Latino/a/x theological discourses in the United States. I know that I am an outsider. I am aware that being the outsider is complex. I seek, however, to honor the theologians who have changed me, and who have changed my classroom. For the life and breath of my faith and my pedagogy have been formed by my community and my social location but also by those you will meet in these pages. Sánchez's work on Northern Ireland paints, in outline, themes present both in Irish theological discourses and Latino/a/x theologies: shifting identities, island homes, experiences of empire, the power of language, the story of accents, the love of family, the need for community, the struggles of women, borders, borderlands, migrations, conflict, violence, walls, and wounds. Yet, faith. Sánchez's work draws me into *teología en conjunto*.

THE CONVERSATION IN THIS BOOK

There is a wealth of resources and materials available on Latino/a/x theologies. You will see the depth and breadth reflected in the bibliography of this book. Yet students, practitioners, and colleagues are often at a loss as to where to begin. This book and this conversation seek to offer one place to begin. The structure and content are guided by the direction and flow of Latino/a/x theologies—what is being addressed, how it is being addressed, why this approach is significant, and where this theology can lead church and society.

In this conversation with Latino/a/x theologies, a question remains. Does a theologian have to be Latino/a/x to be committed to understanding and learning from Latino/a/x theologies? Orlando Espín, in the introduction to the first edition of *The Wiley Blackwell Companion to Latino/a Theology*, argues that Latino/a/x theology is important for the non-Latino/a/x because "it is necessary for the construction of a more just and inclusive world."[6] Theologians cannot ignore the anguish and pain of humanity. Theologians cannot construct theories and theologies that remain distant or aid detachment from human realities. *Teología en conjunto*, theology worked out in collaboration with one another, is theology expressed across difference yet centered on the experiences of Latino/a/x scholars. This book, this conversation, represent my commitment to the construction of the more just and inclusive world pointed to by Espín.

6. Espín, *Wiley Blackwell Companion to Latino/a Theology*, 8.

INTRODUCTION

In each chapter, an engagement with a foundational principle proposed by Latino/a/x theologies is explored: *teología en conjunto, mestizaje, lo cotidiano,* interpreting Scripture *latinamente, la lucha,* and *la justicia.* I have set out to draw from the work that grounds the published theology across decades, and I have also endeavored to incorporate more recent material. In this way, the reader may grasp the development of the work from the outset, and also have a sense of where this theology may lead. Notes provide more detailed information, and resources are suggested to provide the reader with opportunities for further study. As is often the case, key concepts and theological terms remain in Spanish in Latino/a/x theologies. Footnotes on translation and interpretation guide the reader, as needed. Each chapter will close in conversation with a Latino/a/x leader in the church, in response to the theme explored, giving voice to what they consider to be significant and worthy of particular attention for faithful witness today.

In the first chapter, *teología en conjunto* is introduced. This is collaborative, constructive theology that takes place in conversation with one another, in community. The complexities of community and of the histories, stories, cultures, and identities within community bring to prominence the concept of *mestizaje* and its significance for seeing beyond a single narrative in chapter 2. If community is where theology is collaboratively created, then everyday life is when and how that theology is given meaning. In chapter 3, the importance of *lo cotidiano*, the everyday, in Latino/a/x theologies is established. For it is in *lo cotidiano* that a deeper understanding of God and community becomes possible. This deepening of theological understanding in community also draws from the wells of Scripture. In chapter 4, issues arising in the interpretation of Scripture will be discussed and the method of interpreting Scripture *latinamente* will be explored. This approach to Scripture has implications not only in the academy but also in the local church. For if it is necessary to interpret Scripture *latinamente*, then it is also vital to preach and embody biblical teaching *latinamente*. Biblical interpretation can bring life or deny life. In chapter 5 understandings of the struggle or *la lucha*, as expressed through the voices of women in Latino/a/x theologies, is examined. For it is within particularly intricate, interwoven layers of oppression that Latina/x women often live. Undergirding every chapter of this book is the testimony of injustice experienced and justice pursued. Chapter 6, then, brings together the theme of the Spirit of God at work for justice through faith in the public square, and explores remaining theological strands that speak directly to the realities of life in the United States, as conveyed by Latino/a/x theologians. The experiences of *fronteras*, exile and diaspora, the focus on movement, migration and immigration, and the need for further development in queer theologies from Latino/a/x perspectives relate directly to the pursuit of justice. Dominant cultures forestall such justice. In the closing chapter, in conversation with my colleague Altagracia Pérez-Bullard, we ask how might those from the dominant culture be changed through engagement with Latino/a/x theologies and be committed to the necessary work of imagining and realizing resistance and justice?

This is theology that can help communities see more clearly and speak life-giving hope. In the classroom, hands clap, and voices call out "Amen" in response to texts and video clips in which these theologians articulate faith and justice. A space is created for protest and lament as eyes well with tears, and pain is voiced in response to chapters read for a seminar. This is theology that sees clearly. It remembers truthfully. It tells distinct stories. It is theology that testifies to faith and calls for more faithful living. And in response, we are changed.

This book is an offering for a particular audience who want to grow in awareness and want to be changed. It is offered as a foundational text for non-specialists, whether they be students, graduates, or engaged practitioners. I seek to combine academic rigor with readability to encourage the non-specialist to learn from the vitality and depth of Latino/a/x theologies in the United States of America. It is my hope that this work might also lead the informed reader beyond grounding concepts into flourishing theological conversation. If you are new to the field, you will find a foundational overview of the theological themes explored by key Latino/a/x theologians in recent decades. If you have some knowledge of the field, and are seeking to deepen your engagement, I trust you will not only find grounding concepts and conversation with key thinkers but will also be encouraged to explore fresh complexities, intersections, and lesser-known voices. If you are a student or practitioner of Latin American heritage, it is my hope that you will find yourself at the very heart of this conversation.

In the first chapter of *Latino/a Theology and the Bible*, published in 2021, Fernando Segovia recognizes the need for informed and sophisticated conversation with one another. He calls for pointed and confident conversation with dominant religious-theological circles in the past and in the present:

Introduction

> All such work . . . stands as more necessary and urgent than ever. . . . It is an age in which radical nationalist groups have claimed, loudly, and even violently so, an exclusivist hold on the United States. It is an age in which ethnic-racial minoritized groups have been singled out as the culprits behind the perceived decline of the country. It is an age in which the Latino/a population stands as a salient target of such demonization. . . . In such an age, all fields must rally and devise visions of and strategies for resistance and justice.[7]

To be born in Northern Ireland means I am a child raised in a country at war with itself. Police and army on the streets, check points on the roads, security at the doorway of shops. In my childhood, Northern Ireland was a country tearing itself apart. Parents tried to protect us and would switch off the television when the footage was too much. Life went on. This was our normal. But I vividly remember driving home listening to the radio on Saturday 15 August 1998 and hearing the news of a bombing in the market town of Omagh. I remember being blinded by tears. And I remember distinctly being aware, perhaps for the first time, of my own responsibility to learn to live across difference, and to refuse to be formed in hatred. Twenty-nine people lost their lives in the bombing. This included nine children, and a woman pregnant with twins. Three generations of one family were killed.[8] On the memorial for the lives lost in Omagh that day, the words of John 1:5 were inscribed: "The light shines in the darkness and the darkness has not overcome it." This book expresses my commitment to the theological conversation called for by Segovia and the words testified to on the Omagh memorial. This is a conversation that seeks to collaborate, listen, resist, and pursue justice.

FOUNDATIONAL READING

Sánchez, David A. "Troubled Northern Ireland: Talking Walls, Open Wounds." *Political Theology*, March 4, 2019. https://politicaltheology.com/troubled-northern-ireland-talking-walls-open-wounds.

---

7. Segovia and Lozada, *Latino/a Theology and the Bible*, 21.

8. BBC, "Omagh Bomb: The 29 Victims" https://www.bbc.com/news/uk-northern-ireland-45112942 accessed October 14, 2022.

Introduction

Sánchez, David A. *From Patmos to the Barrio: Subverting Imperial Myths*. Minneapolis: Fortress, 2008.

FURTHER READING

Barber, Marian Jean. "How the Irish, Germans and Czechs Became Anglo: Race and Identity in the Texas-Mexico Borderlands." PhD thesis, University of Texas: Austin, 2010.

Davis, Graham. *Land! Irish Pioneers in Mexican and Revolutionary Texas*. College Station: Texas A&M University Press, 2002.

Fanning, Tim. *Paisanos: The Forgotten Irish Who Changed the Face of Latin America*. Dublin: Gill, 2017.

Heaney, Sharon E. *Contextual Theology for Latin America: Liberation Themes in Evangelical Perspective*. Eugene, OR: Wipf and Stock, 2008.

"Irish and Latin American Artists in Conversation." https://www.youtube.com/watch?v=18xPGjCiUDo.

Kirby, Peadar. *Ireland and Latin America, Links and Lessons*. Dublin: Gill and Macmillan, 1993.

———. "Latin America: The Region That Ireland Forgot" *History Ireland* 16.4, Ireland and Latin America (2008) 10–11. https://www.jstor.org/stable/27725822.

Marrow, H. B. "In Ireland 'Latin Americans Are Kind of Cool': Evaluating a National Context of Reception with a Transnational Lens." *Sage Journals* 13.5 (2013) 645–66. https://doi.org/10.1177/1468796812463188 Accessed Sept 20, 2022.

Marshall, Oliver. *English, Irish and Irish-American Pioneer Settlers in Nineteenth-century Brazil*. Oxford: University of Oxford, 2005.

McDevitt, Patrick. "Ireland, Latin America, and an Atlantic Liberation Theology." In *The Atlantic Global History 1500–2000*, edited by Jorge Cañizares-Esguerra and Erik R. Seeman, 248–61. London: Routledge, 2017.

Murray, Edmundo. *Devenir irlandés. Narrativas intimas de la emigración irlandesa a la Argentina (1844–1912)*. Buenos Aires: Editorial Universitaria Buenos Aires, 2000. Available in English as *Becoming Irlandés: Private Narratives of the Irish Emigration to Argentina, 1844–1912*. Buenos Aires: Editorial Universitaria Buenos Aires, 2005.

———. "Ireland and Latin America" *Society for Irish Latin American Studies* 2005 http://www.irlandeses.org/murrayintro.htm.

———. "The Irish in Latin America and Iberia: An Annotated Bibliography." https://hcommons.org/deposits/item/hc:30333.

———. "Secret Diasporas: The Irish in Latin America and the Caribbean." *History Ireland* 4 (Jul/Aug 2008). https://www.historyireland.com/secret-diasporas-the-irish-in-latin-america-and-the-caribbean.

Uenuma, Francine. "During the Mexican-American War, Irish-Americans Fought for Mexico in the 'Saint Patrick's Battalion.'" *Smithsonian Magazine*, March 15, 2019. https://www.smithsonianmag.com/history/mexican-american-war-irish-immigrants-deserted-us-army-fight-against-america-180971713.

1

Teología en conjunto

Collaborative Theologies

[*Caminemos con Jesús*] is also written, however, for others in our church, academy, and society who might find in that heritage a goodness, truth, and beauty which are not limited to U.S. Hispanics but transcend any culture—and which may, thus, aid all of us as we confront the divisiveness and fear that mark a U.S. society on the threshold of the twenty-first century.[1]

—Roberto Goizueta

To be in conversation with published Latino/a/x theologies is to be in conversation with theology that seeks to be constructive, collaborative, and connected in the face of divisiveness and fear.[2] In this chapter, the conversa-

---

1. Goizueta, *Caminemos Con Jesús*, ix.

2. For examples of the collaborative work of Latino/a/x theologians in theology more broadly, see Maynard-Reid, *Diverse Worship*; Pinn and Valentín, *The Ties That Bind*; Aquino and Rosado-Nunes, *Feminist Intercultural Theology*; Pinn and Valentín, *Creating Ourselves*; Floyd-Thomas and Pinn, *Liberation Theologies*. See, in particular, the contributions of Ivone Gebara, Elsa Tamez, Clara Luz Ajo Lázaro, and Maria José Rosado-Nunes in Kwok, *Hope Abundant*, and Kwok, González-Andrieu, and Hopkins, *Teaching Global Theologies*. See the contributions of Maria Clara Lucchetti Bingemer, María Pilar Aquino, and Loida I. Martell in Johnson, *The Strength of Her Witness*. See also Romero and Burris, *Migration, Mission and Ministry*.

tion begins with a recognition of the interruptive power of Latino/a/x theologies seen in the major themes of community, context, and collaboration. Here we name foundational theologians, texts, and concerns, and begin to sketch out how over fifty years this vision and witness has inspired new generations of scholars and practitioners in *teología en conjunto*.

COMMUNITY

Teología en conjunto teaches that theology is best practiced in community with one another.[3] I have been a learner and a teacher in communities across three decades. I have been a local, a host, and a guest in classrooms across three continents. I have always remained a follower of Jesus. It is this call to discipleship and faithful witness that has led me into conversation with Latino/a/x theologies. For this model of *teología en conjunto* continues to challenge my way of being, as a learner, a teacher, and a theologian who seeks to follow Christ. In response to this engagement with one another we are, by God's grace, changed.

It is a humbling and transformative experience to read Latino/a/x theologies in the context of a classroom. Sometimes the response of students is exuberant joy. "Here is what I have been looking for my whole faith journey." Sometimes the response is one of hushed contrition. "Yes, I have said that, done that, believed that, and I need to be changed." Sometimes it is as if a light has shone into the room and a student can see that there might possibly be a way for theologians to converse and discern amid deep complexities. Sometimes tears are shed in the knowledge that at last a student has found a place where they belong, and voices that speak to their experience and witness. These are shared moments on a shared journey in community. Teacher and students are learners together. Disciples.

In many classrooms and churches, dominant theology is presented and taught in categories that have become recognizable, seem familiar, and purport to make sense of the world across the ages. Latino/a/x theologies are born out of resistance to this dominant narrative and survive despite the injustices created by dominant narratives.[4] Latino/a/x theologians

---

3. A commitment to this collaborative, connected approach is evident from the early publications of Latino/a/x or Hispanic theology. See Deck, *Frontiers of Hispanic Theology*; González, *Out of Every Tribe*; Goizueta, *We Are a People!*; Isasi-Díaz and Segovia, *Hispanic/Latino Theology*; Rodríguez and Martell-Otero, *Teología en Conjunto*.

4. For a history and analysis of the development of Hispanic and Latino/a/x theologies

testify to the neglect and exclusion they have experienced in the church and in the academy. Given such experience, this is theology with integrity. It articulates the insufficiency of dominant categories and ways of thinking that have been held up and highly regarded yet fall short.[5] Thinking theologically beyond or outside these categories can make a person from the dominant culture feel at sea. To be shown that such categories are domineering, damaging, and destructive can feel uncomfortable and even shameful. Perhaps one of the hardest things to do in life as a learner or a teacher or a theologian is to be willing to be actively quiet. To be prepared to sit in discomfort and hear the stories and testimonies of others without interrupting is not something that is taught or something that comes naturally to many.

In the quiet, and in seeking to be a listener in the conversation, it becomes clear that there is an interconnectedness present in *teología en conjunto* that sets it apart.[6] Dominant categories are challenged or deconstructed so that a constructive, collaborative, connectedness can be seen. Theological themes are interwoven and overlap in such a way that to create neat classes in a course syllabus or to structure tidy chapters in a book can stand in tension with the complexities and intricacies of the theology being studied.[7] In order to mitigate against imposed categories or oversimplifications, this book is shaped according to themes present in *teología en conjunto* and the scholarship and praxis of Latino/a/x theologians.

Latino/a/x theologians have been interrupting the dominant narrative in the United States of America for decades.[8] Yet many in the church and in the academy do not want to be interrupted. For the dominant narrative grounds communities of faith in histories and stories of the nation of the United States founded on models of a Eurocentric church and a white

---

in the United States from 1972 to 1998, with particular attention given to individual theologians, see Fernández, *La Cosecha*.

5. An early, and clear, articulation of the significance of a minority and theological insight from a Protestant Hispanic position is provided in González, *Mañana*. See also García-Johnson, *Introducción a la teología del nuevo mundo*, in particular chapter 4, "*Por qué la teología sistemática del norte no funciona en el sur*" (Why the systematic theology of the North does not work in the South), 95–116.

6. See Valentín, *New Horizons*; Padilla, Goizueta, and Villafañe, *Hispanic Christian Thought*; Espín, *Building Bridges*.

7. For further examples of such theological reflection, see Espín and Macy, *Futuring Our Past*; De La Torre and Espinosa, *Rethinking Latino(a) Religion and Identity*, and Valentín, *In Our Own Voices*.

8. For a helpful discussion on the context of power, see Pedraja, *Teología*, 15–24.

God. Latino/a/x theologies, however, express understandings of God and humanity that move beyond such Eurocentric frameworks.[9] They bring refreshed ways of reading, of interpreting, and of responding.[10] They model a different form of discipleship.

CONTEXT

Orlando Espín, one of the first generation of published Latino/a/x theologians, describes Latinos and Latinas—who also self-identify as Latinos/as/xs, Latinas/os, Latin@s, Latin@'s, Hispanic, Latinx or Latine—as "the U.S. communities and persons whose cultural and historical roots are to be found in Latin America."[11] Espín is signifying here the complex histories and experiences that shape the context for Latino/a/x theologies. That complexity, and how it acts as interruptive power, might be seen in six grounding principles that he identifies.

First, if we are to understand the rootedness of Latino/a/x theologies in the United States, it is vital to note that at least half of the territory now known as the United States was part of the Spanish colonial world.[12] The story of the United States of America is most often told from east to west. This tends to discount Spanish colonial history and Native American encounter with Spain.[13] To tell the story of the United States of America from south to north brings a very different perspective.[14] These territories "were

---

9. For a broad and constructive collection of essays, see Aponte and De La Torre, *Handbook of Latina/o Theologies*.

10. For a fresh interpretation of the Holy Spirit, the Trinity, Scripture, salvation, eschatology, and the church, see Martell-Otero, Maldonado Pérez, and Conde-Frazier, *Latina Evangélicas*.

11. Espín, introduction to *The Wiley-Blackwell Companion to Latino/a Theology*, 1. For further discussion on the significance of labels and identities, see Mize, *Latina/o Studies*, 1–13, and Scharrón-del Río and Aja, "*Latinx*: Inclusive Language as Liberative Praxis," 7–20.

12. Many modern-day states of the United States of America were part of the Spanish colonial landscape. These included California, Colorado, Nevada, Utah, Arizona, Texas, Oregon, New Mexico, Washington, and Florida. Spanish colonies also included parts of the modern-day states of Louisiana, Kansas, Wyoming, Oklahoma, Idaho, and Montana. See Weber, *The Spanish Frontier*.

13. See Panich and Schneider, eds., *Indigenous Landscapes and Spanish Missions*.

14. A constructive overview is provided in the PBS Series *Latino Americans* produced by Jeff Bieber and Andriana Bosch in 2013; https://www.pbs.org/latino-americans/en/about/index.html, accessed Sept 10, 2022. See also Arreola, *Hispanic Spaces, Latino*

not empty or without history" and the story of their populations is often a story of forced integration into the United States "as conquered peoples."¹⁵

Second, the US Latino/a/x population reached 62.5 million in 2021. Nearly one in five people in the United States, or 19 percent, identify as Latino/a/x. They are the largest "minority" and the fastest-growing group of ethnic/cultural communities in the country. An estimated 34.5 million Hispanic Americans are eligible to vote and were projected to account for over 14 percent of all eligible voters in November 2022. With a strong presence in California, Texas, Florida, New York, and Arizona, these communities are youthful, energetic, and growing in influence. Newborns, rather than immigrants, have driven recent population growth. Four out of every five Latinos/as/xs are US citizens. Those who speak English proficiently now compose over 70 percent, and experience in college education continues to rise. By the year 2030, it is estimated that Latinos/as/xs will make up nearly one third of all students in the United States.¹⁶

Third, it is inaccurate to speak of one Latino/a/x community or culture. There are, rather, a variety of cultural communities, historically and ethnically diverse. Almost twenty-eight million Latinos/as/xs identify as multiracial. While around thirty-seven million people claim Mexican ancestry, almost six million people identify their Puerto Rican descent. The fastest growing populations are from those with origins in Venezuela, the Dominican Republic, Honduras, and Guatemala. Espín explains that while some of the diversity can be explained by the differences in ancestral lands or origins, the actual locations where communities are established within the United States also create a diversity of experience and culture. For example, North Dakota and South Dakota have seen the fastest rate of growth in their Latino/a/x populations since 2010.¹⁷

Places; Chasteen, *Born in Blood and Fire*; Machado, *Of Borders and Margins*; and Vega, *Latino Heartland: Of Borders and Belonging*.

15. Espín, introduction to *The Wiley-Blackwell Companion to Latino/a Theology*, 1.

16. For further details, see https://www.pewresearch.org/fact-tank/2022/09/23/key-facts-about-u-s-latinos-for-national-hispanic-heritage-month/; https://www.pewresearch.org/hispanic/fact-sheet/latinos-in-the-u-s-fact-sheet/; https://www.pewresearch.org/fact-tank/2022/10/12/key-facts-about-hispanic-eligible-voters-in-2022/ and https://www.usatoday.com/in-depth/news/2022/10/11/latino-student-population-us-schools/10426950002/, accessed October 12, 2022.

17. https://www.pewresearch.org/fact-tank/2022/09/23/key-facts-about-u-s-latinos-for-national-hispanic-heritage-month/, accessed October 12, 2022. See the breadth of contributions provided in Nabhan-Warren, *The Oxford Handbook of Latinx Christianities*, including Matovina, "Mexican-Descent Catholics," 15–30; Gonzalez Maldonado,

Fourth, this growing Latino/a/x presence has impacted denominational demographics dramatically in the United States. This is seen in the significant Latino/a/x involvement in the Roman Catholic Church, where they make up between 35 and 40 percent of active, committed participants.[18] Since the year 2000, the contribution of Latino/a/x communities to other church denominations in the US, such as the Episcopal Church, the United Methodist, the American Baptist Convention, and the Assemblies of God, must also be noted.[19]

Fifth, that the majority of Latino/a/x communities identify as Christians, should not occlude the presence of Latino/a/x Jews, Muslims, Lukumí, and Buddhists.[20] In 2014, 18 percent of US Hispanic adults surveyed by the Pew Research Center described themselves as of faith other than Christian, atheist, or agnostic, and 1 percent as "nothing in particular."[21]

Sixth, despite this religious diversity, Espín draws attention to the commonality of the extended family and a popular religious *cosmovision* (worldview) as two of the strongest pillars of Latino/a/x cultures across all differences. He highlights the defining role of older women, particularly in matters ethical and/or religious. He identifies the ways in which bilingualism shapes much of the inclusive understanding of Latino/a/x cultures, and also contributes to the preservation of cultural elements molded during the Spanish colonial era.

Finally, Espín affirms the need for Latino/a/x theologians to be cognizant of the strong contributions of Africans and the "still-living legacy"

"Cuban-Descent Catholics," 31–45; Ortíz Díaz, "Puerto Rican Christianities in the United States," 46–67; Pérez, "Afro-Cuban Catholicisms," 68–86; Menjívar, "The Catholic Church and Central American Immigrants in the United States," 87–108; and Ramos, Martí, and Mulder, "Latino/a Protestantisms," 109–29.

18. See Matovina, *Latino Catholicism: Transformation*. See also https://uscatholic.org/articles/201302/latino-catholics-caught-between-two-worlds/; https://www.pewresearch.org/fact-tank/2014/05/07/fewer-hispanics-are-catholic-so-how-can-more-catholics-be-hispanic/, accessed October 12, 2022.

19. See Maldonado, *Protestantes/Protestants*; Martínez, *Los Protestantes*; Mulder, Ramos and Martí, *Latino Protestants in America*.

20. https://www.pewresearch.org/religion/2014/05/07/chapter-1-religious-affiliation-of-hispanics/, accessed August 20, 2022. To deepen understanding it is also helpful to note the diversity of religion in Puerto Rico, as discussed in Igartua, *Communities of the Soul*.

21. https://www.pewresearch.org/religion/2014/05/07/the-shifting-religious-identity-of-latinos-in-the-united-states/, accessed August 20, 2022.

of the First Peoples of the Americas in Latino/a/x heritage.²² Latino/a/x theologians recognize the need to be attentive to this somewhat neglected aspect of their scholarship in relation to African heritage, in particular. In her groundbreaking interdisciplinary work in 2006, *Afro-Cuban Theology: Religion, Race, Culture and Identity*, Michelle Gonzalez proposed an expansion in understanding the historical intersections between race and religion in the United States. In 2007, Espín began to address this concern directly in his chapter "We Are What We Are" in the book *Grace and Humanness*.²³ In March 2021, around six million US adults identified as Afro-Latino/a/x, speaking to the pertinent significance of this conversation.²⁴

It becomes clear that the contexts shaping Latino/a/x theologies are formed by rich heritage and variegated cultures. This context is a plurality of histories and stories, a diversity of ethnicities and identities, and a vibrancy of traditions. However, this diversity and complexity is not often seen or prized by the dominant culture, or by dominant histories and historiographies. Latino/a/x theologians want to interrupt such dominance.

On the one hand, US American national and religious life was conceived in the rhetoric and ideals of equal and inalienable rights for all people.²⁵ On the other hand, it was conceived in colonial violence against Native American populations, the enslavement of African peoples, the exploitation of Asian peoples, and the disinheritance of Latino/a/x communities.²⁶ Despite the fact that the Latino/a/x presence on the North American continent dates back before the founding of what is now called

22. See https://www.pewresearch.org/fact-tank/2022/05/02/about-6-million-u-s-adults-identify-as-afro-latino/, accessed October 13, 2022.

23. Espín recognizes that in the past Latino/a/x theologians have not paid significant attention to African-ness and slavery in Latino/a/x theologies. He responds directly to this concern in chapter 4, "We Are What We Are," in *Grace and Humanness*, 104–20. See also Gonzalez, *Afro-Cuban Theology*.

24. See for discussion Nolasco, "Doing Latinidad While Black."

25. For a helpful discussion placing issues within a broader imperial context and the recognition that delegates who designed the American Constitution averted their gaze from fundamental questions around enslaved peoples, see Countryman, *Enjoy the Same Liberty*, and also Watkins, *Slavery and Sacred Texts*.

26. See De La Torre, *The Colonial Compromise*; Dunbar-Ortiz and Gilio-Whitaker, *"All the Real Indians Died Off"*; Hoxie, *The Oxford Handbook of American Indian*; Ortiz, *An African American and Latinx History*; Bryant, O'Toole, and Vinson, *Africans to Spanish America*; Gates, *Life upon These Shores*; Kendi and Blain, *Four Hundred Souls*; Reinhard, *Empires and Encounters*; Kidd, *American Colonial History*; Lee, *The Making of Asian America*; Kim, *Invisible: Theology and Experience of Asian American Women*; Park, *A Companion to American Religious History*.

the United States of America, Harold Recinos argues that Latino/a/x communities today are typically viewed by both white Americans and African Americans as "the troublesome outsiders who take jobs away from them, Latin America's social problems on U.S. soil, or simply aliens unwilling to adapt to U.S. society."[27] Anthropologist Leo Chavez names this the "Latino Threat discourse." Rather than portray Latino/a/x communities as the embodiment of "American values" of family and hard work, they are more often portrayed as illegal aliens, criminals, and a burden to society. Tracing individual family lines back many generations cannot protect Latino/a/x families from continually being treated as permanent outsiders.[28] Recinos challenges theologians further by asking why most established Black and white public theologians ignore and avoid engaging Latino/a/x theologians on the subject of white supremacy, the antiracist struggle, social change, and understandings of Jesus.[29]

The Latino-threat narrative has forestalled a recognition of Latino/a/x social, religious, and cultural contributions to society in the United States and to Christian theology.[30] For example, it is the case that "the rich and creative expression of US Latino/a/x Christology that has existed alongside other contextual theologies of racial, ethnic, class and gender construction has been largely unacknowledged."[31] Despite this neglect, the witness of Latino/a/x theologies in the United States may, in fact, provide "the best antidote to exclusionary readings"[32] not only of Scripture but also of history and society (see chapter 4). For Latino/a/x theologies signpost the way to a vision of Jesus that connects Christians to the larger vision of life offered by a peacemaking, community-gathering, boundary-crossing, life-giving God.[33] With the faith communities they represent, Latino/a/x theologians raise a voice that is determined to speak the truth about God, defined most

---

27. Recinos, *Jesus in the Hispanic Community*, ix.

28. Recinos, *Jesus in the Hispanic Community*, x.

29. Recinos, *Jesus in the Hispanic Community*, xii.

30. Benjamin Valentín explores how Hispanic or Latino theology can strengthen its relevance and engagement in society and politics moving to speak to wider issues such as the economy, classism, public policy, and racism. See Valentín, *Mapping Public Theology*.

31. Recinos, *Jesus in the Hispanic Community*, xi.

32. Recinos, *Jesus in the Hispanic Community*, xi.

33. Recinos, *Jesus in the Hispanic Community*, xxi.

faithfully when spoken from within the Latino/a/x communities' struggle for life and justice.³⁴

> For Latinx Christian faith communities, theology becomes the verbal expression of faith as practiced, believed, articulated, and celebrated by Latinx people. It moves beyond the European Enlightenment project that attempts to rationally understand God and communicate this rationality to unbelievers so that they too can believe. Although critical rational appraisals of theology are important and should not be underestimated, for Latinxs, theology is more than dogma or faith formation—it is the daily articulation of life in community where it is known that God and the divine activity move and participate within history to save, liberate and reconcile. . . . In short, Latinx theology is the Latinx voice of faith trying to understand the transcendence within the immanence of Latinx existential contexts.³⁵

COLLABORATION

In the early 1970s, the voice of US Latino/a/x theologians first appeared as published work. As collaborative theology it seeks to create understandings of God and articulate faith from within the shared "experience of social invisibility, cultural marginality, economic inequality, discrimination and everyday struggles for a better life" (see chapter 3).³⁶ To empower rejected and marginalized peoples is foundational. To respond to the racism, sexism, and classism embedded in the narrative of the dominant society and dominant theologies is work that empowers communities (see chapter 6). Arturo Bañuelas explains that God-talk is now being expressed from a new historical point of departure and by new protagonists in that history: Latino/a/x communities struggling for life.³⁷

Reflecting on the early years of Latino/a/x theologies, Espín remembers that "we needed to open 'our' space, speak with 'our' voices, discuss 'our' issues, and very insistently announce that we were not someone else's 'pastoral problem' or 'bibliographic footnote.'"³⁸ Being equals in the theo-

---

34. Bañuelas, *Mestizo Christianity*, 3.
35. De la Torre and Aponte, *Introducing Latinx*, 78.
36. Recinos, *Jesus in the Hispanic Community*, xii.
37. Bañuelas, *Mestizo Christianity*, 1.
38. Espín, introduction to *The Wiley-Blackwell Companion to Latino/a Theology*, 4.

logical conversations meant insisting that particularity and culture, the critique of dominance and white privilege, the articulation of implications for theology, and the defense of Latino/a/x peoples in a social and ecclesial reality adverse to them became and would remain central in this theology. At the heart of this scholarship is the desire to further the goals of Latino/a/x communities—their struggles for equality and dignity, for decent housing, education, and health care.[39] Latino/a/x theology, he suggests, is a movement, a contextual perspective, and a methodological approach to theologizing within (academic) Christian theology.[40]

The importance of collaboration in Latino/a/x theologies is brought into focus when Espín identifies five fundamental aspects of the approach. Firstly, Latino/a/x theology is intent on understanding the cultures, contexts, histories, and needs of the Latino/a/x communities and seeks to empower the daily reality and struggles for justice in a way that honors those cultures, histories, and stories. Secondly, Latino/a/x theology is set apart from other theologies in the sources, approaches, points of departure, perspectives, contexts, and intention present in the work. Thirdly, it models the distinct methodological approach of theology *en conjunto*, demonstrating a reverent passion for the real expressions of life and faith of Latino/a/x persons in their homes, families, and communities.[41] Fourthly, it assumes, honors, and incorporates the searching, the understanding, and the faith of these Latino/a/x communities. Fifthly, Latino/a/x theology is not abstract or removed from the community of faith but rather "it models a scholarly pursuit that is a committed, reasoned understanding of the lives, struggles, and faith of real people in real sociocultural situations that cry out for justice."[42] Latino/a/x theologies, then, are collaborative contextualized theologies for life. Luis Pedraja writes that "to study theology without understanding the context from which it comes is like studying the use of color or set of brushstrokes in a work of art while ignoring the masterpiece itself."[43] Latino/a/x theologies are grounded *desde*, from within, the daily struggles for survival of Latino/a/x communities facing death-dealing obstacles that stand in the way of their flourishing.[44]

---

39. Espín, introduction to *The Wiley-Blackwell Companion to Latino/a Theology*, 6.
40. Espín, introduction to *The Wiley-Blackwell Companion to Latino/a Theology*, 7.
41. Espín, introduction to *The Wiley-Blackwell Companion to Latino/a Theology*, 8.
42. Espín, introduction to *The Wiley-Blackwell Companion to Latino/a Theology*, 8.
43. Pedraja, *Teología: An Introduction*, 13.
44. Bañuelas, *Mestizo Christianity*, 2.

First published in 1995, the volume *Mestizo Christianity: Theology from the Latino Perspective* is a clear demonstration of the five fundamental aspects of the approach, as articulated by Espín. For the contributors firmly grounded the theological reflection in the context of the United States, and through the use of the specific word *mestizo* they identified the many different cultural groups encompassed into the term "Latinos/as/xs" in the United States (see chapter 2). The national and cultural heritages represented include Mexican, Honduran, Salvadoran, Guatemalan, Puerto Rican, Cuban, Chilean, Argentinian, Dominican, Colombian, Venezuelan, Ecuadorian, Bolivian, Peruvian, Panamanian, Costa Rican, and Nicaraguan. Recinos rightly points out: "The full color spectrum of humanity is among them, while they represent various ethnic backgrounds and personally decided racial preferences."[45] Latinos/as/xs who are "new arrivals, aliens on their own land, and poorly understood" are influencing and will continue to change not only the church in the United States but also wider society.[46]

For biblical scholar Francisco Lozada, the unique and vastly diverse social and community experiences brought to bear on theology and biblical interpretation keep the construct "Latino/a/x" "unstable—rarely fixed and always fluid."[47] Fernando Segovia, who led the way in Latino/a/x biblical interpretation, summarizes the reality that "on the one hand, the negative dimensions [of Latino/a/x experience in the United States] may be summarized as across the board marginalization, racial-ethnic othering, and national-political bifurcation and ambiguity. On the other hand, the positive dimensions may be outlined as emphasis on communal-familial solidarity and the presence of radical diversity."[48] While it is important to recognize that shared experiences take place for communities in the United States, it is also vital to acknowledge this breadth and diversity (see chapter 2).

Miguel De La Torre and Edwin Aponte explain that

> this theology arises from the borders—that is, not only geographic borderlands but also from that in-between space that separates privilege from paucity, power from disenfranchisement, whiteness from "colored," wholeness from brokenness. Living on the borders within the United States, Latinx find themselves disjointed both from the culture of their heritage and the culture in which they

---

45. Recinos, *Jesus in the Hispanic Community*, ix.
46. Recinos, *Jesus in the Hispanic Community*, ix.
47. Lozada, *Toward a Latino/a Biblical Interpretation*, 3.
48. Segovia, introduction to Lozada and Segovia, *Latino/a Biblical Hermeneutics*, 13.

reside, outsiders and foreigners to each. . . . From this social location of having one foot in two worlds, Latinx attempt to understand the movement of God.[49]

This mixing or *mestizaje*, which we will explore in the next chapter, is a *locus theologicus* for Latino/a/x theologies. Bañuelas asserts that it should be said from the outset that Latino/a/x theology is not the stepchild of any other theological movement precisely because it is grounded in the daily life-struggles and hopes of Latinos/as/xs. The primary source of reference is the activity of God who, through the liberation of Latinos/as/xs, is fashioning a new human family.[50] De La Torre and Aponte call attention to the fact that while there are similarities and points of contact between Latin American liberation theologies and Latinx theologies—in terms of language, seeking justice, liberation of the poor, interpreting the gospel through lived experience—it would be erroneous to assume that Latinx theological reflection derives exclusively from Latin American theologies:

> Latinx theologies differ by focusing more on the cultural, social, political, and economic issues touching U.S. Latinx communities. Unfortunately, well-meaning theologians—possibly influenced by dominant Euroamerican theological paradigms and uninformed about the U.S. Latinx population or Latinx theological thought, but nonetheless wanting to appear sensitive and inclusive—look to Latin American liberation theologians to be the voice for Latinx theology.[51]

Teología en conjunto is a particular theology grounded in the realities and experiences of Latino/a/x communities living in the United States. From her earliest collaboration with Yolanda Tarango in *Hispanic Women: Prophetic Voice in the Church*, Ada Maria Isasi-Díaz gives voice to Latina women and frames theology in their own stories, with their own words. She writes,

> To *do* theology is to free theology from the exclusive hold of academia; it is also a matter of denouncing the false dichotomy between thought and action so prevalent in Western culture. To do theology is to recognize that the source of theology is human existence, its questions and its concerns as well as its beliefs. To do theology is to validate and uphold the lived experience of the

---

49. De La Torre and Aponte, *Introducing Latinx*, 83.
50. Bañuelas, *Mestizo Christianity*, 3.
51. De La Torre and Aponte, *Introducing Latinx*, 79.

oppressed, since the dominant cultures and countries not only deny its validity, but even question its very existence.⁵²

In the scholarship of Isasi-Díaz, this incorporation of women's voices and stories, and often the inclusion of Spanish-language summaries draws the reader into actual experiences rather than into abstract ideas (see chapter 5). Nancy Pineda-Madrid also firmly grounds her theology in actual experiences. In her work on the atonement and the need for salvation to actively resist evil and pursue justice, she is attentive to the brutal realities of girls and women killed in the borderlands between Texas and Mexico. *Suffering and Salvation in Cuidad Juárez* is deeply rooted in the particular and Pineda-Madrid resists the individualistic interpretations of both salvation and suffering, calling for a reimagining of salvation and theodicy in the face of such evil. For, she argues, "through our response to suffering we learn that community is the condition for the possibility of salvation."⁵³

Teología en conjunto is a collaborative theology that brings communities, churches, and the academy into direct engagement with one another. Elizabeth Conde-Frazier argues that as vocations of faithful service multiply in contemporary society, the dialogical relationships between scholars and church leaders are becoming ever more significant.⁵⁴ In *Sermons from the Latino/a Pulpit*, Eliesar Valentin affirms this and gathers a multiplicity of scholars and church leaders who represent Latino/a/x Christian expression across denominations and roles, thus practicing a "true *teología en conjunto.*" He explains that "only by doing so will we reflect the unity that exists in the One we profess in word and deed."⁵⁵

Teología en conjunto is an interconnected theology that draws on dialogue with Latin American liberation theologies, Latin American contextual theologies, feminist theologies, African American theologies, the social and behavioral sciences, the teachings of Vatican II, new Scripture studies, and the growing ecumenical dialogue. Benjamin Valentín and Anthony Pinn take seriously the need for interlocutors in Latino/a/x and African American scholarship.⁵⁶ Feminist theologians from thirteen countries

---

52. Isasi-Díaz and Tarango, *Hispanic Women: Prophetic*, 2. For further development of this method and commitment, see Isasi-Díaz, *En la Lucha*; Isasi-Díaz, *Mujerista Theology*; and Isasi-Díaz, *La Lucha Continues*.

53. Pineda-Madrid, *Suffering and Salvation*, 7.

54. Conde-Frazier, *Atando Cabos*, 122.

55. Valentin, *Sermons from the Latino/a Pulpit*, xxii.

56. See Pinn and Valentín, *Ties That Bind*; Pinn and Valentín, *Creating Ourselves*; and

across North, Central, and South America model collaborative, interrelated scholarship in their analysis of the relationships between religion, culture, feminism, and power in *Feminist Intercultural Theology: Latina Explorations for a Just World*.[57]

"The cry for justice and the promotion of peace," writes Orlando Costas, "are testimonies to God's love for the world.... To live in the freedom of God's love is to struggle for, demand, and enjoy the space and the blessing of being agents of justice and makers of peace."[58] To be in conversation with *teología en conjunto* is to be in conversation with a constructive theology that gives voice to this pursuit of justice and of peace. This theology is grounded in communities striving for justice and peace. This theology seeks to faithfully declare the ways in which contexts deny justice and peace. This theology calls for a commitment to collaboration, lifting up the voices and experiences of many who testify to the presence of God. This is theology that stands in the face of divisiveness and fear. The foundational theologians, texts, and concerns discussed in this chapter bear witness to this vision and witness over the last fifty years. In the following chapters we will explore themes that have become significant in *teología en conjunto* beginning with the concept of *mestizaje* in chapter 2.

IN CONVERSATION

Omar Rodriguez De La O

> Not all Latinos have the same experience, and therefore not all readings "through Hispanic eyes" are alike.[59]
>
> JUSTO GONZÁLEZ

> *My name is Omar Rodriguez De la O, born in Bayamón Puerto Rico in the year 1981 to a Puerto Rican father born in Arecibo Puerto Rico and a Chicana mother, born in Texas to Mexican parents. I grew up on the island of Boriquen with a mix of customs and traditions in my home that enriched my nuclear family. We could enjoy delicious tacos served with rice and Puerto Rican style beans. In religious life,*

Ortiz, *An African American and Latinx History*.
57. See Aquino and Rosado-Nunes, *Latina Feminist Theology*.
58. Costas, *Liberating News*, 142.
59. González, *Santa Biblia*, 31.

my father had abandoned the faith long before my birth and did not practice it while my mother was always an evangélica believer. I am now a deacon in the Episcopal Diocese of Arizona. (I will be ordained priest by the time this book is published.) I graduated with a MDiv from Virginia Theological Seminary and a BA in biblical studies and theology from the Biblical Institute of Puerto Rico. I have lived in "mainland" United States since 2012 and face the new challenges of being Mexirican in the United States. Everyone knows as a Mexirican that we are half Mexican and half Puerto Rican. Now on the mainland I face new realities that I did not experience in Puerto Rico, some of which are spoken about in this chapter and in this book in general. To be Puerto Rican in the United States carries with it all the dynamics associated with that label. If I were to choose something other than Mexirican or Puerto Rican here, I would choose to identify as Latine. My pronouns are he/him. As Latine in the United States today, one of the challenges we face is holding our own biblical perspectives and theological positions in the midst of white American perspectives. We have to face the imposition of cultural and traditional realities that are not in agreement with our own, and we face the challenge of how Scripture is used to justify this.

Teología en conjunto is a theme for me that speaks directly to my life experience because it speaks to the significance of context, community, and collaboration. It speaks to the diversity of our realities. And it breaks down any idea of a monolithic Latine experience. All are not poor. All are not looking for work. All do not share the same political ideas. Some are wealthy. Some are well educated. We need to hold to a more nuanced understanding of one another—our histories, our cultures, our identities, and our experiences. Then we can begin to understand the complexities within us and within our communities. Those beyond Latine communities can also begin to understand this. *Teología en conjunto* is theology that acknowledges complexity.

I was born and raised in Puerto Rico. This is my community, and it was my context for many years. This brings complexity, therefore, to my story within the United States. I have never "crossed borders" in the ways that people so often assume. I have never walked across a desert in the hope of a better life. I have never been designated as "illegal." I am a US citizen. During my CPE placement, I met a woman whose story moved me to tears. She told me of how she recited Psalm 23 day after day as she journeyed to reach the United States. She experienced the presence of God in her terrifying walk across the desert. I do not have her experience. I have not walked in her shoes. In listening to her, I felt like an outsider because I never experienced this. I read Psalm 23 differently now as I remember her story. In listening to her story, I learned a different lens through which to approach a very familiar text.

I have not experienced immigration like so many. However, I have experienced colonialism in ways that people often do not imagine and very easily forget. I have experienced prejudice and I encounter preconceived ideas about me, my heritage, and our histories. Collaboration calls for listening without prejudice and preconceptions. *Teología en conjunto* calls for listening across difference. It calls for a commitment to understand one another. Experience has taught me that if we can do this together, it bears witness to the Spirit of God at work in the world. *Teología en conjunto* teaches that all of us are needed in the conversation.

Teología en conjunto is an ongoing conversation. It does not end in the classroom. For many it may be a new conversation that begins in the classroom. For some it is the continuation of theology they have already participated in and known. For others it is theology that brings encouragement. We learn from one another in our different stages of the journey. We leave the classroom and move into ministry. We must take *teología en conjunto* with us. It is an ongoing conversation among Latine communities. It is a conversation across cultures, across generations, across denominations, across experiences.

This is a conversation that we need in order to do theology *latinamente*. *Teología en conjunto* offers us a different lens, a different point of view. It stands in contrast to the imposition of a dominant approach to understanding the gospel or Scripture. Sometimes what I am asked to learn simply does not work in my context and does not relate to my context. This is theology that teaches us to look for more ways of understanding. This is why we need ongoing conversation. *Teología en conjunto* motivates us to invite one another to the table. We listen to each other's stories—your story growing up in Ireland and my story growing up in Puerto Rico. We commit to learning to understand one another, and we are not afraid to say "Tell me more about it" when we find we don't agree.

Teología en conjunto is more than conversation. It is praxis. It is a way of doing theology that carries not only educational implications in the classroom but pastoral implications in ministry. We say that we are one body in the church with many parts and we say that all those parts are needed. But how do we understand our complexities? How do we use this understanding to build the kingdom of God together? This theology teaches us to pause and ask, who are we in this congregation? What is our context? How might we be in community with one another? How might we collaborate more fully?

In the United States, bilingual, multicultural communities and congregations are growing. I minister to Spanish speakers and English speakers sharing space, sharing worship. Diverse, they are one body of Christ. This is the collaboration that *teología en conjunto* points to. To be united, we need to understand our complexities. To understand myself and my identity enables me to understand my congregation better. A very practical example is how we communicate across these differences in our congregations. For me, when I am thinking of good communication in my church, and good intercultural leadership, it is often helpful to begin with thinking about effective sermon preparation and delivery in my context. Perhaps we have one congregation and one church service together, or perhaps we have two congregations and several services at different times in different languages. One sermon does not fit all congregations or all services because there is a difference between translation and interpretation. In a multicultural congregation there is a need for both skills to be at work. Just as one sermon does not fit all, one approach in pastoral care and ministry does not fit all. We should ask a bilingual person for their response to our sermon in Spanish and in English, and we should be willing to hear their feedback. In a similar way, we should ask our multicultural congregations for their insight on pastoral care and ministry across differences. Always, we should be willing to incorporate their feedback. *Teología en conjunto* is not simply something that we read or something that we study. We need to make *teología en conjunto* our practice and the core of our commitment to one another.

I appreciate you sharing your story, Sharon. I learned things that I did not know before. You convey how listening to *teología en conjunto* has spoken to you and how this has changed you. We need to continue to tell our stories to one another.[60]

FOUNDATIONAL READING

Aponte, Edwin David, and Miguel A. De La Torre. *Introducing Latinx Theologies.* Maryknoll, NY: Orbis, 2020.

60. Translation and interpretation provided by Sharon E. Heaney.

Espín, Orlando O, ed. *The Wiley-Blackwell Companion to Latino/a Theology*. Chichester, UK: Wiley-Blackwell, 2015.

———, ed. *The Wiley-Blackwell Companion to Latinoax Theology*. 2nd ed. Chichester, UK: Wiley-Blackwell, forthcoming.

Nanko-Fernández, Carmen. *Theologizing en Espanglish*. Maryknoll, NY: Orbis, 2010.

FURTHER READING

Espín, Orlando, ed. *Building Bridges, Doing Justice: Constructing a Latino/a Ecumenical Theology*. Maryknoll, NY: Orbis, 2009.

Nabhan-Warren, Kristy, ed. *The Oxford Handbook of Latinx Christianities in the United States*. New York: Oxford University Press, 2022.

Pinn, A., and B. Valentín, eds. *Creating Ourselves: African Americans and Hispanic Americans on Popular Culture and Religious Expression*. Durham, NC: Duke University Press, 2009.

———, eds. *The Ties That Bind: African American and Hispanic American/Latino/a Theologies in Dialogue*. New York: Continuum, 2001.

Rodríguez, José David, and Loida I. Martell-Otero, eds. *Teología en Conjunto: A Collaborative Hispanic Protestant Theology*. Louisville: Westminster John Knox, 1997.

Ross, Kenneth R., Ana María Bidegain, and Todd M. Johnson, eds. *Christianity in Latin America and the Caribbean*. Edinburgh: Edinburgh University Press, 2022.

2

Mestizaje

The Complexity of Histories, Stories, Cultures, and Identities

> The Irish came here in greater numbers than most immigrant groups. Their history has been tied to America's past from the very beginning. Ireland represented the earliest English frontier: the conquest of Ireland occurred before the colonization of America, and the Irish were the first group that the English called "savages." . . . [T]he Irish were pushed from their homeland by "English tyranny." Here they became construction workers and factory operatives as well as the "maids" of America . . . but they had a distinct advantage: the Naturalization Law of 1790 had reserved citizenship for "whites" only. Their compatible complexion allowed them to assimilate by blending into American society. In making their journey successfully into the mainstream, however, these immigrants from Erin pursued an Irish "ethnic" strategy: they promoted "Irish" solidarity in order to gain political power and also to dominate the skilled blue-collar occupations, often at the expense of the Chinese and blacks.[1]
>
> —Ronald Takaki

1. Takaki, *A Different Mirror*, 9.

THE COMPLEXITIES OF IRISH history, Irish experiences of colonialism, and the Irish presence in the United States invite me to pause. How do I tell the story of the Irish in the United States? On the one hand, the Irish were a people often marginalized and exploited because of their ethnicity, and yet on the other hand in the United States they became a people who found their way to places of power. The nuance of these stories can be difficult to grasp, and the truth of these Irish stories a challenge to untangle.[2] Ronald Takaki, professor emeritus of ethnic studies at the University of California, Berkley, and a preeminent scholar of US race relations articulated the significance of received histories in this multicultural United States of America. He calls each person to examine the received histories that they have believed about the United States and their place in those stories.[3] He calls each person to pay close attention to what they see and in the looking be prepared to see what they have never seen before. The story of the Irish in the US is certainly, as Takaki demonstrates, multivocal. The narratives are complicated and contested, histories are interwoven with the histories of dominant groups and marginalized groups, and identities were often plural and pluralized.[4]

For Latino/a/x theologians, realities of such complicated narratives, interwoven histories, and pluralities of identity are well recognized in their communities. Latino/a/x theology takes seriously the need to examine received histories. In locating their theology in the contemporary landscape of the United States of America they foreground issues of overlapping ethnicities, intermixing cultures, dynamics of power, and changing identities that are at work in defining their communities.[5] These concerns are brought together in *mestizaje*. This a concept that seeks to grapple with the histories, the stories, and the implications of intermixture, blending, fusion, and miscegenation. For Néstor Medina, "*Mestizaje* helps unmask the fallacy behind inherited sanitized notions of history from the vantage point of the victor

---

2. See for further discussion Ignatiev, *How the Irish Became White*, and Roediger, *Working toward Whiteness*.

3. See "Ronald Takaki, Pioneer and Legend in Ethnic Studies, Dies at Age 70," https://newsarchive.berkeley.edu/news/media/releases/2009/05/28_takakiobit.shtml, accessed April 2, 2023.

4. See, for example, Takaki, "Fleeing English Tyranny: The Irish Cross the Atlantic" and "Finding Her Voice for Militant Labor: Elizabeth Gurley Flynn," in *A Larger Memory*, 112–28. See also Young, *The Idea of English Ethnicity*, and Ignatiev, *How the Irish Became White*.

5. A very helpful analysis is provided in Mize, *Latina/o Studies*.

and retrieves the underside of that history. The story always looks different from the side of the vanquished."[6] In this way, *mestizaje* can be a point of departure in Latino/a/x theologies. This chapter will also explore the retelling of the history of the United States in light of *mestizaje*; the truth of personal story to convey *mestizaje*; the testimonies of resistance expressed through *mestizaje*; and the implications of *mestizaje* for Latino/a/x theologies.

MESTIZAJE AS A POINT OF DEPARTURE

Writing *Mestizaje: (Re)Mapping Race, Culture, and Faith in Latina/o Catholicism* in 2009, Néstor Medina recognized that changes in the societal and political landscape in the United States had accelerated to such an extent that ethnic and cultural reconfigurations presented a complex challenge for Latino/a/x theologians. He argues that it is necessary to "review and interrogate U.S. Latina/o theological articulations of ethnic and cultural identity, particularly [the] use of the category of *mestizaje*."[7] As collaborative, constructive, and contextual theology, *teología en conjunto* places such reflection and review at the heart of the theological task. The search for a just theology means not only interrupting dominant theologies but beginning in a different place. A unique point of departure and theological lens for Latino/a/x theologies is this concept of *mestizaje*.

> Originally used to describe the children born from the mixture of indigenous and Spanish and Portuguese peoples in Latin America, today *mestizaje* is used more broadly around the world to describe similar experiences of biological and cultural intermixture. The adoption of *mestizaje* by U.S. Latina/o theologians was not accidental. The initial consideration for adopting *mestizaje* was that the U.S. Latina/o population shared with Latin America the experience of Spanish invasion and conquest that resulted in the original intermixture with the indigenous peoples. . . . U.S. Latina/o theologians' adoption and appropriation of *mestizaje* involved a complex, painful, and creative process of identity formation to name themselves in contrast to the dominant U.S. Anglo culture. A term that was originally used in derogatory ways they redeemed as a term by which to reclaim their ethnic and cultural dignity as a people.[8]

6. Medina, "(De)Ciphering *Mestizaje*," 82.

7. Medina, *Mestizaje*, ix.

8. Medina, *Mestizaje*, xii.

Adopting *mestizaje* amid dominant and domineering stories of the United States was truth-telling that resisted policies to erase the ethnic and cultural heritages of Latino/a/x communities. It was Virgilio Elizondo, committed to articulate the double violence caused by the Spanish colonial enterprise and the expansionist policy of Anglo government in the US, who first employed *mestizaje* theologically.[9] *Mestizaje* was a way to speak theologically about the particular realities of social marginalization, exploitation, and oppression experienced by Latino/a/x theologians and their communities.[10] Applying *mestizaje* as a theological point of departure was recognition of religious resistance and testimony to survival in the face of oppressive powers.[11] Thus, Ada María Isasi-Díaz brought the voices of women to bear on their experiences of marginalization, grounded in the understanding of *mestizaje*.[12] For María Pilar Aquino, *mestizaje* validated the ethnocultural identities of Latinas and she expanded its use to include the witness of others on the periphery who had survived.[13]

Elizondo centered *mestizaje* in his reading of Christ. Considering Jesus as *mestizo* provided a reinterpretation of the Gospel narratives in such a way that the experiences of Mexican Americans were mirrored in the life of the Messiah.[14] Roberto Goizueta reconsidered theological method in light of *mestizaje* highlighting a focus on praxis and the need to pay attention to social location and historicity.[15] Orlando Espín too articulated the ways in which *mestizaje* set Latino/a/x faith communities apart, explaining that "it is what binds them together as a people distinct from all other segments of the U.S. population."[16] If the church honors Latino/a/x cultural

---

9. For early reflections, see Elizondo, *Galilean Journey*, and Elizondo, *The Future Is Mestizo*.

10. Early affirmations of cultural and theological identity in US Latino/a/x theologies are offered in Bañuelas, *Mestizo Christianity*.

11. A constructive overview is provided in Aquino, "*Mestizaje*: The Latina/o Religious Imaginary," 283–312.

12. See Isasi-Díaz, *En la Lucha*, chapter 7, "*Mestizaje*: Symbol of Hispanic Women's Moral Truth-Praxis," 186–204.

13. See Aquino, "Latina Feminist Theology."

14. See Elizondo, "Elements for a Mexican American *Mestizo* Christology," 3–15. Also in this volume, Loida I. Martell offers a constructive engagement with the concept of *mestizaje* from the particularities of a Puerto Rican perspective in her chapter "Encuentro con el Jesús Sato," 74–91.

15. See Goizueta, "The Significance of U.S. Hispanic Experience," 83–103.

16. Espín, "Tradition and Popular Religion," 153.

heritage and traditions, the church can embody inclusion, celebration, and hope. Latino/a/x cultural traditions and popular religious expressions are, in their very essence, intermixed bearing witness to understandings of the divine and demonstrating sustained Christian commitment in the face of suffering.[17]

Medina recognizes that *mestizaje* is a "heavily contested category." He maintains that it is not contested in terms of the possibilities of significance and meaning. "Rather, discussions related to *mestizaje* are often contested because numerous historical experiences of other communities are absent from or ignored by debates and discussions."[18] Jorge Aquino too notes the potential for *mestizaje* to function as a racially exclusionary ideological force privileging some representations above others. No conversation seeking to engage with Latino/a/x theologies, therefore, is possible without giving careful attention to the nuances and implications of *mestizaje* on context, history, and lived experience.

As dominant histories in the United States are framed by power and exclusion, so dominant theologies are framed by power and exclusion. Medina narrates how *mestizaje* first became a foundational category and point of departure for Latina/o theologians in the United States:

> [T]hey drew from the literary tradition of Latin America and borrowed the concept of *mestizaje*. But they turned *mestizaje* upside down by using the term to elucidate what it is to be Latina/o in the United States. By using *mestizaje*, these theologians reclaimed their identity and culture, and gave a sense of symbolic coherence to the communities to which they belong. *Mestizaje* became the useful identity category that glued together these diverse communities as they struggled against social and cultural injustice. U.S. Latina/o theologians used *mestizaje* for naming the complex and dynamic reality of cultural intermixture as present among the U.S. Latina/o experiences and faith expressions.[19]

He demonstrates how this concept has proven theologically subversive and innovative. *Mestizaje* created a powerful framework for theology and expressions of faith within Latino/a/x communities, offering an alternative approach to traditional theological categories and interpretations. Yet he also

---

17. See Gutiérrez, "Indigenous Christianities," 107–27, and Hughes, "Mapping the Autochthonous Indigenous Church," 91–105.

18. Medina, "Ethics, Theology and Mestizaje," 207.

19. Medina, *Mestizaje*, 136. For a concise overview and thorough bibliography, see Medina, "Ethics, Theology and Mestizaje," 207–24.

identifies inherent limitations and contradictions in the term, recognizing the need to articulate the vibrancy and complexity of ethno-cultural and religious identities in contemporary Latina/o communities. As will be explored later in this chapter, Medina recognizes the ways in which *mestizaje* is being reclaimed and reconfigured, with a variety of competing concerns, meanings, and interpretations. *Mestizaje* not only influences the telling of continental histories but is also experienced and retold in personal, family, and community stories. Theologians, therefore, need to engage *mestizaje* in interdisciplinary terms. This they do in relation to historical, social, literary, artistic, economic, and political analyses.[20]

RETELLING THE STORY OF THE UNITED STATES

Daisy Machado maintains that "the telling of national history is really about power and exclusion. This is so because history is the telling of a story told by those who had the power to impose themselves. It is not surprising that those who hold the power to tell their story also hold the power to name themselves and exclude others from that self-definition."[21] Juan González, examining the history of Latinos/as/xs in the USA, recognizes this power of imposition and exclusion. In contrast to the later Eurocentric "American dream" narrative, he journeys through histories of communities experiencing citizenship yet injustice, protection yet abuse, and division leading to disdain and derision. Cognizant of the need to articulate an intricate narrative, he invites his readers to "travel back ... to tear down some walls and begin a new journey through the American story."[22] To tell this story, he employs the metaphor of *las raíces* (the roots), *las ramas* (the branches), and *la cosecha* (the harvest) as a way of broadening the account of North American history narrated in dominant Anglo tradition. He calls attention to the need to retell US American history in such a way that the story is shaped in response to the realities of "borderlands," and so-called "backyard experiences of empire."[23] For communities living with these re-

---

20. For major methodological characteristics, see Aquino, "Latina Feminist Theology," 150. Another helpful example of such interdisciplinary work is Delgadillo, *Spiritual Mestizaje*.

21. Machado, *Of Borders and Margins*, xiii.

22. González, *Harvest of Empire*, xxiv.

23. See, for example, Vega, *Latino Heartland* and Nabhan-Warren, *Meatpacking America*.

alities have deep roots in the story and soil of the contemporary United States.[24] Michelle Gonzalez argues that "standing in the heritage of Latin American liberation theology, Latino/a/x theologians are not new to the ethical dimensions of the theological task. Writing history is a moral (as well as a political, social, and economic) act that must be placed in an ethical framework."[25]

Before the English set out to establish a community at Jamestown in 1607, the Spanish had claimed California in 1542.[26] Before the Mayflower dropped anchor near Cape Cod in 1620, the Spanish colonization of Florida had already begun in 1565 at St. Augustine.[27] One hundred and fifty years before the first wagons attempted the Oregon Trail in 1836, Spanish missions were already established across today's California, Texas, and New Mexico.[28] A history of the United States of America retold from south to north, and from west to east resources what Takaki called the "larger memory."[29] This larger memory gives voice to indigenous communities across the contemporary United States as they retell stories of encounter with Spanish colonialist powers and survival in the face of such encounter.[30] Such work also bears testimony to the significant presence of enslaved Africans in the Americas before the founding of English colonial communities.[31] Enslaved Africans were in Florida as early as 1526.[32] Not only does

---

24. See Breen, *Converging Worlds*, and Kidd, *American Colonial History*. For a crucial contribution by Mexican and North American historians, see Medrano and Kellogg, *Negotiation within Domination*. See also Bryant, O'Toole, and Vinson, *Africans to Spanish America*. For insight on the untold contribution of grassroots faith movements within the histories of the institutional church and secular justice movements, see Salvatierra and Wrencher, *Buried Seeds*.

25. See Gonzalez, *Afro-Cuban Theology*.

26. For thoughtful arguments and innovative perspectives, see Panich and Schneider, *Indigenous Landscapes and Spanish Missions*. See also Peres and Marrinan, *Unearthing the Missions*.

27. For a deeper understanding of the shifting alliances, political competition, and violence during Spanish colonial rule in Florida during the late sixteenth and early seventeenth centuries, see Francis and Kole, *Murder and Martyrdom in Spanish Florida*.

28. For a breadth of discussion encompassing Florida, borderlands of New Mexico and Texas, and California, see Starr, *Continental Ambitions*.

29. See Takaki, *A Larger Memory*.

30. See Lozano, *An American Language*.

31. See McKnight and Garofalo, *Afro-Latino Voices: Narratives*.

32. See Heywood and Thornton, *Central Africans, Atlantic Creoles, and the Foundations of the Americas*, and Guasco, *Slaves and Englishmen*.

this larger memory enrich historiography and history, it also unveils how historiography and history can be used to exclude or marginalize particular experiences and perspectives.[33] As noted, Machado sounds this warning on how power and exclusion often function in the tellings of national history. It is the power of a dominant culture that creates school curricula, writes history textbooks, selects the significant figures, and defines influence.[34] It is this power that enables dominant culture to ignore the contributions of other communities in the growth and development of the United States, denying the fruit of labor and degrading seeds of creativity and survival that sustained life for the nation.[35]

The image of harvest should be one of hope, growth, and fulfillment—and for some, like many Irish Americans mentioned earlier, life in the United States has borne fruit. But the harvest reaped by many Latinos/as/xs in the United States is more often a story bound up in life-denying politics, in unjust systems of immigration, in the disparaging of cultures, and in experiences of inequality within North American borders. Beyond these borders, the harvest has reaped political and economic possession and exploitation:[36]

> [T]he U.S. economic and political domination over Latin America has always been—and continues to be—the underlying reason for the massive Latino presence here. Quite simply, our vast Latino population is the unintended harvest of the U.S. empire. Most of us are uncomfortable thinking of our nation as an empire, even if Wall Street speculators and investment banks have repeatedly shown their ability to wreck entire economies halfway around the

---

33. For helpful discussion on how such power has functioned in the history of literature in the United States, see Lazo and Alemán, *The Latino Nineteenth Century*.

34. For further discussion, see, for example, Madsen, "The West and Manifest Destiny," 369–88, and Woodworth, *Manifest Destinies*. Helpful educational examples include the presentation of a series of maps on the National Geographic page entitled "Westward Expansion," accessed February 5, 2023, https://education.national geographic.org/resource/resource-library-westward-expansion. Online classroom materials at the Library of Congress also include many resources with this emphasis, accessed February 5, 2023, https://www.loc.gov/classroom-materials/?q=westward+expansion.

35. For further reading, see Arreola, *Hispanic Spaces, Latino Places*; De Genova, *Racial Transformations*; Schultze, *Strangers in a Foreign Land*; and Ortiz, *An African American and Latinx History*.

36. Helpful discussion can be found, for example, in Machado, *Of Borders and Margins*; Delgado, *A Puerto Rican Decolonial Theology*; Roorda, Derby, and González, *Dominican Republic Reader*; and Casimir, *The Haitians: A Decolonial History*.

globe in a matter of hours—a power far greater than the Roman or Ottoman empires ever wielded.[37]

González emphasizes that Latinos/as/xs in the United States are not seeking to overthrow or remove others but rather are searching for survival and inclusion. The most dangerous enemy that González identifies is, in fact, "the great wall of ignorance between us."[38] Machado, too, seeks to break down this wall of ignorance in her work to demonstrate that the history of Latino/a/x communities in the United States is not simply about borders crossed "but also very much about racial mixture that includes the *mestizaje* of Indian and Spanish blood, the *mulatez* of Spanish and African, the whiteness of *criollos*, and the brown tones of the indigenous peoples, as well as other racial mixtures that are the reality of human pigmentation in the Americas."[39] In *Brown Church*, Robert Chao Romero traces the stories and influence of Latinos/as/xs in the United States through involvement in social justice, through contribution to theology and through testimony to identity during the last five centuries. The *brown* experience and *brown* theologies have been traditionally pushed to the margins of scholarship. However, in the retelling of the story Chao Romero centers the prophetic testimony of the *brown church* in local congregations who have been living out the gospel and who have been committed to the pursuit of justice in the United States for generations. González emphasizes the need for those from the dominant culture to be in conversation with those who are retelling this story of the United States. This is a story that can no longer be ignored because it is, in fact, as Justo González explains, a story that "is about me who is brown but also about you who are not."[40]

In *Crossing Guadalupe Street*, David Maldonado conveys the complexities of *mestizaje* through biography. He reflects on growing up Hispanic and Protestant in the small town of Seguin in south central Texas during the 1940s and 1950s. He weaves together the experiences of his family, his town, and his Mexican American Methodist church illustrating fragile yet resilient intricacies.[41] *Crossing Guadalupe Street* is the story of a young man

---

37. González, *Harvest of Empire*, xvii.
38. González, *Harvest of Empire*, xxiv.
39. Machado, "History and Latino/a Identity," 35–52.
40. Justo L. González, endorsement of Romero, *Brown Church*. For a broader understanding of Christian communities and their influence, see Ross, Bidegain, and Johnson, *Christianity in Latin America and the Caribbean*.
41. Maldonado is the founding director of the Center for the Study of Latino/a

of Mexican heritage, born in the United States, knowing a deep sense of belonging to his family community and yet also knowing a deep sense of loyalty and service to the United States. This belonging and loyalty to the United States, however, is contrasted by the profound sense of exclusion he experiences from Anglo and African American communities nearby. It is often assumed that Latinos/as/xs are born into Catholic families. *Crossing Guadalupe Street*, however, is the story of being raised in a Protestant family amid the dominance of pre-Vatican II Catholicism.[42] It is the testimony of a family of deep faith who endure exclusion from the dominant expression of Christianity in their community.[43] It tells of a hardworking family, committed to one another, and to education who experience the consequences of poverty given structures of privilege and wealth.[44] It bears witness to the significance of a local community of faith amid the struggle:

> [T]he church gave us self-respect and a sense of worth, social support, positive values, and leadership opportunities as youth that helped us believe in ourselves. As the external environment challenged us because of our ethnicity, the family and church strengthened us internally to survive and to thrive.[45]

Maldonado also narrates the interwoven layers of *mestizaje* in his heritage. His great-grandfather Luis had been a soldier in the army of Porfirio Díaz, the Mexican dictator, and then became an immigrant in the United States. It is possible that his great-grandmother, Amada González, may have been of Apache heritage from the plains of south-central Texas. Maldonado himself is a fourth-generation member of the Methodist Church in Seguin. Within these layers of identity, belonging, and exclusion he captures the essence of his Latino reality:

Christianity and Religions at Perkins School of Theology, SMU. https://www.smu.edu/Perkins/News/News_Archives/Archives2011/Maldonado_Ret.

42. A constructive overview from a sociological perspective is presented in Mulder, Ramos, and Martí, *Latino Protestants in America*.

43. For further insight, see Ramos, Martí, and Mulder, "Latino/a Protestantisms," 109–29, and Barba, "Latina/o Pentecostalisms," 130–50; Barton and Maldonado, *Hispanic Christianity*; and Maldonado, *Protestantes/Protestants*.

44. Such challenges are examined in depth in Reyes, *Nobody Cries When We Die*.

45. Maldonado, *Crossing*, 118. The significance of the local community of faith is explored further in Martínez, *Los Protestantes*; Martínez, *Walking with the People*; and Rodriguez, *A Future for the Latino Church*.

> To be defined as Mexican also meant racial distinction among Anglos. Although in the barrio we used the term "Mexican" to define ourselves as a people with a distinct ancestry, it did not carry the connotation of inferiority. In the Anglo world, to be non-Anglo was to be inferior. This carried distinct social consequences. Social separation was considered important and served as a powerful tool. . . . Ethnic and racial definitions were powerful social constructs. They defined us and determined where we lived, where we went to school, who our friends would be, and the lives of most people from the barrio. It was not something you could outgrow, overcome through study or wages or escape, even if you wanted to. It was a powerful reality in Seguin, in Texas and in the United States.[46]

He names the divisions created and maintained through tradition, ignorance, and lack of mutual trust. Maldonado employs the motif of courageously "crossing the street," which taught him to be bilingual, bicultural, ecumenical, and a citizen of the wider society while always grounded in a larger Hispanic family.[47] "By telling my story," he writes, "I am telling the story of our ancestors and challenging [the next generation] to learn from our experiences."[48]

Resilience in the face of power and exclusion is often captured in literature and the arts, as the memoir of Maldonado demonstrates. To be in conversation with Latino/a/x theologies is to be caught up in deeper and wider conversations with communities who live, breathe, and tell stories about the meaning and consequences of *mestizaje*. For Michelle Gonzalez, "*Mestizaje* and *mulatez* are living terms in our communities, not merely academic constructions."[49] They are living terms because they are concepts that tell and retell stories and histories. These living terms signify the complexities of truth-telling and resistance within frameworks of dominant thought in the church, in the academy, and in wider society in the United States.

---

46. Maldonado, *Crossing*, 139.

47. Maldonado, *Crossing*, 6. These issues are explored further in Nanko-Fernández, *Theologizing en Espanglish*.

48. Maldonado, *Crossing*, 179.

49. Gonzalez, "Who We Are," 73.

ENGAGING LATINO/A/X THEOLOGIES

A TESTIMONY OF RESISTANCE

In *Strangers in Our Own Land*, Hector Avalos turns to the study of religion as portrayed in literature. He considers religion to be a significant interlocutor in the ongoing discussion surrounding what is understood as "American identity."[50] While he distinguishes the variety of ways Latino/a/x authors may find their place of belonging in the United States—some as immigrants and others born and raised here—he recognizes that all "struggle with the majority culture as well as with their own [culture]."[51] In pluralizing the histories and voices in North American literature, Avalos resources a resistant theology that would work against dominant discourses and simplistic assumptions. In a similar way to Romero's tracing of the often unacknowledged influence of the *Brown Church* across the centuries, Avalos reflects on the argument of Luis Leal that Mexican American literature and its influence can be traced back to the sixteenth century. Avalos models what he describes as an *attitudinal* point of departure, examining how literary works express societal attitudes toward religious traditions. He concludes that "most Latinas/os see their roots as a mixture, a *mestizaje*, of indigenous and European blood. But while most Latinas/os are aware that the predominant European heritage is specifically Spanish, there is almost no symmetrical knowledge of the indigenous side."[52] Avalos then examines how reflection on indigenous, African, Catholic, Protestant, Jewish, Islamic, Eastern, and secular approaches to religion will deepen an understanding of *mestizaje*.[53] He provides a critical reading of the interpretations of indigenous religions. In particular, like Machado, he pays attention to power dynamics, and also notes what he names as "colonial impulses":

> I suggest that the Aztecs became the paradigm of the indigenous culture because they exhibit so much of what the Europeans consider "civilization." ... The Europeans valued writing, and the Aztecs had writing. The Europeans were a highly urbanized culture, and so were the Aztecs. The Europeans were imperialistic, and so were the Aztecs. The Europeans even had a soteriology based on the sacrifice of a god, and the Aztecs were no strangers to this idea. The Aztecs may also have had apocalyptic myths of returning

---

50. Avalos, *Strangers*, xiii.
51. Avalos, *Strangers*, xvi.
52. Avalos, *Strangers*, 1.
53. See, for example, chapter 3 on African diaspora religion in Gonzalez, *A Critical Introduction to Religion in the Americas*, 103–26.

deities. In short, the selection of the Aztecs as the paradigm of the "indigenous" still betrays Eurocentric yardsticks for validating a culture.[54]

Awareness of such power dynamics and the implications of colonial attitudes in Christian theology are explored further in *Cultural Memory: Faith, Resistance and Identity*, by Jeanette Rodríguez and Ted Fortier. Avalos points to religious expressions present in literature as powerful incarnations of resistance to destruction and denigration. Such religious expressions, often handed down through generations, become defining experiences for communities. Rodríguez and Fortier describe this as "cultural memory." For a community that has been oppressed, the spirit of resistance is the very essence of cultural memory—a remembering of histories and stories disparaged by dominant culture, and a testifying to faith that endures despite devastation. Rodríguez and Fortier examine four distinct case studies: the image of and devotion to Our Lady of Guadalupe among Mexican Americans; the role of secrecy and ceremony among the Yaqui Indians of Arizona; the evolving narrative expressed by the church of the poor in San Salvador around the martyrdom of Archbishop Oscar Romero; and what they refer to as the syncretism of the Catholic Tzeltal Mayans in Mexico. In Latino/a/x theologies, such studies of resistance show how communities have subverted dominance. Despite oppression and injustice, these religious expressions are forms of cultural memory and devotion to faith which have preserved the spirit of a particular people. This is the kind of work that Avalos calls for—work that pays attention not only to the Spanish roots of religious expression in the United States but also work that carefully examines the indigenous roots. Rodríguez and Fortier elucidate further:

> The definition of culture flows from an understanding that people develop unique sets of categories, including languages, political organizations, and rituals and ceremonies. Historically marginalized groups have additional categories that reveal the cultural forces that have resisted annihilation from dominant groups by accessing forms of spiritual resistance. These are the issues of people who have historically had to fight for their community and maintain a social construct to exist in the world. . . . [L]ife is a struggle to find a place—that is, establish their presence in the world today and make known their rights not only to survive but to flourish

54. Avalos, *Strangers*, 7.

apart from the dominant cultures—in a globalized world that has marginalized them.[55]

The cultural memory of Our Lady of Guadalupe has become one of the most recognizable expressions of religious devotion within Latino/a/x communities in the United States and illustrates the intricate layers of *mestizaje*.[56] From the story of her appearances on December 9 and December 12, 1531, to a peasant Juan Diego on the Tepeyac hillside, a number of traditions have emerged surrounding her feast day. Understanding this story and these celebrations also provides deeper insight into the devotion offered to other figures brought to the United States—Our Lady of Charity of El Cobre from Cuba, and Our Lady of Divine Providence from Puerto Rico, for example. Firstly, Rodríguez and Fortier argue that Our Lady of Guadalupe identifies herself with the supreme creative power, "the true God through whom one lives." Secondly, Guadalupe symbolizes a new creation, a new people revealing the power of God to reverse the shame of conquest. Thirdly, Guadalupe is a deep response to the need for dignity, a restoration of belief in all human beings created with inherent worth as those made in the image and likeness of the Creator. Fourthly, Guadalupe symbolizes a reversal of power. In the face of violence and injustice, such figures declare that God cares, and that God is faithful to God's people. In this passing on of cultural memory, the promises of God are recalled, and people experience hope. The image and memory of Our Lady of Guadalupe can be seen and can be touched.[57] She represents both a symbol of death and a symbol of resurrection. In her role as mother to Jesus Christ, she is a reminder that God was willing to take on human form to enter into a divine-human dialogue. Here is that very message of love, compassion, help, and protection as an affirmation of a particular people in salvation history. The iconography of Our Lady of Guadalupe carries eschatological hope, not only bringing healing but calling people to stand up for themselves. Such hope and healing drawn from within the culture of Mexican American communities has also become meaningful for other Latino/a/x communities across the United States:

---

55. Rodríguez and Fortier, *Cultural Memory*, 2.

56. See Aquino, "*Mestizaje*: The Latina/o Religious Imaginary," 283. For further reading, see Rodríguez, *Our Lady of Guadalupe*; Castillo, *Goddess of the Americas*; and Sison, *The Art of Indigenous Inculturation*.

57. Rodríguez and Fortier, *Cultural Memory*, 28.

> To put it succinctly, cultural memory continues to exist because it feeds a basic need for identity, salvation, hope and resistance to annihilation. The cultural memory of the Guadalupe event exists because there is a need for it. The story speaks of the restoration of human dignity in a voice once silenced and now restored. It speaks of restoration of a lost language and a way of perceiving the divine. It speaks of accessing lost symbols and transforming them in a new time. Ultimately, it speaks and continues to speak of a shared experience of a people—a people who suffer. The Guadalupe event resurrected the Nahuatl cultural memory at a time when everything in the world of the Nahuatl people had been destroyed. By activating their cultural memory, Our Lady of Guadalupe empowered and renewed the life of that people.[58]

Rodríguez and Fortier present six distinct aspects of cultural memory. *Identity* means that careful attention is paid to ethnicity. *Reconstruction* is the task of understanding the past to enable meaningful existence in the present. *Enculturation* is the practice of learning ethnic identity and passing this on from generation to generation. *Transmission* creates structures that convey this cultural memory through image, narrative, rituals, or syncretism modes. *Obligations* or moral imperatives, shaped by the values of a particular community's culture, ensure resilience. *Reflexivity* nurtures the conscious ability to "ground the everyday with the interpretation of the meta-memory."[59] Because many marginalized, struggling communities and "ethnic enclaves" are denied a place in the world, Rodríguez and Fortier conclude that to value and practice cultural memory establishes place, legitimacy, and voice.[60]

Place, legitimacy, and voice have theological significance and speak to the complexities explored through *mestizaje*, as it is conveyed in the work of Latino/a/x theologians. Christian theology, more broadly, is plurivocal and contextually complex. Latino/a/x theologies articulate this reality. As Rodríguez and Fortier affirm:

---

58. Rodríguez and Fortier, *Cultural Memory*, 23. For reflection on beauty expressed in such devotion, see García-Rivera, *The Community of the Beautiful*. Further helpful discussions can be found in Harris, *Carnival and Other Christian Festivals*; Romero, *Hispanic Devotional Piety*; Elizondo and Matovina, *Mestizo Worship*; Candelaria, *Popular Religion and Liberation*; and Aponte, *¡Santo!*.

59. Rodríguez and Fortier, *Cultural Memory*, 14.

60. Rodríguez and Fortier, *Cultural Memory*, 111.

Theologies are not pure, uncontaminated intellectual enterprises; they are influenced by a variety of interests. They cannot be intelligently studied apart from other writings coming out of the same tradition taken as a whole. To make complete sense, they have to be contextualized in the economic, social, political, and artistic life of the social groups from which they sprang.[61]

IMPLICATIONS FOR LATINO/A/X THEOLOGIES

While recognizing the foundational significance of *mestizaje* for the retelling of histories, the exploration of personal stories, and the nature of testimony as resistance, as noted earlier the concept of *mestizaje* can also be a contested category. Medina explains that

> the term evokes the long-standing history of five centuries of ethnocultural and racialized relations. It includes violent power moves and countermoves, the profound negotiations that resulted when radically different enthocultural backgrounds were thrown together by colonization, as well as how people come together now because of migration and physical attraction.[62]

Despite the contested and complicated nature of the term, Medina does not abandon *mestizaje*. He argues that to do so would be to abandon historical complexities and foundational issues in Latino/a/x theologies. He also resists replacing *mestizaje* with the postcolonial term "hybridity." For *mestizaje* has historical and experiential specificity that must not be elided. It is "the semantic, cultural, and critical analytical malleability of *mestizaje* that makes it at once a promising and risky category."[63] Medina maintains that other terms offered such as *ajiaco, sata/o,* and *nepantla* enrich the glossary to communicate particular senses of intermixture and in-betweenness but they fail to encompass the depth that *mestizaje* communicates.[64]

Concerns arise around the romanticization of *mestizaje*, the veiled racial hierarchies at work in the idea, the limited categories of identity provided within *mestizaje*, the disquiet around a single narrative of the

---

61. Rodríguez and Fortier, *Cultural Memory*, 29.
62. Medina, "Ethics, Theology and Mestizaje," 208.
63. Medina, "Ethics: The Latina/o Religious Imaginary," 208.
64. See Manuel A. Vásquez, "Rethinking *Mestizaje*," 129–57, and Miguel A. De La Torre, "Rethinking *Mulatez*," 158–75, in De La Torre and Espinosa, *Rethinking Latino(a) Religion and Identity*.

experience, and the potential dangers of a simplistic application of it. Medina admits that "*mestizaje* may be both our poison and our cure."[65] He expands further:

> We see this double function in *mestizaje*, in the multiple ways it was utilized and broadened by LatinaXo scholars and theologians. By adopting *mestizaje*, these scholars reinvented theological method, redrew the limits of theological sources, and reconfigured the theological task even while remaining within the structures of traditional theological frames. But they also reinscribed inherited forms of articulating community which discounted and excluded the multiple diverse ethnocultural presences in their communities.[66]

Jorge Aquino shares the concerns Medina articulates when he provides an overview of what he considers to be the three generations of thought regarding *mestizaje* in Latino/a/x theologies.[67] The first generation (1980–99), beginning with Elizondo, set the scene for ethno-racial thinking in the field. Arturo Bañuelas and the contributors to *Mestizo Christianity: Theology from the Latino Perspective* in 1995 provide a landmark volume. They relate theology to cultural identity, they offer a grounding methodology, and they explore key themes that include popular religiosity, voices of women, social ethics, spirituality, and ecumenism.[68] Ada María Isasi-Díaz is considered by Aquino to be a transitional figure between the first and second generations of reflection on *mestizaje*. For Isasi-Díaz *mestizaje* signifies the diversity of social, religious, and familial experiences for Latina women and compels a practical response of solidarity. Indigenous theologians, Afro-Latino/a/x theologians, and women theologians dispel any naïve notions of a harmonious and peaceful *mestizaje*. They unveil the ongoing and often violent struggles amid racial, ethnic, cultural, economic, and class realities. Despite the expansive nature of her concern, it should also be noted that Isasi-Díaz has faced some criticism. For some, she essentializes *mestizaje* to the extent that the understandings of *mestizaje* and *mulatez* are collapsed into a single category. Aquino warns that the constructive and creative potential of *mestizaje* may veil the risk that the

---

65. Medina, "Ethics, Theology and Mestizaje," 208.

66. Medina, "Ethics, Theology and Mestizaje," 208.

67. Aquino, "Mestizaje: The Latina/o Religious Imaginary," 286–91.

68. Helpful background on ecumenism can be found in Medina, "Latin America," 527–35.

concept could play "an exclusionary role in unwittingly racist politics" and reduce the acknowledgment of indigenous and African heritage.[69]

Aquino dates the second generation of theologians concerned with *mestizaje* to the early 2000s. Miguel De La Torre, Michelle Gonzalez, Manuel Vásquez, Rubén Rosario-Rodríguez, and Néstor Medina (already mentioned) offer a critical rethinking of *mestizaje*. They grapple with the tensions in a changing US American sociopolitical, ethnic, cultural, and economic landscape. They warn of the risks of racial nationalism, racial segregation, and racism in theology and provide nuanced engagement with *mestizaje*. A central concern is that simplistic notions of *mestizaje* can contribute to structures of oppressive power by preserving notions of whiteness at the top of a "racialized pyramid." In such a construction, people of lighter skin are portrayed as "purer" or "less mixed."[70]

> In privileging certain representations of the "*mestizo*" or "*mestiza*," a community may end up marginalizing other elements in the supposedly inclusive *mestiza* community. This dark side of *mestizaje* is a commonly experienced phenomenon of exclusion, one that falls with particular force on pure-blood indigenous and Afro-descended peoples. And while the discourse of *mestizaje* was widely embraced by US Latin@ theologians of Caribbean descent, this has taken place despite the fact that social movements self-identifying as "*mestizo*" are all but unknown in the Spanish Caribbean.[71]

As a third-generation contributor, Aquino recognizes that while *mestizaje* began as a "critical, anti-racist analytic," weak historical sensibility and theoretical apparatus has done little to esteem Africans and the Amerindians. He calls, therefore, for a more penetrating and prophetic critique that points to the common engine of capitalism. He writes, "For theology to confront the deeper challenges of *mestizaje*, it must confront the historical role that racism has played in the construction of the subaltern labor classes that are intrinsic to capitalism. This means examining the class structure of the United States in terms of the ever-changing tropes of racial identity and racial privilege."[72]

---

69. Aquino, "Mestizaje: The Latina/o Religious Imaginary," 290 and 291.
70. Medina, *Mestizaje*, 137.
71. Aquino, "Mestizaje: The Latina/o Religious Imaginary," 285.
72. Aquino, "Mestizaje: The Latina/o Religious Imaginary," 304.

Mestizaje

In conclusion, Medina proposes that a reconfiguration of *mestizaje* in future Latino/a/x theological thought is necessary. For *mestizaje* cannot signify a single experience of intermixture shared by all Latinos/as/xs. Rather it must reflect a plurality of experiences, histories, stories, and identities. This method of pluralizing *mestizaje* is an intellectual reorientation that can be a means for Latinos/as/xs to break away from "the cycle of colonialism and Europe's indelible mark of white intellectual frames."[73] Such pluralizing recognizes that no one category can encompass everyone's reality, identity, and experience and it recognizes the need for the ongoing narration of such reality, identity, and experience. A distinctive strength of *teología en conjunto* is the priority given to communities to tell their own stories of *mestizaje*. Communities will articulate the impact this has had on their faith, on their understanding of God, and on their interpretation of Scripture. Medina urges theologians to be attentive to Latinos/as/xs who are voicing the complex character of faith as experienced in the United States.

Harold Recinos is correct: "American society desperately needs to come to terms with its plural self."[74] Latino/a/x theologians demonstrate how to draw on multiple diverse religious experiences, symbols, and ethnic traditions. In Latino/a/x theologies, *people* are at the center of the theological task. Their concrete expressions of faith in God are a form of resistance to the assimilationist power of the dominant Anglo-culture in the US:

> *Mestizaje* continues to be a useful theological category which elucidates the divine dismantling of structures of racialized, cultural and religious power. At its best, it also constitutes an ethical praxis and ethos unwilling to succumb to easy recipes of "inclusion," "unity," and "hospitality." Instead, it is used to celebrate and wrestle with complex and fluid multicultural, multilingual, and multinational history and ancestral lines for which it is a cipher . . . [T]he adoption of *mestizaje* was and is itself an ethical choice. It is an attempt to actively reject social, cultural, and economic structures of discrimination, racism, and marginalization. It also rejects intellectual frames which undermine the rich cultural, contextual, and experiential component of lived faith experiences as part of human activity and struggles for justice.[75]

---

73. Medina, *Mestizaje*, 138.

74. Recinos, *Good News from the Barrio*, 6. See also chapter 5 and the discussion on the imperative for Christians to embrace cultural pluralism.

75. Medina, "Ethics, Theology and Mestizaje," 217.

When people are empowered to express and articulate the nuances of their experiences of *mestizaje*, and when this understanding of *mestizaje* is brought into dialogue with the concerns raised by second- and third-generation scholars, then such theology *en conjunto* opens up the possibility of encountering the divine in "refreshingly new ways." It is possible, also, that those who have experienced the complexities of *mestizaje* will find in God "a source of strength to resist oppressive forces."[76]

Daily life for Latino/a/x theologians and their communities is most often the multicultural, multilingual, multinational reality described by Medina and signified by the term *mestizaje*. The active rejection of discrimination and racism, and the active pursuit of justice are, therefore, central commitments for Latino/a/x theologies. From such commitments in the everyday, deeper understandings of God and faith arise. In the next chapter, then, we shall explore how Latino/a/x theologies are firmly rooted in *lo cotidiano*.

IN CONVERSATION

Yoimel González Hernández

Porque donde esté tu tesoro, allí estará también tu corazón.

MATEO 6:21

I am originally from Cuba where I was born, grew up, and began my theological studies. I am a proud Latino and Cuban American. I am a priest in the Episcopal Diocese of Washington, serving in St. Alban's, a multicultural parish in DC. I am also dean of the Diocesan Latino Deacon's School. I am passionate about multicultural ministries, the Bible, and formation in my ministry. I have enjoyed contributing to church publishing by proofreading and translating books into Spanish.

In my experience of life and ministry, it is vital to appreciate and understand complexity. *Mestizaje* is important for clergy and leaders to understand because if you want to plant or grow a church it will be about more than just inviting the Latino/a community into the building. If you are serious, and genuine, you need to look deeply into categories of culture, identity, race, and gender, as discussed in this chapter. *Mestizaje* is

---

76. Medina, *Mestizaje*, x.

a reminder to be attentive to mixed boundaries as opposed to the fixed boundaries of identity so often set by the US context. I see a temptation sometimes to focus on the Mexican American experience as the defining experience for all Latino/a communities. But we are not a monolith. Look for the "cultures" within what is categorized as "Latino/a" culture. Look for the complexities not only in your Spanish-language congregation but also within your Anglo congregations. In your community, in your classrooms, in your pews, there is much more cultural complexity than you imagine.

To establish meaningful pastoral relationships is to recognize and honor the cultural heritage and roots present in our communities and in our congregations. In my culture, we acknowledge the whole person, and we care about who they are and their story. This is intercultural competency—to acknowledge and to connect with one another. I have a family who faithfully attend our English-language service. If I want to create a meaningful pastoral relationship with them, I need to recognize that this family has a unique story. Their contribution and participation in church has a cultural component in the way they make connections and in the way I convey care about who they are. I need to acknowledge their whole reality. If I treat them as an Anglo family without honoring their Latin American cultural roots, they will not feel seen.

Some time back I was speaking at a formal black-tie event in the city. I saw this particular family from my parish at one of the tables during the event. We saw one another and acknowledged one another with a smile. In that moment of acknowledgment, I was not only their priest; I was part of their family. To acknowledge one another, even in such a formal setting, was a sign of relational depth. They said that they felt proud to see me there. In such ways, we are very close to our people.

Boundaries in an US American church, dominated by white people, can feel very fixed. These boundaries are more often closed beyond church, or beyond Sunday morning. The priest–people relationship in my heritage is more intimate. For those with Latin American heritage, there are expectations of connection and relationship with clergy and church leaders. We are offered invitations to celebrations like *quinceñeras*. We are welcomed into community, culture, and fellowship that is deeply rooted. Sometimes I have to eat food or accept drinks that I don't like at these events! If I don't accept the hospitality, I send a message that I don't like your culture, and deeper still, that I don't like you. In a similar way, the coffee and the meals so often served after church for the community in these cultures is often more important than the service itself in terms of connection and pastoral care.

I have families then who find meaning in the English-language services but in terms of a pastoral response, I need to be aware of their cultural heritage and identity. I need to be aware of the implications of inculturation. People may be speaking English or attending English-language events and services, but their hearts are so often speaking a different culture. We need to address these cultural components in our pastoral and community relationships. Our multicultural congregations have a capacity to live across cultures, to move competently between communities, and to flourish. This is a matter of survival and enables them to find meaning for their spiritual lives and their family lives. *Mestizaje* reminds us to let people name themselves, to tell their story, to describe themselves in their own terms. *Mestizaje* expresses the diversity of voices and identities. It speaks to the importance of the places people come from, their need for legitimacy and the significance of voice. This is part of the richness of this theologizing.

Mestizaje teaches us that histories and stories make meaning. So often this meaning is expressed in the popular practices of faith. I am reminded of my grandmother, who would pray for us at our bedsides when we were children if we were sick. Her prayers were so natural. They made meaning. They testified to the authenticity of the faith she was passing on. Being from Cuba, I don't come from a heritage that celebrates Our Lady of Guadalupe. Yet, I have learned so much from the aesthetic of devotion and celebration that is talked about in this chapter. In my experience we have such different perspectives on beauty. How Anglos often perceive this celebration is not how we perceive it. These places of religiosity in our background, often sustained by women like my grandmother, speak both to supernatural realities and our difficult experiences. The love, compassion, help, and protection experienced in Latino/a communities through devotion to Our Lady of Guadalupe, as mentioned in this chapter, testifies to divine beauty amid human histories. While some in the dominant culture may see popular practices as tacky or events as crowded, there is in fact a beauty being expressed that connects us to the divine. It is beauty in the face of the dryness of life. It is beauty in contrast to the world in which we find ourselves. Finding meaning in these realities is a means to survival. I appreciate that *mestizaje* acknowledges this and does not romanticize our heritage and histories.

On a practical level, the implications of the theology in this chapter speak to expectations of clergy and church leaders. It speaks to how we make meaningful connections in our communities and congregations. It reminds us of the importance of celebrations, family events, community activities, coffee, and meals together. For these moments point to heritages that honor such relationships and care. It may be the case that pastoral care is conducted in English, but for pastoral relationships to be meaningful, the cultural components need to be addressed and understood. Do not be isolated as clergy and leaders. Stay for coffee at the break. Stay for the meals after church. Accept the invitation to family occasions. This is so often where and how relationships are nurtured, and meaning is made across cultures.

I loved the introduction you wrote in this book, Sharon. I loved to hear your story. I love to tell my story. Our stories need to be personal. Our stories make meaning. We need to know who is speaking to us. We need to know the whole person to whom we are speaking.

FOUNDATIONAL READING

Gonzalez, Michelle A. "Are We All Mestizos?" In *Afro-Cuban Theology: Religion, Race, Culture and Identity*, 15–33. Gainesville: University Press of Florida, 2006.

Medina, Néstor. "(De)Ciphering *Mestizaje*: Encrypting Lived Faith." In *The Word Became Culture*, edited by Miguel H. Díaz, 71–92. Maryknoll, NY: Orbis, 2020.

———. "Ethics, Theology and Mestizaje." In *The Oxford Handbook of Latinx Christianities in the United States*, edited by Kristy Nabhan-Warren, 207–24. Oxford: Oxford University Press, 2022.

Rodríguez, Rubén Rosario. *Racism and God-Talk: A Latino/a Perspective*. New York: New York University Press, 2008.

FURTHER READING

Alcoff, Linda Martín. *Visible Identities: Race, Gender and the Self*. Oxford: Oxford University Press, 2006.

Aquino, Jorge A. "*Mestizaje*: The Latina/o Religious Imaginary in the North American Racial Crucible." In *The Wiley-Blackwell Companion to Latino/a Theology*, edited by Orlando Espín, 283–312. Chichester, UK: Wiley & Sons, 2015.

Delgadillo, Theresa. *Spiritual Mestizaje: Religion, Gender, Race and Nation in Chicana Narrative*. Durham, NC: Duke University Press, 2011.

Elizondo, Virgilio. *The Future Is Mestizo: Life Where Cultures Meet*. Oak Park, IL: Meyer-Stone, 1988.

García-Johnson, Oscar. *Mestizo/a Community of the Spirit: A Postmodern Latino/a Ecclesiology*. Eugene, OR: Pickwick, 2009.

González, Justo L. *The Mestizo Augustine: A Theologian between Two Cultures*. Downers Grove, IL: IVP Academic, 2016.

3

Lo Cotidiano

Understanding God and Community in the Every Day

> Some would like to dismiss this careful concern for identity and its construction from rich and varied pieces and experiences of life; but for Latin@' theologians it is an ethical responsibility to be self-aware, especially for those who seek to articulate, signify, and make meaning from within faith communities.[1]
>
> —Carmen Nanko-Fernández

TEOLOGÍA EN CONJUNTO (CHAPTER 1) is collaborative, constructive, and grounded in a community of voices, accountable to one another. In grappling with the concept of *mestizaje* (chapter 2), Latino/a/x theologies demonstrate the necessity of attending to a plurality of histories and stories that honor a diversity of cultures, traditions, and identities. To be grounded in community and to attend to the retelling of stories brings community life and lived experience into the very heart of theology. The place of *lo cotidiano* in Latino/a/x theologies makes clear that daily life, lived in communities who tell their own stories, is a privileged place for understanding God. For believers and communities bear testimony to faith in God in the everyday

---

1. Nanko-Fernández, "Lo Cotidiano as Locus Theologicus," 15–33, at 16. See also Nanko-Fernández, "Playing en los Márgenes," 93–114.

experiences and moments of life.² This testimony unveils histories of conquest and theologies of colonialism. This testimony includes critique of a nation that would claim to honor God while building systems of exclusion.³ As will be seen, this testimony bears witness to suffering, resilience, and growth in the service of renewed understandings of the life-giving God at work in the witness of Jesus Christ.⁴ In this chapter, the privileged place of *lo cotidiano* (the everyday) in Latino/a/x theologies will be outlined. How *lo cotidiano* relates to the experiences of conquest and to liberative understandings of God will be explored. Finally, the hope and promise of God incarnate in *lo cotidiano* will be considered.

PRIVILEGING *LO COTIDIANO*

Frameworks for thinking about God in dominant theologies are often constructed with histories and methods drawn from Western, male-dominated, white, European conceptions.⁵ Such frameworks tend to veil location and trade on abstractions.

> The dominant group ... being blind to its own privilege, has created epistemic hegemony: an epistemic hegemony that makes it possible for those in the dominant group to ignore or disavow their epistemic hegemony. Little or no effort has been made to facilitate and encourage the elaboration of knowledge that does not use the dominant episteme, that is, the dominant system of understanding and the ideas that emerge from the experience of the dominant group. The center continues to hold ... and, therefore, it continues to oppress.⁶

---

2. For a full discussion on the meaning of *lo cotidiano*, see "Lo Cotidiano," in Isasi-Díaz, *La Lucha Continues*, 91–106, at 95.

3. De La Torre, *Decolonizing Christianity*.

4. See, for example, Espinosa, Elizondo, and Miranda, *Latino Religions and Civic Activism*; De La Torre, *Trails of Hope and Terror*; Reyes, *Nobody Cries When We Die*, 138–80; Pineda-Madrid, foreword to Theuring, *Fragile Resurrection: Practicing Hope*, ix-xii; and Salvatierra and Wrencher, *Buried Seeds*.

5. Isasi-Díaz and Mendieta, *Decolonizing Epistemologies*, 6. See also Isasi-Díaz, "Mujerista Theology: A Challenge to Traditional Theology," in *Mujerista Theology*, 59–85; Barreto and Sirvent, *Decolonial Christianities*, 7–13; Kwok Pui-lan, introduction to Kwok, *Hope Abundant*, 1–16; Schroeder and Taylor, "Restore Me That Am Lost," introduction to *Voices Long Silenced*, xi-xiv.

6. Isasi-Díaz and Mendieta, *Decolonizing Epistemologies*, 3. See also chapter 2, "The Story of Puerto Rican Oppression and Resistance," in Delgado, *A Puerto Rican Decolonial*

A theology that is grounded in *lo cotidiano* confronts such oppression and provides not only a renewed understanding of God, but distinct categories of thought. Of course, Latino/a/x theologians do not simply jettison the so-called traditional understandings of God. Latino/a/x systematic theologians engage them fully. But they set out to do more than that and in the process they "inform and challenge the traditional normative discourse held to be a self-evident 'objective' orthodoxy against which everything else is measured."[7]

> Rereading the traditions is not necessarily a rejection of the essential claims of the tradition (although this may happen). Rereading means honestly stating what every generation does, that is, try to make sense of what has been passed on to it. Second, rereading the tradition means taking the tradition seriously. Third, rereading the tradition means a commitment to be contextual, without which any received tradition becomes lifeless and a museum piece.[8]

In a foundational text like the *Handbook of Latina/o Theologies* categories of revelation, Scripture, Christology, pneumatology, ecclesiology, sin, salvation, eschatology, and sacraments are at work. Yet, on the very cover of the book, dominance is challenged. For the male adjective *latino* is relativized to *latina/o* and the collection opens up to a plurality of *Latina/o Theologies*. This very title of the volume illustrates the awareness that *lo cotidiano* is experienced beyond a single narrative. The daily life of the communities represented by the contributors is intercultural, ecumenical, and interreligious with multiple understandings of identities and cultural locations.

In 2020, Aponte and De La Torre demonstrate what, in practice, rereading means. Cognizant of changing times, changing contexts, and changing relationships in *lo cotidiano*, they update *Introducing Latino/a Theologies* (first published in 2001) to *Introducing Latinx Theologies*. They acknowledge the twenty years of joys and struggles of genuine encounter and theological collaboration in real life, noting that

> *comunidad*/community is relational, with all the messiness of life that interpersonal interaction implies. When *comunidad* is evoked without relational commitments and the associated risks, then it can become highly wrought mythological rhetoric, self-deception,

---

Theology, 21–59.

7. Aponte and De La Torre, *Handbook of Latina/o Theologies*, 2.
8. Aponte and De La Torre, *Handbook of Latina/o Theologies*, 6.

and the basis of oppression of others. When commitment perseveres through disappointments, misunderstandings, and persecution . . . then the reality of *comunidad* is experienced and the potential for working toward the good and just is unlimited.[9]

The everyday, for Aponte and De La Torre, is about contexts and experiences that are always in flux. Oppressive structures remain but manifest themselves differently for each generation. If theology is closely bound to local faith communities, then as the circumstances surrounding Latinx peoples change, theological interpretations and responses must recognize and respond to those changes.[10] Such an ongoing process calls for discernment that connects crucial concepts articulated in the past with the realities contemporary communities are dealing with in anticipation of challenges to come.

> If theology is to remain an active, relevant component of the lives of Latinx peoples in the United States in order to illuminate how the Deity makes Godself known to a people, then religious views must be updated to include the changing ethos of Latinxs. If all religious perspectives and theologies serve a particular people for a specific moment in time, then religious perspectives and theologies must always be giving way to newer understandings that can help communities, specifically marginalized communities, to better understand the movement of God in their midst. . . . [E]ach new Latinx generation must wrestle with and define for themselves the complex intersectionality of their social location, their spirituality, and the overall society in which they find themselves.[11]

The Wiley-Blackwell Companion to Latino/a Theology, published in 2015 with a new edition forthcoming, demonstrates how this awareness of context as *lo cotidiano* is foundational in Latino/a/x theologies.[12] In the opening chapter of both editions, Carmen Nanko-Fernández grounds the reader in the principles of *"Lo cotidiano* as Locus Theologicus."[13] Beginning with the contexts of the everyday, of history and identity, of methods and of ecumenical encounters, scholars engage with the theological

---

9. Aponte and De La Torre, *Introducing Latinx*, xvi.
10. Aponte and De La Torre, *Introducing Latinx*, 150.
11. Aponte and De La Torre, *Introducing Latinx*, 150.
12. I am grateful to the volume editor Orlando Espín for a valuable conversation on April 14, 2023, in which he elaborated on the updates and revisions that will be seen in the forthcoming second edition of *The Wiley-Blackwell Companion to Latinox Theology*.
13. Nanko Fernández, "Lo Cotidiano," 15–33.

tradition inherited, and then make constructive moves beyond that tradition to respond theologically to the realities encountered by Latinos/as/xs in the United States.[14] Nanko-Fernández explains:

> For any number of Latin@' theologians lo cotidiano functions as locus theologicus. In other words, ordinary living is privileged as source, provides context, particularizes context, and marks the spaces and place(s) from which Latin@'s *do* theology. Such theologizing avoids abstraction and is admittedly polyvocal and fluid.[15]

Theology grounded in *lo cotidiano* challenges the tendency toward abstraction and resists any moves toward homogeneity. Complexity is honored in humility, and place is acknowledged in honesty. Generational considerations are taken into account. The breadth of religious expressions and ecumenical challenges are given attention. The joys and sorrows of shaping collaborative theologies, in light of contemporary concerns, are voiced. To affirm *lo cotidiano* as theological locus, then, requires naming situatedness and location. It requires a willingness to broaden the vision through interdisciplinary work. It requires a capacity to be self-aware and self-critical. Aponte and De La Torre, for example, openly examine Intra-Latinx oppression, the challenges presented by new "undocumented" immigrants, the considerations brought by postcolonial thought and the queering of Latinx religious thought. This is the current and changing "everyday" for Latino/a/x theologies.[16]

Lo cotidiano as theological site (and sight) evokes a sense of *convivencia*, living together. Indeed, Nanko-Fernández names this lived reality as source for divine revelation, content for theologizing, and place of theologizing:

> Lo cotidiano as lived in nuestros barrios and nuestros casas, en comunidades and familias, in the particular and in the local, from the underside, peripheries, and grassroots is a dynamic matrix of sin, grace, and ambiguity, of the perceived presence of God as well as of the perceived absence of the divine.[17]

---

14. See Espín, *The Wiley-Blackwell Companion*, vii–ix, for an overview of this approach. See also, for helpful examples of constructive turns, Martell-Otero, Maldonado Pérez, and Conde-Frazier, *Latina Evangélicas*, in particular "Dancing with the Wild Child: *Evangélicas* and the Holy Spirit," 14–32, and "The Trinity *es y son familia*," 52–72.

15. Nanko Fernández, "Lo Cotidiano," 15.

16. Aponte and De La Torre, *Introducing Latinx*, 149–84.

17. Nanko-Fernández, "Lo Cotidiano," 16.

Lo Cotidiano

Convivencia, living together, and by implication theologizing together, demands an ethical and a creative response.[18] Some have considered this awareness of relationships, influences, experiences, biases, and preferences to be an expectation only of so-called "contextual theologians." For Latino/a/x theologies, however, such self-awareness carries an ethical responsibility for all those theologizing. It is necessary for every theologian to acknowledge the interrelated and interdependent nature of theology and life.[19]

Centering *lo cotidiano* is to pay attention not only to particular personal stories and realities but it is also to pay attention to the histories and stories of how this experience of daily life came to be for a particular community. It is a commitment to intentional interdisciplinary and intercultural dialogue in order to comprehend the complexities that a Latino/a/x community may face on a daily basis. It is an ethical obligation to examine the roles that the church and the academy have played for good and for ill. To center *lo cotidiano* involves a careful listening to the testimony of communities that voice the injustices visited on their peoples across generations, in the name of God, by the church and by the academy. It means theological reflection on the everyday realities of generations past, reflection on everyday realities for contemporary communities, and it is anticipation on what the everyday might hold in the future:

> If future demographic forecasts are correct and Latinx peoples represent over a quarter of the U.S. population by 2040, their traditions and customs will move from the margins towards the mainstream. What we call Hispanic or Latinx religion, religiosity, and spirituality may cease to be an "interesting perspective" and become, instead, one of the central voices within North American civil and theological discourses. As Latinx peoples move from society's margins, their theologies—as a reflection of how they understand the Deity and identify meaning and purpose in life from their varied and intersectional spaces—can also be expected to change.[20]

---

18. See De Anda and Medina, "*Convivencias*: What Have We Learned?," 185–96.

19. Nanko-Fernández quotes the renowned biblical scholar Fernando Segovia here when he describes his life story as foundational to his work as a biblical scholar and theologian. Nanko-Fernández, "Lo Cotidiano," 17.

20. Aponte and De La Torre, *Introducing Latinx*, 186.

THE GOD OF CONQUEST AND *LO COTIDIANO*

Contemporary and future communities need to be cognizant of the part conquest played in determining *lo cotidiano* for past generations. As seen in chapter 2, the histories and the heritages of Latin America, the Caribbean, and North American Latino/a/x communities took place, for the vast majority of peoples, under brutal conquest and cruel oppression. This was their daily experience, and this was their *locus theologicus*.[21] If such an everyday is to be acknowledged as a source of divine revelation, then a key question comes into view—how can God be understood in the histories that shaped the Americas? Espín writes: "No one seems to have questioned the concept or images of God in the legitimization arguments employed to justify the colonial system. Indeed, the Christian God was the 'conqueror,' victorious over the traditional deities, as well as the mighty foundation for the authority and shape of colonial rule."[22]

The violence and the power of conquest was too often justified by the might of the Spanish God who defeated the gods of the peoples. This mighty God granted the *conquistadores* authority in God's name. In his study of the spiritual history of Spain and South America, John MacKay observes:

> Spain received a sense of mission.... She felt herself to be a "chosen vessel," the "arm of the Lord," to establish His righteousness upon earth.... Christianity during Spain's greatest age had a decided Old Testament flavour. God was above all else a God of battles. The favorite New Testament text seems to have been the words of Jesus: "I came not to send peace but a sword." The sword and the cross entered into partnership.[23]

Thus, the first encounter with Christianity was an encounter with a conquering God. On the island of Hispaniola (Haiti and the Dominican Republic today) on Friday 12 October 1492 Christopher Columbus took possession of the land in the name of this God.[24] González and González note that his attitude marked deeply held European views. These views were embodied time and again as multiple civilizations, and cultures were

---

21. See, for example, Delgado, *A Puerto Rican Decolonial Theology*.
22. Espín, *The Faith of the People*, 37.
23. McKay, *The Other Spanish Christ*, 26.
24. A thorough overview is provided in González and González, *Christianity in Latin America*, 1–38. See also Lynch, *New Worlds*, 1–28. See also Casimir, *The Haitians: A Decolonial History*, and Roorda, Derby, and González, *Dominican Republic Reader*.

encountered and decimated "from the nomadic peoples of the southern pampas and the North American plains to the high civilizations of the Andes (the Incas) and the central valley of Mexico (the Aztecs)."[25]

As the colonial administration was set up, so too was the systematic enslavement of African peoples and Amerindians in the *encomienda* system, beginning with Hispaniola and then expanding to Puerto Rico, Cuba, and across the Spanish colonies.[26] Spanish settlers were granted the legal right to extract forced labor and tribute from indigenous tribes. In return, the Europeans were to offer military protection for their laborers and provide religious guidance by encouraging conversion to Christianity and by funding parish priests. What kind of God was this? Concerns over the harshness and inhumanity of this *encomienda* system resulted in the creation of the Laws of Burgos in 1512 and the New Laws of 1542. This represented attempts to reconcile the system of labor with evangelization and codify a more "benevolent" approach.[27] What kind of God was being testified to in such apparent change?

As the slow and often violent *mestizaje* took place, God's authority and order were again used to justify racially based legal codes of privilege and discrimination:

> Christian society became more complex. Spanish America was being transformed by social change. By 1600 the first generation of American-born Spaniards had taken root and occupied dominant positions as landowners, manufacturers, merchants, and capitalists. Spanish American whites now called themselves *criollos* and were conscious of a difference between themselves and *peninsulares*. These attitudes were mirrored in the ranks of the clergy and religious orders. . . . Yet the American Church was now a multiracial Church, and as bishops looked out from their palaces and priests from their pulpits they saw a faithful composed not even

---

25. González and González, *Christianity in Latin America*, 13.

26. For an in-depth discussion, see González and González, *Christianity in Latin America*, 29–30, 31, 47; Lynch, *New Worlds*, 25–26, 33–35. The voices of the Dominican priests Antonio de Montesinos and Bartolomé de Las Casas in opposition to the *encomienda* system should be noted. See Rivera-Pagán, "The Political Praxis of Bartolomé de Las Casas," 131–45.

27. See Lynch, *New Worlds*, 34–35. It is also important to pay attention to the implications for enslaved African peoples who were often used to replace dwindling Indian populations in the labor system.

mainly of pure whites, but of mestizos, mulattos, zambos (black-Indian mixture), and other racial groups.[28]

As discussed in the previous chapter, it is necessary to continually hold in tension the complexities and the contradictions of this often violent, religio-cultural intermixing. Doing *teología en conjunto* is to name such oppression, marginalization, and exclusion. It is to ask particular questions about God. It is to offer understandings of God grounded in the experience of *lo cotidiano* of the underside. Thus, for Sixto Garcia, Latino/a/x theology emerging from such loci will be theodicy since "the belief in a God of justice and mercy in the Latino/a communities hinges on the community's awareness that in the midst of the tsunamis of racism, prejudice, and exclusion, God stands not on the side of the oppressor and the racist, but on their side."[29]

THEOLOGICAL COUNTER-TESTIMONY FROM *LO COTIDIANO*

Latino/a/x theologians reject the vanquishing God of conquest, enslavement, and destruction. Theological counter-testimony that bears witness to a different vision of God is required. Espín provides two grounding assertions that shape a Latino/a/x vision of the divine. Firstly, he asserts that it is necessary to look to God as revealed through the human experience of Jesus Christ. Secondly, he maintains it is essential to reflect on the experience of Jesus as the revelation of God. He affirms that contemporary scholarship widely agrees that Jesus of Nazareth centered his teaching around the theme of the reign of God in contrast to the dominant reign of empire. For Jesus, God is a compassionate God who intervenes in human life. The prophetic preaching and the just ministry of Jesus end in the apparent "failure" of the crucifixion. God in Christ, then, cares for humanity in compassionate historical intervention and this same God encounters failure, rejection, and destruction. To claim otherwise, Espín argues, is to sanitize or "colonize" the witness of Jesus.

In *lo cotidiano*, popular spiritualities express the faith and the understandings of God held by individuals, families, and communities who have not known power or authority or unmerited reward. Rather, like Jesus, and

---

28. Lynch, *New Worlds*, 38.
29. García, "Theodicy," 147.

like the generations living the daily reality of conquest and colonialization, these are people who, in the words of Espín, experience "vanquishment."[30] The revelation of God in Jesus does not, however, end in vanquishment. Jesus subverts the vision of lordship associated with conquest and colonialization. The self-giving witness of Christ directly challenges any construction of deity associated with imperial or colonial might and conquest. For in Christ:

> God encounters failure, rejection and the victimizing treatment given the politically and religiously insignificant. Belief in the resurrection necessarily implies the affirmation of the ultimate significance and success of Jesus's experience and the ultimate truthfulness of the perception of who God is as sensed through the experience of Jesus.[31]

Contemporary Latino/a/x communities see their daily experience reflected in the life and ministry of Christ. The person of Jesus Christ stands over and against the God of conquest. Testifying to the brutality experienced in conquest, and recognizing a similar brutality experienced by Jesus at the hands of empire provides a necessary counter-testimony. Espín demonstrates what can be learned when church history, church dogmatics, and systematic theology based on traditional understandings of God are challenged by those who experienced conquest and theological visions of God complicit in conquest.[32] Espín explores understandings of God brought to the New World and how such understandings of God were taught or conveyed by Catholic priests and teachers of that time. Given this historical work, he examines understandings of God developed over subsequent generations. He asks what kind of God is testified to in contemporary religious expression that is also, in some sense, in continuity with the counter-testimonies emerging from *lo cotidiano* shaped by colonialism?

The fundamental theological category of God was shaped by the everyday. Espín observes that understandings of the Christian God were enculturated through early portrayals of the divine from the late 1500s. Espín recognizes challenges of communication between the early Christian brothers and those they sought to evangelize. The faith being received was not necessarily being received in the ways the Europeans had intended.

---

30. For further insight beyond the field of theology, see Candelaria, *The Latino Christ*.
31. Espín, *The Faith of the People*, 15.
32. See in particular Agosto, "Revelation," 91–110, and Garcia, "The Latino/a Theology of God as the Future of Theodicy," 129–54.

For example, in enculturated images God was associated with feather-like emanations and rays of light that did not necessarily communicate divine oneness. Received understandings of God were being interpreted and reinterpreted by the peoples who were being taught about God and who had a particular experience of life at the hands of those who followed this God. Thus, interpretation and reinterpretation were not simply about cultural expression of Christian faith. It was about discerning a God associated not with the dominant cultures of Europe but a God on the side of the vanquished.[33] The peoples in the Americas were, in other words, constructing a form of resistant enculturation in dialogue with their own family and social experiences. This was distinct from a doctrine of God framed by conquest and domineering lordship.[34]

In 1992, many in Europe and in the Americas celebrated the five hundredth anniversary of the arrival of Columbus on the shores of the Caribbean. In contrast to such celebration, Elizondo marked the year by editing a volume called *Way of the Cross: The Passion of Christ in the Americas*.

> I think there is no better way to commemorate the past five hundred years than through the clash between the powers of darkness and the divine power of light on that first Good Friday. That is the supreme moment in revealing both the wickedness of sinful humanity and the power of God's love. On the cross Jesus was glorified! In the crucifixion of the Americans the new humanity, despised and rejected up to today, will be glorified. . . . Far from justifying the injustices of our world, the Way of the Cross from Jesus' day to our day continues to rip away the sacred curtain around what is deemed good, attractive, just and even holy in this world. It shows those things for what they really are: ugly, rotten, even Satanic. At the same time it reveals the ones who are truly God's good and holy ones: those who freely love to the point of giving their lives for others, even for people who betray, abandon, and condemn them to death. They are unjustly condemned to death but those who feel threatened by God's limitless love. The Way of the Cross continues to reveal the persistent malice of a world dominated by sin and the inexhaustible love of a God who seeks to save us in spite of ourselves.[35]

---

33. See Espín, "The God of the Vanquished: Foundations for a Latino Spirituality," in *The Faith of the People*.

34. For a series of meditations reflecting on the passion of Christ against the background of conquest, see Elizondo, *The Way of the Cross*.

35. Elizondo, *Way of the Cross*, xi–xiv.

Lo Cotidiano

For Espín, popular expressions of spirituality such as *Via Crucis* when the Latino/a/x community gathers during the reenactment of the Passion narrative to walk alongside Jesus, remain one major component of Latino/a/x cultural reality that have not been colonized by the Euro-American dominant culture.[36] As seen in the work of Rodríguez and Fortier in chapter 2, these expressions of faith are a testimony to resistance and survival. In this way, popular spiritualities and expressions of faith in Christ still act as indispensable and resistant bearers of values, traditions, and symbols among Latino/a/x communities in the United States. Goizueta, however, is careful when he writes:

> The source of strength and liberation is not the *Via Crucis* itself, not the values behind this religious ritual, but the God of Jesus Christ, the God whose Son suffered torture and crucifixion with us, and so continues today to suffer torture and crucifixion with us. . . . [W]hat empowers and liberates is not the *experience*, not the ritual or the performance or the symbols, not the meaning behind the symbols, but *God*, and not just any god but *this* God, the God whose Son conquers death by dying on the cross, the God who dies accompanied by his sorrowful mother.[37]

Espín maintains that the importance of cultural self-determination and self-preservation in such popular religiosity cannot be exaggerated. The God as expressed in the spiritualities of the people contrasts with and stands as counter-testimony to the God brought by the Spanish *conquistadores*. Espín turns to forms of both popular Catholicism and popular Protestantism to discern what is distinctive about these particular understandings of the God found through Jesus Christ. Woven into the fabric of *lo cotidiano*, God is present. God journeys with humanity. Now. In this moment. In this world of evil, violence, and hatred, God is *cariñoso* (the one who cares). In the face of evil, suffering, and exclusion, God is experienced as *amor* and God is *amoroso*. God is not distant and removed but rather is *Diosito*—the one who knows human beings intimately and can be known by them, as testified to in the incarnational love and ministry of Christ. Amid the uncertainty and fears of daily life, God is *el buen amigo*, the trusted and trustworthy friend.

Such themes are particularly at work in *coritos*, informal worship songs. Javier Alanís notes that "*coritos* are concrete vehicles that express

---

36. De La Torre, *Politics of Jesús*, 47.
37. Goizueta, *Christ Our Companion*, 92.

hope, faith, and empowerment rooted in Scripture and in lived experiences of the community. They allow the community the freedom to give voice to their understanding of God."[38] He affirms that Latino/a/x communities do not experience God as an "exclusive metaphysical reality" but rather as a "personal and communal God who journeys with the people in daily life."[39] Alanís maintains that Latinos/as/xs understand themselves to be created in the image and likeness of *Diosito*. Popular *coritos* capture this sense of the sacred Other who knows each one and calls each one by name. Amid radical diversity, all people are welcomed. No person is a stranger before *Diosito*, who is both *amigo* and *amante*, friend and beloved.[40] Expressions of faith in daily interactions convey these understandings of God in everyday life. Testimonies of God that powerfully counter the testimonies about God in dominant theologies are woven through families, homes, and communities. In the everyday, Latino/a/x theologies reveal a God of relationships within a community of relationships. With Espín, Loida Martell traces this cultural expression of relational faith—with a focus on one another rather than a focus on task or schedule—back to *lo cotidiano* of centuries past. "And so, you don't rush us," she explains, "We're not rushed to get some place. We're not attentive to time because we're attentive to relationships and to people. And that comes from our indigenous roots."[41]

When an understanding of *lo cotidiano* is privileged, attention is given not only to the moment Latino/a/x communities are in but how those communities came to be in this moment. The everyday of conquest and colonialism impacts the everyday of contemporary Latino/a/x communities in the United States. The everyday of ancestral communities with indigenous and African roots was often an experience of a dominant victor. Yet a counter-testimony of the living God incarnate in Christ and in *lo cotidiano* emerges.

38. Alanís, "God," 11–17 at 15.
39. Alanís, "God," 11.
40. Alanís, "God," 16.
41. Loida I. Martell, "Relationships," https://www.youtube.com/watch?v=aUqIwVuTJc4, accessed August 4, 2022.

CHRIST AND *LO COTIDIANO*

For Roberto Goizueta, to love God is to love Jesus of Nazareth. "God can no more be loved in the abstract than human beings can."[42] This focus on the person of Jesus, and on *lo cotidiano* as experienced and lived by Jesus, and how this speaks to the lived experience of Latino/a/x communities is foundational to Latino/a/x theological scholarship.[43] In *Galilean Journey*, published in 1983, Virgilio Elizondo demonstrates the relationship between Christ and context when he argues that "we will never truly appreciate the full meaning and significance of Jesus as savior and liberator unless we are keenly aware of our own historical and existential reality."[44] For Elizondo this contextual and Christological work is intricately connected to belonging and identities. He affirms that "we have a soul of our own. To be made in the image and likeness of God does *not* require the finishing touches of Anglo-American melting-pot assimilation."[45]

As a Galilean, Elizondo observes, Jesus would already have been considered among the ignorant, insignificant, and despised of the world. *Lo cotidiano* of Jesus, then, was a struggle against the power of the establishment. The community of Jesus experienced rejection in society, persevered to uphold their own identity, and strived to belong to a different kingdom. The pronunciation of his words and the very accent of Jesus meant he was mocked and laughed at by educated people.[46] As Maldonado shares in *Crossing Guadalupe Street*, Latinos/as/xs can empathize with how it feels when their place of family origin already marks them out as unacceptable to some or "less than" to others.[47] Elizondo notes that the seemingly ordinary yet charismatic and prophetic personality of Jesus, and also the personality of John the Baptist, were shocking and provocative to official Judaism. Jesus and John knew that confrontation with the structures of

---

42. Goizueta, *Caminemos con Jesús*, 196.

43. Neomi De Anda provides a further fifteen themes present in Latino/a/x christologies, including *mestizo* Jesus, *mulato* Jesus, walking with Jesus in the *barrio*, exiled and migrant Jesus, and relational Christology. See "Jesus the Christ," 155–72. See also Gonzalez, "Jesus," 17–24.

44. Elizondo, *Galilean*, 1.

45. Elizondo, *Galilean*, 2.

46. For an in-depth discussion on the religious and political context of Jesus, with further insights on the implications of *mestizaje* in the experience of Jesus, see Rodríguez, *Racism*, 176–211.

47. Maldonado, *Crossing*, 13.

power could lead to death. Yet this was the path Jesus walked to overcome evil.[48] In turn, disciples of Jesus must enter into a struggle against the root and causes of oppression for "it is not sufficient to do good and avoid evil: the disciple must do good and *struggle against* evil."[49] This message of Jesus was embodied in the new life of his followers who moved from marginalization to new creation. De La Torre explores the daily realities of Jesus as a colonized man, as one with a questionable genealogy, as a migrant, as one of the poor. He notes that "putting on flesh means Jesús is one of us, living with us in *lo cotidiano*."[50] Coined by Elizondo as the "Galilean principle," this focus underlines the fundamental dignity of those treated with indignity: for "what human beings reject, God chooses as his very own."[51] The everyday experienced by Jesus speaks deeply to the everyday experienced by contemporary Latino/a/x communities. Not only that, but the truths lived out by Jesus confront and stand in opposition to exclusion, exploitation, and evil. So too Latino/a/x theologies offer counter-testimony. Martell writes:

> For *evangélicas*, then, *Jesús sato* is not an appeasement for a wrathful God. Rather, he is the embodied evidence that God knows them and loves them, because, like them, God in Jesus has experienced and confronted the sinful structures of the world. They recognize that through Jesus, God understands what it means to be wounded and to suffer. Like them, *Jesús jíbaro* suffered death and abandonment. Like them, he was dehumanized, *tratado como un perro* (treated like a dog).... God faced the worst of the world, but was not overcome by the sin of the world. Suffering, abandonment, cruelty, and death do not have dominion. The resurrection is God's "No" to the rejection of the *satas* of this world. It is God's resounding "No" to death-dealing institutional forces, whether social, political, economic, religious, or familial, that destroy bodies and communities.... The resurrection is evidence that in the eyes of God, those whom the world rejects as *satas*, God considers *santas* (saints). They are not *sobraja*, persons of no worth, but children of the Living God.[52]

48. Matthew 16:21–28; Luke 22:39–44.
49. Elizondo, *Galilean*, 72.
50. De La Torre, *Politics of Jesús*, 45.
51. Elizondo, *Galilean*, 91.
52. Martell-Otero, "From *Satas* to *Santas*—*Sobrajas* No More," 232–42, at 236. *Evangélicas* refers to Latina Protestants. In Puerto Rico, *jíbaro* refers to a peasant, laborer, or rural worker. The term *sata* was originally slang for a mongrel dog in Puerto Rico and

Lo Cotidiano

In his work, *Caminemos con Jesús: Toward a Hispanic/Latino Theology of Accompaniment*, Goizueta expresses his gratitude to those Hispanic communities "whose lives have borne witness—and continue to bear witness—to the liberating power of a God who walks with us."[53] The hermeneutical circle at work for Goizueta moves from *experience* of social locations, histories, and communal relationships, to *analysis* of those experiences, to a *theology* grounded in the *praxis* of taking a preferential option for the faith of the poor as a process of accompaniment.[54]

> This Jesus is a concrete, historical, *flesh-and-blood* person, who, as such, is known in and through his *relationships*: he is the Son of God, son of Mary, our Lord, brother, friend and *compañero*.... Jesus reveals to us not only who God is (theology) but also who we are (anthropology).... This Jesus is the one who accompanies us in our suffering and whom we, in turn, accompany in his. This Jesus is, thus, the source of our community; we are one insofar as we all accompany Jesus together. This Jesus is, consequently, the source of those communal bonds which constitute us as persons and as a people, thereby giving us the strength to confront life's vicissitudes.[55]

In *Jesus Is My Uncle: Christology from a Hispanic Perspective*, Luis Pedraja also roots Christology in Latino/a/x communities with this particular emphasis on relationships and context:

> Jesus is my uncle. He also was my next-door neighbor, a boy in my school, and a deacon in my church. Jesus is not just the name of God's son, it is also the name of many of my friends, relatives and neighbors in the Hispanic community. When well-meaning missionaries periodically came by the house to ask us if we knew Jesus, they were surprised when we would answer, "Yes, he lives in that house across the street." Unlike my English-speaking friends who considered it sacrilegious to name someone after God's son,

---

has expanded to denote a person of low morals or indecent behavior. Martell writes, "I use *sata* as a theological metaphor to connote the existential pluriform and peripheral experience of Latinas" (235). *Sobraja* is a person at the bottom rung of society, a nobody, a leftover.

53. Goizueta, *Caminemos con Jesús*, ix.
54. Goizueta, *Caminemos con Jesús*, xi.
55. Goizueta, *Caminemos con Jesús*, 67.

Hispanics consider it an honor and a constant reminder of God's nearness.[56]

Speaking of Jesus as one who is near reflects the sense of intimacy and solidarity that is felt with Jesus, who knows what it is like to hope and love yet suffer and die. For "we felt he knew what it was like to be human, poor, and powerless. Jesus knew what it was like to be one of us."[57] This nearness of Jesus is expressed in experience, language, faith, ritual, symbol, sacred space, or through the experience of the indwelling of the Holy Spirit. Such expressions contextualize the deep reality that "our very existence is the fruit of God's love, creating us and bringing us to life."[58] Jesus remains present in the "flesh-and-blood reality" of those who serve in love. God's love, through Jesus, is encountered through incarnational, active expression in community.[59] Christology, then, must be grounded in the midst of human life: "Through countless ages, humanity has sought God in the heavens and high places. We expected to find God in the midst of awe-striking power and majesty, yet the Incarnation proved otherwise."[60] The incarnation then forces theology and Christology to turn toward humanity and see.[61] As Goizueta writes, "In Jesus Christ's own cry of abandonment, and his intractable hope against all hope, we hear our own cry and discover our own hope."[62]

56. Pedraja, *Jesus*.

57. Pedraja, *Jesus*, 28. See also the specific examples of suffering and death experienced by Latino/a/x communities listed in Nanko-Fernández, *Theologizing en Espanglish*, 56–57.

58. Pedraja, *Jesus*, 56.

59. For a diverse collection of essays demonstrating constructive theological engagement with the person of Jesus and significant examples from popular religion, see Recinos, and Magallanes, *Jesus in the Hispanic Community*. Miguel H. Díaz explores the significance of life-giving encounters in the life of Jesus and in experiences of Guadalupe which lead to hope-filled communal relationships in "The Word That Crosses: Life-Giving Encounters with the Markan Jesus and Guadalupe," in Díaz, *The Word Became Culture*, 1–24.

60. Pedraja, *Jesus*, 62.

61. Michael Lee proposes three insights that signal key changes in how Christology must be done in the future: (i) reconsidering the transmission of traditional sources, (ii) a focus on the ministry of Jesus, (iii) reorienting theology to allow the experience of the poor to serve as a lens to understand Jesus. See Lee, "A Way Forward for Latino/a Christology," 112–32. Miguel De La Torre presents a powerful biography of Jesus told from the margins, challenging his audience to see the oppression caused by the Jesus of dominant culture and the need to move the study of Jesús into the reality of the global present, see De La Torre, *Politics of Jesús*.

62. Goizueta, *Caminemos con Jesús*, 84. See also Nanko-Fernández, *Theologizing en Espanglish*, 56, and "Jesus or Jesús?," introduction to De La Torre, *Politics of Jesús*, 1–19.

Lo Cotidiano

The very language of *encarnación*, *carne*, and *carnal* in Spanish creates a more expansive understanding of the place of embodied love in the everyday realities of the flesh. Pedraja explores the implications of the translation of John 1:1 in Spanish "*En el principio era el Verbo.*" In Spanish, Jesus is not just God's "Word." Jesus is God's living and active "Verb." This principle leads Latino/a/x theologians to ask what Jesus specifically reveals about God's love, and how the humanity lived out by Jesus reveals what God is like. For Jesus, in word and in action, bears God's image on earth.[63] De La Torre explains, "Because Jesús experienced humanity in the flesh of the poor, the ethical is perceived not by ethereal philosophizing but by determined experiences. . . . I argue for an ethics rooted in the experiences of the marginalized, an experience that was, and continues to be, shared by God."[64] The incarnation and the Trinity exemplify the self-giving, sharing love of God and, notes Martell, point to incarnational justice.[65] Consequently, glimpses of the kingdom of God can be seen in the community of faith on earth imitating God's love as "being-for-others." For "as we enact God's love for humanity, we also embody the principles of Christology."[66]

The focus on *lo cotidiano* as a source in Latino/a/x theologies centers discipleship and faith, on relationship and community as loci for encountering and understanding God. Nanko-Fernández offers the reminder that "our God-talk, in our vernacular, requires us to read in nuanced ways the context and the contours of our situated humanity—in relationship. After all, theologies are the humble articulations of the perennially tongue-tied in the presence of mystery."[67] At the same time, *lo cotidiano* unveils the insufficiency of doctrine that might have had dogmatic coherency but was all but mute in the face of brutal violence and destruction.[68] Indeed, such theology could cast God as domineering power. A renewed emphasis on the person of Christ brings a renewed understanding of God grounded in the realities of the everyday of history and in the ever-changing realities

---

63. For a further discussion on the translation of Jesus as *Verbo*, see Pedraja, *Jesus*, 89–106.

64. De La Torre, *Politics of Jesús*, 82.

65. Martell-Otero, "From *Satas* to *Santas*," 241.

66. Pedraja, *Jesus*, 124. See also Bedford, *Who Was Jesus?*

67. See chapter 4, "The *Imago Dei* in the Vernacular," in Nanko-Fernández, *Theologizing en Espanglish*, 51–60, at 51.

68. Nanko-Fernández, *Theologizing en Espanglish*, 55. De La Torre also explores the Christological articulations within traditional Eurocentric Christian institutions that tends to justify and normalize oppression. See De La Torre, *Politics of Jesús*, 144–47.

of life in this time. No engagement with Latino/a/x theologies, therefore, would be complete without a careful examination of the understanding of the Holy Spirit at work in the church and in the world. We will explore this further in chapter 6.[69] In the meantime, we must explore the theme of *lo cotidiano* further.

We turn next to examine how faithful witness in *lo cotidiano* renews not only an understanding of God but also leads to renewed approaches to reading, interpreting, and preaching Scripture to a particular community of faith. This reading of Scripture *latinamente* illustrates the principles we have begun to explore already. For Scripture is to be read, interpreted, and preached collaboratively in community, in light of the histories and stories of those communities, and with a commitment to discern afresh the word of God for today. For as Martell maintains:

> When interwoven with prayers, *testimonios* (witnessing, or telling personal stories), and *coritos* (short refrains based on scriptural texts, or indigenously generated songs of lamentation and joy), biblical texts provide *evangélicas* with a sense of self and agency. These interweavings articulate an experiential faith, a historical encounter with God from the margins that narrates a holistic experience of salvation in the everyday.[70]

IN CONVERSATION

Omar Cisneros

> Being part of the life of our people, sharing their sufferings and joys, their concerns and their struggles, as well as the faith and hope that they live as a Christian community—all this is not a formality required if one is to do theology; it is a requirement for being a Christian.[71]
>
> GUSTAVO GUTIÉRREZ

I am a priest in the Diocese of Oklahoma and a Virginia Theological Seminary graduate. Growing up, I spent my summers in Mexico with my extended family, and this became foundational to my faith

---

69. For an exploration of the foundations of Spirit Christology, see Alfaro, *Divino Compañero*, and Benavides, "The Spirit," 25–32.

70. Martell-Ortero, "From *Satas* to *Santas*," 238.

71. Gutiérrez, *A Theology of Liberation*, xxxii.

Lo Cotidiano

and spiritual formation. Latino/a theologies are important to me because they are intrinsically a part of my faith and cultural context. Latino/a theologians have put into words what I have always felt and perceived about my own theological context. I am passionate about uplifting the different theologies of the margins and bringing them to the center of the contemporary theological discourse. Before becoming a priest, I spent almost ten years as a community organizer in various roles and causes. I enjoy spending time with my wife Karina, reading, cracking jokes, and practicing Judo and Jiu-Jitsu in my spare time.

It is easy to think about *lo cotidiano* as attempting to theologize mundane tasks. Some might consider it to be a looking toward the "folksy" aspects of Latin American spirituality and giving it a Western theological spin. We might go as far as to give theological meaning to the work of impoverished communities who are, in reality, simply trying to survive. We must take care that we do not move from seeking to honor the work of people in other cultures, into an attitude that may become patronizing. In reality, *lo cotidiano* is about understanding that the mystery of God can be found in daily life.

Latinos/as/xs, in particular, understand that the mystery of God can be found in daily life because, I believe, our communities were formed and continue to exist in chaos and strife. Latinos/as/xs from around the world are struggling to find their identity. Some look to our European, indigenous, and African ethnicities. Some look to our precolonial spiritualities. Some look to Christianity. The religious structures that dominated much of Latin America for centuries were ones in which you went to the parish church to be "sacramentalized and not evangelized." Therefore, the spiritualization or the meaning of faith had to be found beyond such structures, and it was found in the theologizing of *lo cotidiano*. This is clearly seen in the understanding of work as a blessing from God. A farmer's toiling in the fields is seen as a blessing because it means that the farmer fed not only his family but also countless members of his community. If you work in the city, it gives you an opportunity to be charitable through your work, which God would honor. If you give away some of your labor for free to help a stranger, for example, God will bless you and your work. In my experience, it is very common to pay a street vendor in Mexico and for that street vendor to take your money and then make a sign of the cross with it before putting it away. It is common for all types of stores to have shrines to particular saints, and for city buses to be marked with *oraciones populares*, prayers of everyday people. God is ever-present in the daily lives of workers. God is blessing their work, so they in turn may be a blessing to others.

Lo cotidiano brings joy in everyday life because tasks that might seem repetitive and dry are transformed by this understanding into a gift from God, a gift to God and a gift to your neighbor. It gives meaning to hard but critical tasks. It transforms seemingly insignificant or unseen tasks into hidden blessings that are, in fact, undertakings on behalf of the kingdom of God. Seeing your role in life as a blessing and a blessing to others makes *lo cotidiano* become spiritually powerful: how a shoe shiner tells you a story or joke, or the way a local butcher takes a few moments to inquire about your family even if he has never met them. There is joy in everyday tasks and everyday encounters because they are gifts from God and because the Spirit of God gives them special significance. This redefines daily moments and mundane tasks, making them powerful catalysts of transformation. In busy cities and vast fields, we catch glimpses of the kingdom of God breaking in.

When I think about theologizing *lo cotidiano* I am reminded of the story of Jesus and the Samaritan women at the well in John 4. Drawing water from a well is just about one of the most tedious jobs one can do. I know because I have done it. However, in this rather mundane act, the Samaritan woman meets Jesus. In this boring chore, she encounters the person of Jesus Christ, she understands who Jesus is, and she learns what Jesus means for her life. We, too, come back to the well again in the moments of everyday life as we understand and learn more about God. It is when we come to the "wells of our lives" that we encounter Jesus Christ. This is the interweaving of the world with the church. It is a spiritually profound way to see the world, for in this way we connect every small fiber of God to the moments, tasks, and obligations of every day.

In my personal experience, much of the theologizing in *lo cotidiano* is led by women and this is a noteworthy feature. However, much of Latin American culture and heritage is structured within chauvinistic frameworks and male-dominated hierarchies. Women come together to make sense of what is going on in their families and in their communities. They gather to share how God is responding to their needs and the needs of their loved ones. Women often organize wakes or social gatherings of family and loved ones to watch over the body of a deceased person, for example. The minister or priest will show up and play his role, but it is the women who plan, organize, and lead this function. It is the women who attempt to find meaning in the death of a loved one. It is the women who feed their guests and host those gathered. It is the women who take their responsibility as heads of the household seriously and lead their community in love and in mourning. From the outside, some may see this as simply fulfilling a gender role. But within the structures of a male-dominated culture, these women offer a powerful witness to faith in *lo cotidiano*.

Centering *lo cotidiano* forces us to reflect on God closely and personally. In theology, there is a tendency to want to wrestle with God at a distance, to grapple with God in the abstract, to deconstruct God. *Lo cotidiano*, in contrast, is about experiencing God in new and refreshing ways *todos los dias*. Having conversations about God in the experiences of daily life is, in fact, much more complicated than first imagined. Having conversations about God in the experiences of daily life forces us to search for God in and through our everyday moments. In the parish, for example, when we encounter communities from El Salvador we need to listen to their theologizing of their experiences. For their stories and their witness teach us about central questions of the Christian faith. It is imperative that we listen. I have learned to understand more about the reign of God through the testimonies of people who risked it all to be in this country. Their experiences and these realities demand a different way of doing theology.

Centering *lo cotidiano* helps to peel back the layers of life and to find meaning in what is often chaotic, senseless, and without a beginning or end. Centering *lo cotidiano* gives value and meaning to work and play. It allows God to enter, and to be present in all aspects of our lives. God is not relegated to be present only in the spaces designated for "worship." *Lo cotidiano* makes sense of what feels like a cruel and unjust world by bringing together the shattered pieces of our histories and asking where the Spirit of God is at work in a way that heals. A theology that honors *lo cotidiano*, for me, is a theology that looks outward and demonstrates community awareness.

In my experience, this is theology that exemplifies the priesthood of all believers in action. In this sense the word "priest" becomes a verb. In *lo cotidiano* there are no "big" questions but only questions that need a theological response. For in these seemingly insignificant moments, in these seemingly insignificant places, we proclaim the Risen Christ. These are pastoral moments where God is revealed in the everyday. To understand the theological significance of *lo cotidiano*, then, is to understand the theological and pastoral significance of life at a local level. This means we need to become good at listening to people when they tell their stories. This means we need to be good at community organizing. This means we need to help our congregations and communities search for their "why" as they find reason in life, and as they organize for a better, just future. *Lo cotidiano* offers us opportunities to catch glimpses of the kingdom of God and the Spirit of God at work. I have often noticed that those with privilege, those who are educated, those who are learned, those who are wealthy miss the significance of the Spirit of God moving among us at the local level. A commitment to *lo cotidiano* is a commitment to remedy this. For *lo cotidiano* forces us to think of the reign of God not as an abstraction but as a slow-burning event that is present in this moment, in our daily lives.

FOUNDATIONAL READING

Alanís, Javier. "God." In *Handbook of Latina/o Theologies*, edited by Edwin David Aponte and Miguel A. De La Torre, 11–17. St. Louis: Chalice, 2006.

De Anda, Neomi. "Jesus the Christ." In *The Wiley-Blackwell Companion to Latino/a Theology*, edited by Orlando Espín, 155–72. Chichester, UK: Wiley-Blackwell, 2015.

De La Torre, Miguel. *The Politics of Jesús: A Hispanic Political Theology*. Lanham, MD: Rowman & Littlefield, 2015.

Martell-Otero, Loida I. "From *Satas* to *Santas—Sobrajas* No More: Salvation in the Spaces of the Everyday." In *The Strength of Her Witness: Jesus Christ in the Global Voices of Women*, edited by Elizabeth Johnson, 232–42. Maryknoll, NY: Orbis, 2016.

Nanko-Fernández, Carmen. "Lo Cotidiano as Locus Theologicus." In *The Wiley-Blackwell Companion to Latino/a Theology*, edited by Orlando Espín, 15–33. Chichester, UK: Wiley-Blackwell, 2015.

FURTHER READING

Alfaro, Sammy. *Divino Compañero: Toward a Hispanic Pentecostal Christology*. Eugene, OR: Pickwick, 2010.

Delgado, Teresa. *A Puerto Rican Decolonial Theology: Prophesy Freedom*. New York: Palgrave Macmillan, 2017.

Goizueta, Roberto S. *Christ Our Companion: Toward a Theological Aesthetics of Liberation*. Maryknoll, NY: Orbis, 2009.

Isasi-Díaz, Ada María. *La Lucha Continues: Mujerista Theology*. Maryknoll, NY: Orbis, 2004.

Recinos, Harold J., and Hugo Magallanes, eds. *Jesus in the Hispanic Community: Images of Christ from Theology to Popular Religion*. Louisville: Westminster John Knox, 2009.

4

Santa Biblia

Interpreting Scripture *latinamente*

> At a time when representing difference (i.e. a Latino/a identity) and different ways of being (ontology) and knowing (epistemology) are coming under attack as belonging to specific groups or as purely biased in their interpretations, the task of understanding as many types of cultural biblical interpretation as possible is important. This is not to say that Latino/a biblical interpretation is without its limitations but listening to the demands of the present as well as the voice of the text can bring about transformation and liberation to all God's people in the present.[1]
> —Francisco Lozada Jr.

TEOLOGÍA EN CONJUNTO (CHAPTER 1) is a commitment to a collaborative, constructive, and communitarian approach in theology. *Mestizaje* (chapter 2) testifies to the complexities of Latino/a/x communities and their intermixing pluralities of histories, stories, cultures, traditions, and identities. Latino/a/x theologians privilege *lo cotidiano* (chapter 3) in their search to understand God, through relationship in community and through the presence of God in the experiences of everyday life. Such "demands of the present," as Francisco Lozada articulates, require serious attention

1. Lozada, *Toward a Latino/a Biblical Interpretation*, 18.

and authentic dialogue with the voice of Scripture. For a central act of a witnessing Christian community is reading, interpreting, and hearing the Bible faithfully proclaimed. To read, interpret, and communicate Scripture *latinamente* is a particular homiletical and hermeneutical approach characterized by collaboration that honors complexity in community and centers life on the margins. To center the experiences of communities on the margins demands an awareness of the horrors that communities face. Conde-Frazier notes that given what may often be considered "biblical horrors" actually remain ever present in the contemporary world means that the "challenge of the text becomes the imperative for readers today. To respond to the imperative is to become a skilled interpreter of the text."[2] In short, in Latino/a/x theologies, reading Scripture *latinamente* is reading for justice. In this chapter, we will explore what it means to interpret Scripture *latinamente*, how Scripture might be preached and heard *latinamente*, and finally, why complexity not only describes contexts but also defines an ongoing hermeneutical imperative for the sake of doing justice *latinamente*.

INTERPRETING SCRIPTURE *LATINAMENTE*

Early published biblical scholarship through a Latino/a/x lens is often located in collaborative, edited volumes that do not exist simply to resource academic study.[3] Latino/a/x theologians, biblical scholars, and preachers not only interpret the text for those in the academy but also for the growth of the church and for the good of the whole community. Furthermore, to interpret Scripture *latinamente* is not only for the nurture of Latino/a/x churches and communities but is for the benefit of the whole church and the good of the wider human community.[4] Lozada is particularly careful to acknowledge the complexities of the question of who is interpreting Scripture *latinamente*.[5]

---

2. Conde-Frazier, "Evangélicas Reading Scriptures: Readings from within and beyond the Tradition," in Martell-Otero, Maldonado Pérez, and Conde-Frazier, *Evangélicas*, 82.

3. See, for example, González, "Visions of the Word," in González, *Out of Every Tribe and Nation*, 38–60; Segovia, "Hispanic American Theology and the Bible," in Goizueta, *We Are a People!*, 21–50; García, "Sources and Loci of Hispanic Theology," in Bañuelas, *Mestizo Christianity*, 104–24; Jiménez, "The Bible: A Hispanic Perspective," in Rodríguez, and Martell-Otero, *Teología en Conjunto*, 66–79.

4. González, *Santa Biblia*, 19. See also chapter 5, "Reading the Bible in Spanish," in González, *Mañana*, 75–88.

5. Lozada, *Toward a Latino/a Biblical Interpretation*, 28–29.

For Lozada, Latino/a/x biblical interpretation is an integral part of the history of biblical interpretation. As Latino/a/x interpretation it presupposes the history and tradition of biblical interpretation, reacts contextually to this history and tradition, and builds upon and moves beyond previous interpretations.[6] He is convinced that studying Latino/a/x biblical hermeneutics or interpretation, and by implication Latino/a/x theologies, leads to a fuller vision of Latino/a/x communities, and will lead to a better understanding of the character of Latino/a/x interpretation. Without taking this critical and constructive agenda into account, an understanding of interpreting Scripture *lantinamente* is incomplete, and without taking into account Latino/a/x interpretations of Scripture an understanding of Christian biblical interpretation is incomplete.[7]

Latino/a/x approaches to interpretation, argues Lozada, nurture a much-needed open-mindedness and receptiveness toward difference in a time when difference is "feared and rebuked."[8] Attentiveness to minoritized hermeneutics nurtures respect and understanding for "the other" without undermining one's convictions in how the biblical traditions are read and received. Interpreting Scripture *latinamente* is a call to live creatively with difference.[9] Two principles begin to provide an understanding of a Latino/a/x theological approach to scriptural interpretation. First, Lozada emphasizes the foregrounding of Latino/a/x identities. To comprehend the histories, the diversities (see chapter 2), the stories, and the testimonies of communities (see chapter 3) is essential to biblical interpretation that prioritizes context. Second, Lozada traces the transformation of Latino/a/x communities. In more recent histories, and in some contexts, Latino/a/x communities have experienced transformation away from previous forms of marginality in the political sphere toward greater degrees of representation or belongingness in various mainstream institutions. Such transformation includes changes in religious communities and institutions (see chapter 6).[10]

---

6. For a Protestant perspective, see Conde-Frazier, "Evangélicas Reading Scriptures: Readings from within and beyond the Tradition," in Martell-Otero, Maldonado Pérez and Conde-Frazier, *Evangélicas*, 73–89.

7. It is also important to be attentive to the perspective brought by Michelle A. Gonzalez Maldonado when she addresses the question "Biblical Silence: Where Is the Bible in Latino/a Theology?," in Lozada and Segovia, *Latino/a Theology and the Bible*, 73–88.

8. Lozada, *Toward a Latino/a Biblical Interpretation*, 2.

9. Lozada, *Toward a Latino/a Biblical Interpretation*, 2.

10. See Lozada, *Toward a Latino/a Biblical Interpretation*, 22.

For Jean-Pierre Ruiz, those who engage in biblical interpretation *latinamente* are "born and reborn as a matter of deliberately claiming their particularity."[11] To illustrate that Latino/a/x biblical scholars are "*both* born and made" he traces his own personal journey and the journey of renowned Cuban American biblical scholar Fernando Segovia.[12] Ruiz describes the years that it took for Segovia to become acutely conscious of "the complex and pluriform minorizations" that he and other Latinos/as/xs would face as biblical scholars:

> It came . . . from people who thought that "someone like me" shouldn't waste my time bothering with academic pursuits since—according to them—what I really needed to do was to work directly with "my people." Another sort of minorization came from the gatekeepers of the academy, who actively patrolled the borders of biblical studies to keep the discipline safe from the incursions of those who would threaten the supposed objectivity of its historical and literary critical analyses. Woe to the flesh-and-blood, socially located readers of the Bible whose real-world concerns are far from the artificial cares of the implied reader who bleeds only the uncoagulated jargon of the literary critic.[13]

Segovia argues that behind any exercise in minority criticism—and minority biblical criticism, in particular—lies a desire for self-assertion and self-introjection in the face of marginalization and erasure. When Segovia uses the term *minority*, he explains that he means *minoritized*. That is to say, Latino/a/x scholars are not only a minority voice but also that the dominant voices set out intentionally to keep it this way. Segovia expresses the desire "to break through the gaze-patrol of dominant culture and society," interrupting such dialectics of minoritization by transgressing established and "establishment" ways of thinking.[14] In light of his lifetime in biblical scholarship, Segovia is well placed to provide an astute analysis of power relations, the process of minorization, and the work toward hermeneutical transformation.[15] Given the struggle toward transformation, waged over

---

11. Ruiz, "The Bible and Latino/a Theology," 118.
12. Ruiz, "The Bible and Latino/a Theology," 111–28.
13. Ruiz, "The Bible and Latino/a Theology," 115.
14. Segovia, introduction to Lozada and Segovia, *Latino/a Biblical Hermeneutics*, 3.
15. See Liew and Segovia, *Reading Biblical Texts Together*. This volume is dedicated to David Sánchez and his essay "'It Is No Longer Because of Your Words . . .': Interrogating John 4 through the Lens of *Malinchismo* and the Vanquished Woman Motif" is included, 309–22.

decades by scholars like Segovia, Ruiz can propose three defining elements for interpreting the Bible *latinamente*.[16] Firstly, it is *collaborative*. Secondly, it is *connected*. Thirdly, it is *committed*.

Collaborative interpretation

Collaborative interpretation, exhibited through *teología en conjunto*, resists individualism and centers biblical interpretation on the "*us*" of Latino/a/x community. This is the "community of interpretation" for Latino/a/x biblical studies.[17] Sammy Alfaro identifies the faith-community context in which Scripture is being interpreted and he is careful to articulate how, in his experience, Pentecostal congregations approach and employ the Bible.[18] In the local church, and across church traditions, the collaborative emphasis espoused by Latino/a/x biblical scholars is put into practice. Conde-Frazier also observes:

> This reflects how the Bible is read from lived reality, with the purpose of interpreting and finding both meaning and God in the midst of it. Finding God is important, not because God is considered absent, but because God is the refuge of the poor when evildoers frustrate their plans (Ps. 14:6), and God has not despised or disdained the suffering of the afflicted or hidden his face from them but has listened to their cry (Ps. 22:24). Strength is a part of empowerment but does not fully define it.[19]

She provides a poignant example of how a group of Latina women in the bathroom of a Pentecostal church in New England privately reread and respond to the narrative of the woman with the issue of blood in Mark 5. In their commitment to one another, that creates a space in which it is safe to break silence on sensitive issues, they are able to approach the text through the lens of sexual assault. Personal truths are shared, and healing

---

16. For further discussion, see Ruiz, "Beyond Borders and Boundaries," 25–48, at 27–35.

17. Garcia-Treto, "Reading the Hyphens: An Emerging Biblical Hermeneutics for Latino/Hispanic U.S. Protestants," in Maldonado, *Protestantes/Protestants*, 161, 164. See also the intentionally collaborative volume Bailey, Liew, and Segovia, *They Were All Together in One Place*, written by African American, Asian American, and Latino/a/x scholars.

18. Alfaro, "Reading and Hearing Scripture in the Latina/o Pentecostal Community," 34–38.

19. Conde-Frazier, "Evangélicas Reading Scriptures," 78.

comes in response to the power of Scripture interpreted from lived reality. Through their communal approach and narrative, "La verdad trae justicia. Truth brings justice."[20]

In her work, Isasi-Díaz too recognizes that for many Hispanic women it is "women's experience and our struggle for survival, not the Bible, [that] are the source of our theology and the starting point for how we should interpret, appropriate, and use the Bible."[21] She proposes three fundamental aspects of *mujerista* biblical interpretation—(i) women engage Scripture in response to their own need; (ii) the struggle for liberation is the critical, hermeneutical lens; and (iii) interpretation by women for women in the service of liberation is the outcome always in view. She writes, "It is not that the integrity of the text is not important; it is that the need to survive takes precedence."[22] While coming from different wings of the church, both Conde-Frazier and Isasi-Díaz—in giving voice to Latina women's struggles, Latina women's biblical stories, and Latina women's lives—demonstrate the collaborative principle that Ruiz names.

> The study and interpretation of Scripture by Hispanic women is a revolutionary act for neither our churches nor the academy consider us capable of doing it, consider that we have something to contribute to this field. Therefore, doing biblical exegesis is a way of claiming our right to think, to know critically—it is an element in our self-definition. We must also insist on theology, biblical exegesis included, as a communal task. The values and needs of the community must play a central role in *mujerista* biblical hermeneutics, and the only way to make sure this is so is by doing theology as a community of faith and struggle.[23]

Connected interpretation

To say that Latino/a/x biblical interpretation is *connected* is to recognize and demonstrate that *la vida cotidiana* (daily lived experience as seen in

---

20. Conde-Frazier, "Evangélicas Reading Scriptures," 88. For the story and full interpretation, see Elizabeth Conde-Frazier, "Latina Women and Immigration." Martell too reflects on the suffering and abuse of Latina women at the hands of doctors and a health service that has often been racist and culturally insensitive. See Martell, "Reading," 115.

21. Isasi-Díaz, *Mujerista Theology*, 149.

22. Isasi-Díaz, *Mujerista Theology*, 152.

23. Isasi-Díaz, *Mujerista Theology*, 154–55.

chapter 3) is a point of departure for interpretation or a constant focus or a guiding principle. The themes that shape and form Latino/a/x hermeneutics, therefore, include the sights and sounds of *fiesta*, the celebration of all things *santo*, the heartbeat of *familia*, and the concerns of *conviviencia* (living together) as active communities in the *barrio*. As discussed earlier, religiosity is most often expressed in Latino/a/x communities through customs and traditions. This "grassroots mixed methodology" of ritual and reading is explored further, for example, in the work of David Sánchez, who connects resistance in the book of Revelation with the powerful, imaginative depictions of the Virgin of Guadalupe found in the murals of East Los Angeles.[24] Sánchez does this correlating work by offering cross-cultural analysis of imperial myths. He leads his readers from the island of Patmos in the first century, where John inverts Roman imperial mythology in Revelation 12, to Mexico in the seventeenth century, where indigenous peoples appropriate Spanish symbol and myth, to the inspirational figure of the Virgin of Guadalupe for contemporary Chicana resistance movements.

Martell studies connectedness in interpreting Scripture *latinamente* through the work of Latina *evangélicas* and their reading of the Bible in relation to *testimonios* and *coritos*. This communal storytelling in word and song "reveal that for them Scripture is not simply a book to be read, but a living testament that is to be interpreted and incorporated into their daily lives. It is an incarnational, pneumatological, and praxis-centered reading."[25] Martell argues that it is in these communal narratives that God is encountered. God speaks through Scripture. At the same time, Scripture is interrogated by the concerns that arise in daily life from the perspective of social location and particular experience. Martell confronts what she refers to as "normatizing myths" used to define often nameless and powerless people in the biblical text. She coins this phrase to point to the stereotypes created by those with privilege and power who articulate "often-coded public discourses about those conceived as 'other'" in Scripture. With these myths in place the text can be interpreted in the service of those with excessive privilege and power. The Samaritan woman in the Johannine account (John 4:4–42), for example, is often portrayed as a woman who has prostituted herself many times over rather than a woman who has been exploited

---

24. Sánchez, *From Patmos to the Barrio*. See also Sánchez, "Interpretive World Making," 246–62. For further discussion on the book of Revelation and apocalyptic legacy, see Sánchez, "The Apocalyptic Legacy of Early Christianity," 63–82.

25. Martell, "Reading against the Grain," 103–26, at 114.

and abused. The woman who enters the house of Simon and weeps tears on the feet of Jesus (Luke 7:36–50) is most often assumed to be a sinner and prostitute. "Reading against the grain," argues Martell, "from the perspective of the marginalized, the poor, the voiceless; of women treated as *sobrajas*, discounted and invisible—provides a hermeneutic of suspicion against such interpretation."[26] For Latinas resonate with these stories of being maligned, stereotyped, and ridiculed. Martell gives voice to the subversive reversal of a Jesus who upholds the dignity and worth of the woman in contrast to the unworthy actions of Simon and those who think they are superior because of class or gender (Luke 7:44–47). For Martell, upholding the women's dignity in the text and in interpretation is transformative for Latinas. It speaks hope and it speaks shalom to those who have walked in the shoes of this woman. It speaks of a hermeneutical connectedness to daily life in today's world. "Thus, the communal narratives of Scripture, testimonio, and coritos bring to light the falsehood of normatizing myths and assert the humanity of the dehumanized."[27]

Committed interpretation

The third concept of *commitment* that Ruiz identifies in Latino/a/x biblical interpretation is clear in Martell's work. For her hermeneutics exhibit "the way in which the interpretive task is driven, animated, and nourished by the ethical imperative to side with those brothers and sisters in the human family who have been shoved to the very edges of society, often to the very edge of survival."[28] That such a reading is contextual or particular does not mean, however, that it is limited. De La Torre and Aponte write:

> [T]he biblical text is to be read from the margins—that is, from the perspective of the disenfranchised and dispossessed—using John 10:10 ("I come that they may have life, and have it abundantly") as the primary lens for interpretation. Simply stated, if a textual interpretation prevents the experience of abundant life by any segment of the population—or worse, if it brings death—then said interpretation is anti-gospel and anti-Christ. Biblical interpretations

---

26. Martell, "Reading against the Grain," 117.
27. Martell, "Reading against the Grain," 117.
28. Ruiz, "The Bible and Latino/a Theology," 117.

closer to the meaning of the text are those that enhance and expand the abundant life for all of God's creation.[29]

To read Scripture *latinamente*, then, is to interpret the text embodied, contextualized, and socially located for the sake of God's church and God's world. In this, Ruiz recognizes Latino/a/x biblical interpretation's debt to Latin American theologies of liberation, embracing as they do "the important alliance . . . between epistemology and ethics, between knowing and doing, between interpretation and the effects of interpretation."[30] Scripture and its interpretation cannot be separated from *lo cotidiano* and the witness to God lived out faithfully in the everyday for the sake of those denied life in all its fullness.[31]

In the contemporary United States, as will be discussed further in chapter 6, Latino/a/x theologies pursue justice on many fronts where life in all its fullness is denied. This pursuit of justice is deeply rooted in an interpretation of Scripture that anticipates ethical responsibility and action. In *Reading from the Edges: The Bible and People on the Move*, Ruiz explores public theology and the case of US immigration reform. He provides a rereading of the encounter between the "Migrant Jesus" and the Greek Syrophoenician woman (Mark 7:24–30) in conversation with Sharon Ringe. Ringe's work articulates the necessity of unmasking crucial issues of gender, ethnicity, language, and harmful views of "the other." In response, Ruiz suggests a move away from the academic practice of private Scripture-reading. He calls for a return to the practice of reading *en voz alta*. This "reading aloud," together, and across difference requires open minds, active listening, and respectful awareness. To practice such reading "must include a broad range of voices, especially those whose voices have been minoritized and thereby reduced to whispers from the margins by those who effectively control reading practices in the academy, in the churches, and in society at large."[32] These voices whose testimonies are reduced to whispers, for Ruiz, include those who must cross borders to survive, those living in exile, those

---

29. De La Torre and Aponte, *Introducing Latinx*, 85.

30. Ruiz, "The Bible and Latino/a Theology," 117.

31. For further discussion on the preferential option for the poor and the hermeneutical privilege of the poor, see chapter 2 in Ruiz, *Readings from the Edges*, 24–34. See also Dávila, "A 'Preferential Option': A Challenge to Faith," 49–70.

32. Ruiz, *Readings from the Edges*, 52. See also De La Torre, *Reading the Bible from the Margins*, in which he recognizes those on the margins due to race, class, the patriarchy, homophobia, and family dysfunction.

who do not yet speak the dominant language, those forced to assimilate, those who live in the liminal space between cultures, and immigrant laborers among others. Biblical texts speak to the whispered testimonies Ruiz names. His close readings of such texts evidence his demand for biblical scholarship that exhibits ethical responsibility.[33] Ruiz models how to read *latinamente* in his interpretation of the border-crossing experiences of Abram and Sarai in Genesis 12, in his postcolonial exploration of the exile experience in Ezekiel 20, and in his application of the parable of the day laborers in Matthew 20 to the daily struggle of immigrant workers across the United States.[34] Such contextual work rethinks method and rereads Scripture in light of the *"lectores de carne y hueso"* both past and present. The "flesh-and-blood readers" matter.[35]

Ruiz is a Catholic scholar who nonetheless consistently recognizes the ethical commitment to reading Scripture *latinamente* across denominations. He highlights the "patient and even-tempered" approach of respected evangelical biblical scholar M. Daniel Carroll R., who has already reached beyond the Protestant audience he addresses and, according to Ruiz, deserves to be engaged further by other church traditions.[36] For in his work Carroll R. exemplifies this commitment to flesh-and-blood communities. Amid the controversial issues surrounding immigration for the contemporary church in the United States, Carroll R. authored *Christians at the Border: Immigration, the Church and the Bible* (2008) and *The Bible and Borders: Hearing God's Word on Immigration* (2020). In these texts, Carroll R. offers guidance from Scripture framed by understandings of the law, the sojourner, and the stranger. Firmly grounded in the understanding of human beings created in the image of God, with a nuance for complexity and complication in the texts and in the contemporary world, he draws on the stories of migration and exile in the Old Testament (Genesis, 1 and 2 Kings, Daniel, Ruth, Ezra, Nehemiah), practices of hospitality (Genesis 18; 2 Kings 4:8–10; Job 31:32; Isaiah 58:6–7), legislation in the ancient world stemming

---

33. Ruiz specifically engages Genesis 12:10–20, Ezekiel 12:1–16, Ezekiel 20, Nehemiah 13, and Matthew 20:1–16. See Ruiz, *Readings from the Edges*, part II, "Looking to the Texts," 57–122. See also Ruiz's reading *latinamente* of Ruth 1:16–17 in "Beyond Borders and Boundaries," 35–47.

34. For these topics and more, see Ruiz, *Readings from the Edges*.

35. Ruiz, "Beyond Borders and Boundaries," 25–48, at 26.

36. Ruiz, *Readings from the Edges*, 41. For further discussion on Latino/a/x Protestant interpretation of Scripture, see Agosto, "*Sola Scriptura* and Latino/a Protestant Hermeneutics," 69–90.

from Genesis 12 (where the patriarch is told his descendants will be the channel of God's blessing), and hospitality or care for the stranger in the New Testament (Matthew 25; Luke 10; 1 Corinthians 16:5–12; Galatians 4:13–14). Demonstrating that there is a consistent ethic of hospitality and welcome toward the outsider across both Testaments, Carroll R. recognizes that "Christian traditions regularly affirm that the Bible is foundational for faith and practice, but living out this conviction well is a never-ending challenge."[37]

Reading Scripture *latinamente* requires ongoing ethical commitment in dialogue with Scripture, marginalized experience, and the vision of a fuller life for all communities. To communicate the implications of these principles of collaboration, connectedness, and commitment in biblical interpretation means that Latino/a/x theologies also take seriously the preaching of Scripture *latinamente*.

PREACHING AND HEARING SCRIPTURE *LATINAMENTE*

In Latino/a/x theologies, the role and interpretation of Scripture is not siloed within the field of biblical studies. Rather, scriptural interpretation is a communicative endeavor across communities and disciplines. Segovia, for example, notes the early and influential contribution of Justo González, theologian and church historian, to the work.[38] In his foundational text *Santa Biblia: The Bible through Hispanic Eyes*, González holds up the importance of seeing and hearing differently:

> Precisely because perspective cannot be avoided, when it is not explicitly acknowledged the result is that a particular perspective takes on an aura of universality. Thus it happens that theology from a male perspective claims to be generally human, and that North

---

37. Carroll R., *The Bible and Borders*, 117. See also Carroll R., "The Image and Mission of God," 37–52.

38. Segovia provides a constructive overview of the challenges González has brought to Latino/a/x biblical scholarship. See Lozada and Segovia, *Latino/a Biblical Hermeneutics*, 14–20. Similarly, Loida Martell points to the early call of Protestant theologians such as Orlando Costas and Justo González to provide a reading of Scripture and history that was "Hispanically oriented." Martell, "Reading against the Grain," 108. See also González, "A Latino Perspective," 113–43. Ruiz also addresses similar issues in chapter 1, "Good Fences and Good Neighbors? Biblical Scholars and Theologians," in *Readings from the Edges*, 13–23.

Atlantic white theology believes itself to be "normal," while theologies from the so-called Third World or from ethnic minorities in the North Atlantic are taken to be contextual or perspectival. Just as important for our purposes is the second point, namely, that the matter of perspective should not be avoided. The reason for this is not simply that we delude ourselves when we believe that ours is not a particular perspective. The reason is rather that, unless the text addresses us where we are, it does not really address us.[39]

By 1980, published Latino/a/x theologians were interrupting dominant models of biblical interpretation and of preaching. Justo González and Catherine G. González published *Liberation Preaching: The Pulpit and the Oppressed* in which they explored a liberationist approach and process for homiletics.[40] They examined the difficulties of hearing the text in dominant, traditional voices, and they unveiled the often-forgotten interpreters of Scripture living and bearing witness on the margins of society beyond the academy. Pointing toward a *teología en conjunto*, they challenged their readers to ask the political questions, to reassign the cast of biblical characters in a way that gives significance to those often deemed insignificant, to imagine a different setting, to consider the direction of the action, and be willing to face uncomfortable issues. They invited their readers to become aware of the powerless who are present and the powerless who are absent. They warned that "to be a liberation preacher . . . is to embark on a long and costly journey, with no guarantee that those who are traveling with you really wish to travel that road—and perhaps not even that you yourself wish to travel it."[41] At the very least, commitment to a liberationist homiletics will demand change toward life-giving practice/praxis, and the awareness that what is life-giving may change over time in response to contexts and communities. González and González do not simply gesture toward such awareness, they practice it. By 1994, they had thoroughly revised their work in *The Liberating Pulpit*. Justo González explains that "the very act of 'retiring' those older sermons and studies forced us to turn to other biblical texts, and thus to be both enriched in our preaching and in our lives."[42]

---

39. González, *Santa Biblia*, 16.

40. For more current reflection, see Lozano, "Is It Truly a 'Good' Book?," 89–102; Rodríguez, "Liberation Hermeneutics in Jewish, Christian and Muslim Exegesis,"169–88; Ruiz, "The Bible and Liberation: Between the Preferential Option for the Poor and the Hermeneutical Privilege of the Poor," in *Readings from the Edges*, 24–33.

41. González and González, *Liberation Preaching*, 112.

42. González and González, *The Liberating Pulpit*, 11.

The revised edition is a conscious commitment to enrich the ministries of minoritized preachers. This willingness to be changed, to reread, to see again the limitations of dominant models of interpretation, and the disposition to be prepared to transform engagement and practice in direct response to the particular needs and concerns of Latino/a/x communities of faith is what it means to read, interpret, and preach Scripture *latinamente*.

A decade later, in 2005, Justo González and Pablo Jiménez present a more expansive exploration and exposition of Hispanic preaching in their collaborative work *Púlpito*.[43] Their approach models an active awareness of place, location, and otherness in the histories, contexts, and concerns of congregations in the United States. It illustrates Hispanic homiletics in practice by providing a selection of biblical passages and the texts of accompanying sermons. This collection of sermons demonstrates ecumenical commitment, provides sermons preached by both women and men, and draws widely from scriptures across the Old and New Testaments.[44] As Alfaro describes it in his Pentecostal tradition, there is a "burning desire for God to communicate a fresh Word to his people."[45]

Through their reflections in *Púlpito*, González and Jiménez share their life experience with the Bible, provoking questions that raise self-awareness in response to the interpretation and application of Scripture. They invite their readers to consider marginalization as an entry point. Through the lenses of marginality, social location, and solidarity they seek to discern points of contact with their Latino/a/x communities. As they describe the landscapes in which Latino/a/x congregations find themselves, they invite their readers to see how this might influence the ways in which a biblical text is interpreted, preached, and heard. They maintain that this kind of renewed approach to scriptural interpretation speaks directly to Latino/a/x communities because it challenges the dominant narrative, and this contextual reading and proclamation ring true.[46] González was taught much

---

43. González and Jiménez, *Púlpito*.

44. The collection includes Carcaño, "Child of God (Luke 1:57–66)"; Conde-Frazier, "True Worship (Isaiah, Psalms, Hebrews 11, and Luke 12)"; Elizondo, "Seven Last Words"; Martínez, "Come to the Jordan Moments (Luke 3:21–22)"; Pupo-Ortiz, "The Spirituality of the Cross (Matthew 10)"; Rivera, "Sacrifice on Mount Moriah (Genesis 21:1–2)" and several sermons by González and Jiménez illustrating their insight put into practice.

45. Alfaro, "Reading and Hearing Scripture in the Latina/o Pentecostal Community," 29–45, at 37.

46. González and Jiménez, *Púlpito*, 39–69.

about poverty, for example, that he has learned is not true. He argues that it is not true that poverty is the product of laziness. Poverty is not willed by God. God did not destine some to be rich and some to be poor. The rich, or non-poor, are not closer to God. To strive for a better life, to resist the powers, or to rebel against injustice is not ungodly. On the contrary, González maintains that fundamental to a Latino/a/x hermeneutical model is the understanding of the Bible as a *liberating* text. The Bible "speaks directly" to the "struggles and hopes" of many Latino/a/x communities of faith.[47] Thus, proclamation from the pulpit will mean consistent reading practices that honor survival in the face of great suffering, embody resistance, speak judgment, and enunciate interruptive hope.[48] De La Torre too demonstrates how Scripture can speak directly in response to contemporary struggles against racism, classism, sexism, economics, justice, and family dysfunction in *Reading the Bible from the Margins*.[49]

González and Jiménez trace the history of the homiletical tradition across Latin American and the Caribbean, and into the United States. They reframe Latino/a/x theologies as affirmation, solidarity, and eschatological subversion, emphasizing that the purpose is not simply to gain a fresh interpretation of the biblical text. Rather, the purpose is that the text interprets the reader, finds the reader, and finds the reader out.[50] They speak to the challenges of culture and language in preaching. They acknowledge that social, economic, and political location affect listening. They name the realities of exile, immigration, and identity on congregations gathered.[51] They are convinced that while these issues may most concern contemporary Latino/a/x communities, they are, in fact, issues that impact all human communities and should concern all humans. Taking account of such

---

47. González, *Santa Biblia*, 28, 118.

48. For further understandings of survival, memory, and witness, see Hidalgo, *Latina/o/x Studies*, 40–44.

49. De La Torre, *Reading the Bible from the Margins*.

50. González and Jiménez, *Púlpito*, 27. See also Jiménez, "Toward a Postcolonial Homiletic: Justo L. Gonzalez's Contribution to Hispanic Preaching," in Padilla, Goizueta, and Villafañe, *Hispanic Christian Thought*, 159–67.

51. See in particular chapters on Scripture and marginalization, such as Agosto, "Marginality and Solidarity in 1 Corinthians," 11–21; Garcia-Treto, "Genesis 1:1—2:4 *Apuntes* for a Hispanic/Latina/o Reading," 22–29; Ramírez-Muñoz, "'It Is These You ought to have practiced, without neglecting others': Life in a Healthy Tension—An Alternative Model to Live in Community," 47–54, and Segovia, "Towards a Hermeneutic of Diaspora: A Hermeneutics of Otherness and Engagement," 55–68, in Padilla, Goizueta, and Villafañe, *Hispanic Christian Thought*.

issues, therefore, is the call of the whole church as it is called to proclaim the word of God.[52]

For González and Jiménez, standing in the pulpit and preaching is a communal event. It is a bilingual, bicultural, and often multicultural practice.[53] It calls for awareness of class, gender, and status.[54] More recently, Elieser Valentin edited the volume *Sermons from the Latino/a Pulpit* where Latino/a/x scholars, teachers, priests, and practitioners bring to life Scripture *latinamente*. This collection exhibits *teología en conjunto* as sermons speak powerfully from context and across contexts, demonstrating the ecumenical, interdisciplinary, and practical approach called for by González and Jiménez. This is an anthology that Valentin argues takes seriously the contextual nature of proclamation and reflection, paying close attention to the creative and prophetic expression of hope emanating from the Latino/a/x pulpit. More than a "how to" manual, this collection is an opportunity to "listen to."

> Not having a seat at the table means that Latino/a voices go unheard or, worse yet, are purposely muted. It is out of this reality that Latinos/as/xs live, work, theologize, and preach. What does God say to those in conditions of despair? What does God *do* when God's people are pushed to the margins of society? What does the Bible have to say about it?[55]

Orlando Espín asks, "Who do people say that I am?" in response to Mark 8. Through Ruth 4, Liliana Da Valle explores survival against all odds. Through Rachel's tears in Jeremiah 31:15 and Matthew 2:18, Jean-Pierre Ruiz responds to the tragic death and soul-wrenching image of three-year-old Aylan Kurdi lying face down on a Turkish beach. Mireya Alvarez continues to explore the biblical motif of migration and the immigrant through Matthew 25:35. Pablo Jiménez deals with experiences of invisibility—how the other is invisible and how Jesus renders the other visible in Mark 1:29–39. Efrain Agosto explores the impact of gratitude in building well-being,

---

52. For the wider significance of multiethnic readings of Scripture, see also Carroll R., "Reading the Bible through Other Lenses," 5–26.

53. See Conde-Frazier, Kang, and Parrett, *A Many Colored Kingdom*; Badillo, *Latinos and the New Immigrant Church*; and Rodríguez, *A Future for the Latino Church*. These issues are also noted by Rodríguez in "Between Two Worlds: Hispanic Youth in the United States," in Medina and Alfaro, *Pentecostals and Charismatics*, 127–40.

54. See Pilarski, "A Latina Biblical Critic and Intellectual: At the Intersection of Ethnicity, Gender, Hermeneutics and Faith," in *Latino/a Biblical Hermeneutics*, 231–48.

55. Valentin, *Sermons from the Latino/a Pulpit*, xix.

faith, and the *shalom* of all in our communities through Luke 17. Leopoldo Sánchez approaches the same text from the perspective of borders and border crossings. In welcoming the stranger (Deuteronomy 10:17–19; Psalm 146:9; Wisdom of Solomon 19:13–14; and Matthew 23:34–40) Sr. Teresa Maya calls her audience to be the face of mercy. Carmen Nanko-Fernández shapes *¡Una Pneumatología de Basta Ya!* in light of Isaiah 61:1–2 and Luke 4:16–21. This is an unsettling spirituality of "enough already!" in the face of injustice. Miguel Alvarez too speaks from Luke 4 articulating the "Galilean Manifesto" in the liberating mission of Jesus. Valentin closes the collection echoing this straightforward message of Jesus in Luke 4 in light of the promise of the Holy Spirit in Acts 2. Testifying that God is a God of life, he calls his listeners to be witnesses to such a God.

When M. T. Dávila offers her sermon on "Extravagant Interruption" in this volume, she recounts a story from her youth in Puerto Rico when the actions of a friend, who took notice of another teenager working at the house where they were relaxing and eating pizza, profoundly interrupted her assumptions and habits in a way that modelled justice and grace. She writes, "With this extravagant act of interruption, my friend upturned my expectations of inclusion, hospitality, shared table, identity, solidarity."[56] So too traditional expectations of inclusion, hospitality, shared table, identity, and solidarity can be profoundly interrupted through hearing the biblical text preached *latinamente*. These sermons are an interruption that leads toward justice. In response to such homiletical tradition, listeners, congregations, and communities are changed. Alfaro narrates the significance of this change in response to the proclamation of Scripture for Latino/a/x Pentecostal communities:

> [G]reat emphasis is placed on reading and hearing Scripture through the witness of the Spirit. It is the text of the Bible, read and activated by the Spirit, that becomes a living text for the Pentecostal community, and, as such, serves to guide—on an individual basis—and to direct the congregation in everyday decision-making.[57]

If the Spirit of God bears witness through Scripture, then Latino/a/x theologians recognize that the text needs to be read, interpreted, and preached with care. This is an interdisciplinary and intercultural conversation that models effective and constructive dialogue between theologians, church

---

56. Valentin, *Sermons from the Latino/a Pulpit*, 68.
57. Alfaro, "Reading and Hearing," 29.

historians, biblical scholars, ministers, and practitioners. The work of Jared Alcántara speaks to such homiletical commitment and practice in what he refers to as "Crossover preaching." He argues that crossover preachers will decenter the hegemonic impulses of Western homiletical discourse and cross borders of difference for the sake of the gospel: "By transgressing divides, they imitate Christ."[58] He emphasizes that it is essential to preach convictionally, contextually, clearly, concretely, and creatively.[59] In *Predicadores: Hispanic Preaching and Immigrant Identity*, published in 2021, Tito Madrazo employs the commitments of collaborative ethnography and testifies to the ethical and moral responsibilities involved in such research. He moves beyond the earlier work of González and Jiménez and points toward the fluid and varied approaches to preaching that will be needed to sustain authenticity. These new preaching voices will "reflect the lived experiences of both ministers and congregations in contextually faithful and life-giving ways."[60] Such ongoing conversation is necessary amid the nuanced realities of the contemporary United States.[61]

EMBRACING COMPLEXITY *LATINAMENTE*

Latino/a/x theologies take the Bible seriously. Latino/a/x theologies read, interpret, proclaim, and listen to the Bible in the various contexts that define the richness and diversity of Latino/a/x communities. Reading Scripture *latinamente* is a complex task amid complicated realities. Established and emerging Latino/a/x scholars are writing in response to issues at the intersection of biblical studies, cultural studies, and theological studies. Conde-Frazier recognizes the complexities:

> [W]e need not only the usual tools of theology and Bible but also the tools of sociology, psychology, economics, ecology, and medicine to analyze the situation responsibly and to be able to give an incarnated, wise public witness of our faith in the public square,

---

58. Alcántara, *Crossover Preaching*, 308.
59. See Alcántara, *The Practices of Christian Preaching*.
60. Madrazo, *Predicadores: Hispanic Preaching and Immigrant Identity*, 162.
61. See Madrazo, "Preaching and the Wounds of Migration," 45–50, and Madrazo and Ruiz, "Preaching from Sanctuary," in Ottoni-Wilhelm, *Preaching the Fear of God in a Fear-Filled World*, 119–33. See the variety of scholars invited to contribute to *Latino/a Theology and the Bible* and *Sermons from the Latino/a Pulpit*, as previously mentioned. See also the work of Jared E. Alcántara in *Let the Legends Preach* and *How to Preach Proverbs*.

where persons wonder where God is. It is in the public square that we might already find the new things of God taking place. And it is the church that needs to seek after the Lord, who is found in spaces the church sometimes does not imagine itself to be.[62]

Latino/a/x scholars continue to rise to this challenge. *Latino/a Biblical Hermeneutics: Problematics, Objectives and Strategies*, published in 2014, illustrates the vulnerable nuances of *mestizaje* as scholars are invited to reflect on what it actually means to be a Latino/a/x biblical scholar in the academy today and how such identities might function in the interpretive process.[63] Among others, David Sánchez seeks to formulate a space for critical Latino/a/x cultural and biblical discourse. Ahida Calderón Pilarski explores the intersection of ethnicity, gender, hermeneutics, and faith. Jaqueline Hidalgo approaches issues of hybridity and ambivalence in reading the Scriptures from "no place." Osvaldo D. Vena proposes dialogue between Latin American and Latino/a/x hermeneutics. The diversity of experiences and expressions in this volume honors the commitments explored in this chapter.

Latinxs, the Bible, and Migration avoids abstraction and romanticization in a collection published in 2018. It addresses issues arising in association with global migration, gender violence, masculinity, the well-being of children, food security, and environmental concerns, among others, through engagement with complex and ambiguous biblical texts.[64] "We consider the Christian Bible as a space of migrant urgency. Fundamentally, we read with migrant humanity, alongside migrant perspectives, and for the humanization of migrants in broader discourse."[65] Standing against the vilification of immigrants and testifying to the dehumanizing perceptions that migrants encounter, these scholars examine the complexities that arise globally through war, politics, economics, and human-caused climate change. Recognizing that religions often shape and are shaped by human migrations, they argue that in the context of the United States, the study of religion has underscored the importance of place:

> Because the United States is a settler colonial state, the various peoples who have migrated here or who were forcibly brought to these shores have had to grapple with either making home or surviving

---

62. Conde-Frazier, *Atando Cabos*, 105.
63. Lozada and Segovia, *Latino/a Biblical Hermeneutics*.
64. Agosto and Hidalgo, *Latinxs*.
65. Agosto and Hidalgo, *Latinxs*, 2.

in this new land. Meanwhile Native populations were forced to transform their religious relationships with the landscape, and settler colonists forced many Native populations to migrate to regions of this continent far from their ancestral homelands. Even as dominant Euro-diasporic settler colonists sacralized their home-making processes in this hemisphere, minoritized communities in particular have turned to religion as they struggled to make home. Religious traditions have often supplied crucial practices, material cultures, and mythic traditions for this space making.[66]

Although not the focus of the volume, Agosto and Hidalgo acknowledge the importance of articulating how the Bible has been a text of domination in this hemisphere, generating violence and structuring unequal power dynamics for women and LGBTQ+ migrants. They note "In this way ... sometimes the Bible too is a border that must be crossed."[67]

Released in 2021, *Latino/a Theology and the Bible: Ethnic-Racial Reflections on Interpretation* is an exploration of theological construction and biblical criticism in an ethno-racial key. This volume encompasses a wide range of biblical scholarship, including a Latino/a/x perspective on inter-religious discussion, Pentecostal and *evangélica* approaches to Scripture, critical and constructive responses to the Bible and liberation, Scripture conveyed through popular expressions of religiosity, and reinterpretations of allegory and imagery.[68] Such interdisciplinary biblical scholarship demonstrates a sustained commitment to collaboration, connectedness, and pursuit of justice.

Lozada suggests that one of the most significant challenges in the future of biblical scholarship is not simply the ongoing development of contextual interpretations of the Bible. Rather, he points to the need to expand more complex notions of context within Scripture itself, and across Christian theology more widely. In the pluralizing contexts of the contemporary world, he calls on scholars, teachers, and students to challenge master narratives evident in the ethos and orientation of dominant pedagogical discourses and practices. Without complicating and pluralizing narrative frames, contextual readings will remain marginalized. Master narratives, he argues, shut down pluralist perspectives and therefore must continually be resisted by reading *latinamente*:

---

66. Agosto and Hidalgo, *Latinxs*, 9.
67. Agosto and Hidalgo, *Latinxs*, 15.
68. Lozada and Segovia, *Latino/a Theology and the Bible*.

Textbooks that continue to employ master narratives are simultaneously requiring readers to remain invisible during the reading of the narrative. By engaging and challenging the master narrative via perspectives from ethnic/racial studies, postcolonial studies, and feminist studies, and by proposing multiple perspectives and histories, we may allow the text to begin to reveal more about the people and communities of the Gospel—and perhaps even reveal something about ourselves.[69]

From the perspective of postcolonial studies, Lozada acknowledges that complex questions continue to be raised for Latino/a/x scholars in particular. One of these questions concerns the relationship between binaries expressed in biblical scholarship: the center and the periphery, the majority and the margins, the powerful and the powerless, or the imperialist and the colonized, for example.[70] Inadvertently to depend on such binaries, he suggests, might embed, and not dislodge these master narratives. In contrast, proposing and examining diverse perspectives and histories (that include reading Scripture *latinamente*) will free communities to engage the text, and engage one another, in broader and deeper ways. This push toward embracing complexity and multiple perspectives transforms not only the ethos and orientation of biblical studies and biblical interpretation. It transforms teaching, preaching, ministry, and pastoral care in congregations. It

---

69. Lozada, "Teaching the New Testament: Toward an Expanded Contextual Approach," in Lozada and Carey, *Soundings in Cultural Criticism*, 151–64.

70. Lozada, "Teaching the New Testament."

transforms attitudes, pedagogies, and curricula in theological education.[71] It is consistently a turn toward justice in every sphere.[72]

For many years, Justo González argued that Latino/a/x communities were reading and rereading Scripture from multiple places. This complexity empowered them and continues to empower them to unveil realities, experiences, and interpretations of marginality, poverty, *mestizaje*, *mulatez*, exile, oppression, solidarity, and much more.[73] In his contribution to postcolonial biblical criticism, Segovia asks how Scripture has been used to enforce and reinforce structures of colonialism, which have led to the sufferings that González names. Segovia probes the assumptions of the colonizers, who often use Scripture to serve self and justify their actions, asserting that

> Latinxs are in a unique position to hear God's word in the context of their own sufferings, making their oppressed existence part of the text's interpretation. This subversive reading of the text uses what is known as the "hermeneutical privilege of the oppressed," who have learned how to function without power in a realm constructed by those with privilege, know more about the overall U.S. culture than those with power, who only know their own protected space. This does not confer truth exclusively on those who are oppressed. It only states that they are in a better position

---

71. For further discussion on implications for theological education, see Conde-Frazier, *Atando Cabos*; Fernandez, *Teaching for a Culturally Diverse and Racially Just World*, in particular chapters by Martell-Otero, "From Foreign Bodies in Teacher Space to Embodied Spirit in *Personas Educadas*: or, How to Prevent 'Tourists of Diversity' in Education," 52–68; Conde-Frazier, "Thoughts on Curriculum as Formational Praxis for Faculty, Students and Their Communities," 126–246; and Maldonado, "Institutional Life and Governance: Realities and Challenges for Racial-Ethnic Leadership within Historically White Theological Schools," 202–18. See also De La Torre, "Identity Cross-Dressing while Teaching in a Global Context," 75–90, and Martell-Otero, "*Hablando Se Entiende la Gente*: Tower of Babble or Gift of Tongues," 143–62, in Kwok, González-Andrieu, and Hopkins, *Teaching Global Theologies*. For implications on the teaching of homiletics specifically, see Alcántara, "Pedagogy That Purifies the Air: Recognizing and Reducing 'Stereotype Threat' in the Preaching Classroom," 20–30; Alcántara, "Sermons with 'Local Soil': Cultivating Contextually Responsive Preachers," 185–98, and Alcántara, "'I Can't Breathe': The Adverse Impact of Racialization on Seminarians of Color and Its Import for the Homiletics Classroom," 30–65.

72. See the trajectory of Latino/a/x biblical criticism in Lozada and Segovia, *Latino/a Biblical Hermeneutics*, 4–10.

73. González, *Santa Biblia*, 28–29.

to understand the biblical call for justice than those who deceive themselves into thinking that justice already exists.[74]

Consequently, to interpret Scripture *latinamente* is to embrace complexity *latinamente*. It is ongoing work for justice grounded in place, in social location, and in genuine experience. It is ongoing work in the complexities of intersecting places, social locations, and genuine experiences.

In the context of the United States specifically, if this pursuit of justice is to be grounded in the complexities of place, social location, and genuine experiences then it is necessary to engage with language. For language in biblical interpretation, in homiletics, in the church, and in the classroom is also a justice issue. In *Theologizing in Espanglish*, Nanko-Fernández is careful to point out that "the significance of language in the navigation of boundaries and in the negotiation of identities within and across generations emerges as a legitimate and necessary locus for theological reflection."[75] To be attentive to language is to be attentive to power dynamics. Isasi-Díaz too raises serious concerns regarding power in interpretation. She demonstrates how an authoritative interpretation of Scripture emphasizing a seemingly collective Latino/a/x reading may, in fact, continue to veil repression experienced by those within the community, at the hands of those leading the community. Such challenges brought by *mujerista* theology and by women scholars bring a necessary critique to the theological conversation, as will be seen in chapter 5.

IN CONVERSATION

Luis Hernández Rivas

Ya no los llamo siervos, porque el siervo no está al tanto de lo que hace su amo; los he llamado amigos, porque todo lo que a mi Padre le oí decir se lo he dado a conocer a ustedes.

JUAN 15:15

I am a Latino transitional deacon in the Diocese of New York. I was born and raised in Cuba. I studied philosophy and education in the Dominican Republic. While being raised in the city, my weekly visits to our family's farm shaped many of my experiences of life,

74. De La Torre and Aponte, *Introducing Latinx*, 87.
75. Nanko-Fernández, *Theologizing en Espanglish*, 62.

the world, and community. I was baptized as a teenager. One of my favorite memories is seeing the water run down my face during my baptism and thinking I could now fully call God "Father." A member of the Community of Francis and Clare, a Christian community in the Episcopal Church, I strive to follow Jesus in Franciscan minority.

As a Latino reading your life-experience in the introduction, Sharon, I was deeply moved. We share experiences of shifting identities. We share the unveiling of questions when people seem to be simply asking your name. I really loved your story. In my life-experience, Scripture is also about storytelling. We hear Scripture first in the voices and stories of our *abuelitas*, women who through hardship and endurance have earned the authority to speak on the things of faith. And so, in listening and hearing these stories we learn how to relate to Scripture *latinamente*. My Anglo friends often talk about "reading" Bible stories at bedtime. In my oral culture, we listened as the stories were told to us. There is a different form of cultural communication happening. We value the *testimonio* and the storytelling more than the academic framework. Authenticity is conveyed in the storytelling, and when sermons are "told" this connects very intimately with how we first heard Scripture in our homes.

I really value the emphasis in this chapter on the collaborative, connected, and committed nature of approaching Scripture *latinamente*. For my community it is the urgency of today, the here and now, that is most important. When we look at Scripture, right away we begin with our context, the needs of our communities, and we look for the ethical implications. We are not rejecting literary criticism in scriptural interpretation. But we are drawn immediately to priorities that shape a different framework so that Scripture speaks to our reality. This has implications for theological education, ministry, and pastoral care.

In my experience, we read Scripture from the perspective of the cross and suffering, on our way toward the hopes of liberation. This hermeneutic of suffering is the lens through which we read, we interpret, we preach, and we listen. When I preach to an Anglo congregation in the United States, they are conditioned to believe that suffering is not for them. Suffering is something that happens to other people. It is often an uphill battle for me to actually communicate the reality of suffering there. Latino congregations, on the other hand, experience suffering as part of life. It is not something that can be denied or rejected. Latinos hold to the images of suffering and the cross in the Bible. In this way, Scripture inspires endurance and

Scripture also requires an ethical, just response. We are a people of the cross. White Americans, shaped by triumphalism and manifest destiny, in my experience do not see themselves as people of the cross. We do not read Scripture in the same way.

As we look through the lens of suffering, and hold to the image of the cross, in my culture we also read Scripture looking for an experience of the fatherhood of God. Of course, I am aware this mingles with the complex realities of patriarchy. But in my community, I often hear people reading and interpreting Scripture with this understanding of God in mind—*Papa Dios*. God is a good and loving father, *Diosito*. God, who is present in Scripture, protects and cares for God's people. God who is present in Scripture also walks with us, is present with us, in this moment today. God will protect us and care for us. Scripture is embodied, contextualized, and socially located for our Latino communities.

Given our different contexts and social locations and given the differences in cultural communication and frameworks of thinking, we naturally interpret and preach Scripture differently to the dominant culture. This chapter is a reminder that dominant theology can no longer dictate the approach or the way to correctly interpret Scripture. I wish that we could talk more about these other ways of thinking in our biblical studies and in our homiletics. We need to encourage one another to learn other ways of reading, interpreting, exegeting, and preaching. In preaching, I have always been encouraged to find my own voice. But people's experience of me finding my own voice is always framed by their own experience. My home culture, for example, appreciates it when I speak to them through story and preach without a transcript. To preach without notes communicates care and understanding to them. Yet for my Anglo congregation, writing my sermon out and offering a literary word study is often what communicates care and good understanding to them. Many white Americans are primed to tell good stories, but they do not use this skill in the pulpit when they preach to Latino congregations. "Can you translate my sermon?" they will often ask me. "Sure, I can," I will answer. But the question remains—if I translate the sermon for you, is it going to land? In multicultural ministry we need to acknowledge the dominant culture at work. We need to be aware of different ways of communicating. We need to be competent in different ways of preaching. We need to be storytellers. We need to tell stories that speak to today. We need to affirm ethical responsibilities in light of Scripture. We need to lift our eyes up from our notes. If we are committed to feeding the souls of our congregations, and if we have two services, we will need to write two sermons.

This chapter also encouraged me to think of the importance of our foundational practice of *lectura orante de la Palabra de Dios*, a prayerful reading of Scripture, often used in Latino congregations. People love to read Scripture in this way. People value having their voices heard. They often bring perspectives and wisdom that I may never have thought of before. This is a grounded approach to Scripture that is collaborative and connected. We are committed to reading Scripture in commitment to one another. This lay-led reading of Scripture is often the foundation of our churches. We plant churches through a prayer group or a Bible study cell that begins with this practice. This is a way to plant a church and grow a whole new church community. This is our way—small groups, gathering in homes, sharing food, and prayerfully responding to Scripture. This is where the church is made.

I find it encouraging that this chapter also speaks to people beyond Latino communities. These frameworks for critical thinking and these topics are important as we look to the future. Among those born in the United States today many feel marginalized, many feel conflicts of identity, and many recognize concerns of belonging in relation to this land. In the years that lie ahead, immigration, migration, and diasporic conversations in our ministries and pastoral care will become ever more significant. We need to hear the voices of theologians who recognize the limitations of dominant cultural approaches to Scripture, who inspire us to broaden our understanding, and who strive for more. All the while, we carry in our hearts the stories our *abuelitas* told us so many years ago.

FOUNDATIONAL READING

Carroll R., M. Daniel. *Christians at the Border: Immigration, the Church and the Bible*. 2nd ed. Grand Rapids: Brazos, 2013.

Conde-Frazier, Elizabeth. "*Evangélicas* Reading Scriptures: Readings from within and beyond the Tradition." In *Latina Evangélicas: A Theological Survey from the Margins*, edited by Loida I. Martell-Otero, Zaida Maldonado Pérez, and Elizabeth Conde-Frazier, 73–89. Eugene, OR: Cascade, 2013.

Hidalgo, Jacqueline M. *Latina/o/x Studies and Biblical Studies*. Leiden: Brill, 2020.

Lozada, Francisco. *Toward a Latino/a Biblical Interpretation*. Atlanta: SBL, 2017.

Madrazo, Tito. *Predicadores: Hispanic Preaching and Immigrant Identity*. Waco, TX: Baylor University Press, 2021.

Ruiz, Jean-Pierre. "The Bible and Latino/a Theology." In *The Wiley-Blackwell Companion to Latino/a Theology*, edited by Orlando O. Espín, 111–28. Chichester, UK: Wiley-Blackwell, 2015.

Valentin, Elieser, ed. *Sermons from the Latino/a Pulpit*. Eugene, OR: Wipf and Stock, 2017.

FURTHER READING

Alcántara, Jared E. *Crossover Preaching: Intercultural-Improvisational Homiletics in Conversation with Gardner C. Taylor*. Downers Grove, IL: IVP Academic, 2015.

———. *The Practices of Christian Preaching: Essentials for Effective Proclamation*. Grand Rapids: Baker Academic, 2019.

Lozada, Francisco, and Fernando F. Segovia, eds. *Latino/a Biblical Hermeneutics: Problematics, Objectives, Strategies*. Atlanta: SBL, 2014.

———, eds. *Latino/a Theology and the Bible: Ethnic-Racial Reflections on Interpretation*. Lanham, MD: Lexington/Fortress, 2021.

Ruiz, Jean-Pierre. *Readings from the Edges: The Bible and People on the Move*. Maryknoll, NY: Orbis, 2011.

5

En la Lucha

Voices of Women in the Struggle

> To name oneself is one of the most powerful acts a person can do. A name is not just a word by which one is identified. A name also provides the conceptual framework, the point of reference, the mental constructs that are used in thinking, understanding, and relating to a person, an idea, a movement. It is with this in mind that a group of us Latinas who live in the United States and who are keenly aware of how sexism, ethnic prejudice, and economic oppression subjugate Latinas, started to use the word *mujerista* to refer to ourselves and to use *mujerista* theology to refer to the explanations of our faith and its role in our struggle for liberation.[1]
> —Ada María Isasi-Díaz

IN THE FACE OF violent colonialism,[2] the voices of women in Latina theologies declare that "struggle is a name for hope."[3] Women testify to the resilience and strength required to live and to flourish in *lo cotidiano*.

---

1. Isasi-Díaz, *Mujerista Theology*, 60.

2. Foundational reading would include Moraga and Anzaldúa, *This Bridge Called My Back*, and Pitts, *Nos/Otras: Gloria Anzaldúa, Multiplicitous Agency and Resistance*.

3. See the title to part I in Aquino and Fiorenza, *In the Power of Wisdom: Feminist Spiritualities of Struggle*, 5.

Michelle Gonzalez maintains that "when Latinas locate the sacred in the everyday, spirituality saturates every aspect of their lives. Through their spirituality, Latinas lament their struggles and sufferings while simultaneously celebrating their full humanity as created in God's image."[4] It is in this daily struggle, then, that Latina women bring renewed understandings of God, refreshed interpretations of the life of Jesus, and reinterpretations of Scripture *latinamente*. Encapsulated by the phrase *en la lucha*, Latina women in theology acknowledge the particularity of their struggle and the complexities of their experience. As Neomi De Anda frames it, they both "engage the particular and highlight the importance of difference."[5] Nancy Pineda-Madrid notes that "a dynamic and evolving matrix of interlocking dimensions shape each Latina's life experience so distinctly that treating Latina's experience as a universal, singular reality severely compromises this theology's commitment to emancipatory praxis."[6] Bearing witness in every sphere, women are the lifeblood and soul of Latino/a/x communities and, therefore, women are at the very heart of *teología en conjunto*. Elisabeth Fiorenza recognizes that Latina theologies see "possibilities for articulating a political Wisdom spirituality that sustains rather than mutes struggles for survival and liberation."[7] This is theology that gives Latina women and their communities voice. "Central to Latina spirituality are the struggles that Latinas encounter in their everyday lives," writes Gonzalez. "Through their spiritual practices, Latinas are able to express and denounce those oppressive forces which deny their full humanity."[8]

This is theology in which Latina women and their communities find freedom to use their own words and their own interpretations.[9] In this chapter, the particularities of their theologies and how these theologians choose to name themselves will guide the conversation. For "when someone else names you," Loida Martell maintains, "they have the power to objectify you

---

4. Gonzalez, *Embracing*, 26.

5. De Anda, "Latina Feminist and *Mujerista* Theologies as Political Theologies?," 271–84, at 273.

6. Pineda-Madrid, "Feminist Theory and Latina Feminist/Mujerista Theologizing," 346–63, at 357.

7. Aquino and Fiorenza, *In the Power of Wisdom: Feminist Spiritualities of Struggle*, 7.

8. Gonzalez, *Embracing*, 77.

9. For examples of a communal model of theological conversation and interpretation, see Rodriguez, *Stories We Live/Cuentos Que Vivimos*; Isasi-Díaz and Tarango, *Hispanic Women*; Conde-Frazier, "Latina Women and Immigration," 54–75, at 68–74.

and create you in whatever image they desire."[10] De Anda too considers self-naming to be significant. For she recognizes that being named by others has been part of the historical oppression and marginalization experienced by Latinas. At worst, she notes, "Latinas have not been named at all."[11]

Gonzalez argues that Latinos/as/xs must be aware of how they and their communities are grouped and categorized by others. She explains that the way in which a community functions within the dominant culture may even be distinct from and in tension with the understanding of community and family ascribed to that very community.[12] Similarly, she clearly articulates the complexities involved in attempting to name or categorize women theologians. She cautions against an essentialized understanding of the nature and writings of women for she recognizes that this often leads toward segregating women's contributions. She warns against ignoring the tensions that may exist when a theologian chooses to name herself in a particular way. She expresses concern about framing theology as either *mujerista* or as Latina feminist, and in doing so making the latter non-*mujerista*. Gonzalez also accepts the challenges brought by *mujeres evangélicas* who advocate for theology written by women who are not within the Roman Catholic tradition. "It is clear to me now, more than ever," she argues, "that we need to open the doors of dialogue among all Latinas, for the manifold divisions among us can only enrich our theological projects."[13]

The contribution of women theologians of Latin American and Latino/a/x heritage is found throughout Latino/a/x theologies and therefore permeates each chapter in this book. This chapter is a conversation that will focus specifically on listening to the broader dialogue among Latinas. First, the significance of *mujerista* theology will be explored. Second, the focus of Latina feminist and feminist intercultural theology will be examined. Third, attention will be given to theology offered by Latina *evangélicas*. Fourth, the emergence of *abuelita* theology will be discussed. Finally, the ways in which such theologies resource concern for the whole of humanity will be considered.

---

10. Martell-Otero, *Latina Evangélicas*, 3.
11. De Anda, "Latina Feminist and *Mujerista* Theologies," 273.
12. Gonzalez, "Who We Are," 64–84, at 73.
13. Gonzalez, "Rethinking Latina Feminist Theologian," in De La Torre and Espinosa, *Rethinking Latino(a) Religion and Identity*, 176–99, at 190.

MISSING VOICES

Pineda-Madrid observes that most Latino theologians write ignoring the many contributions of Latina feminist or *mujerista* theologians. "These theologies are either, at worst, ignored, or, at best, treated as an addendum to the *real* theological work, meaning work done by Latino men."[14] She notes that engagement with feminist theory has sharpened approaches in the scholarship of women, and this has led to a more mature discourse for all. Pineda-Madrid examines the significance and necessity, not only of privileging the experience of women, but of centering these particular experiences in Latina theology. Firstly, she maintains that women's lives have long been ignored as a subject worthy of critical reflection. Secondly, she argues that by critically analyzing the lives of women, a vulnerable segment of the population is privileged, and by extension, the lives of others who are also overlooked and marginalized will benefit because theology is being more attentive to the whole community. She recognizes the interlocking nature of multiple forms of oppression, including classism, racism, heterosexism, militarism, ageism, and discrimination against the disabled, in the reality of the stories of Latinas. Thirdly, she affirms that this theological work envisions the flourishing of women's lives, thus supporting women as active agents and empowered subjects. Fourthly, this is a theological approach that listens to the stories and narratives of all women and is, therefore, attentive to a vast diversity of expressions and experiences. Isasi-Díaz observes,

> What is missing in the respect some of us Hispanic Women receive is engagement. The respect we are given does not seem to include being taken seriously. It does not recognize that what one says about oneself cannot ignore others and their struggles. That is precisely what engagement is all about. For engagement to happen, difference has to be recognized as an asset and not a problem.[15]

With María Lugones, the Argentine feminist philosopher and activist,[16] Isasi-Díaz proposes that difference should be an asset because those who

---

14. Pineda-Madrid, "Feminist Theory and Latina Feminist/Mujerista Theologizing," 348. See also Gonzalez, "Rethinking Latina Feminist Theologian," 177–88; Isasi-Díaz and Tarango, *Hispanic Women*, 1–12.

15. Isasi-Díaz, *En la Lucha*, 197.

16. See, for example, Lugones, *Pilgrimages/Peregrinajes*; Espinosa-Miñoso, Lugones, and Maldonado-Torres, *Decolonial Feminism*; DiPietro, McWeeny, and Roshanravan, *Speaking Face to Face*; and Pitts, Ortega, and Medina, *Theories of the Flesh*. For further

are different "are mirrors in which you can see yourselves as no other mirror shows you.... What we reveal to you is... something that may in itself be frightening to you. But the self we reveal to you is also one that you are not eager to know...."[17] Such engagement, then, takes courage and trust.

Inspired by the fundamental question, "What would theology look like if it was genuinely life-giving or liberating for Latinas?"[18] Latina theologians have provided, and continue to develop, a variety of approaches that speak to a shared struggle and yet at the same time acknowledge different experiences of struggle. Jeanette Rodríguez maintains:

> Women and those who are in a constant state of oppression have decided to define themselves. They want to express in their own words their particular way of experiencing God and their particular way of living their faith. In the midst of a reality in which women are doubly or triply oppressed, doing liberation theology from a woman's perspective is not a luxury, but a necessity and a right to be claimed.[19]

In the very name *mujerista* theology, Isasi-Díaz centers women at the heart of theology and theology at the heart of realities for women—their experiences of history, family, community, faith, the church, and God. Latina feminist theology brings a different perspective and also offers a crucial critique of the dominance of the white feminist voice.[20] Close attention to the testimonies of women within the Protestant traditions is provided especially by Latina *evangélicas*, who are a minority within a minority. The awareness of what is shared and yet what might be particular to some has led to a breadth of intercultural interpretations and responses that speak to themes ranging from the traumatic to the beautiful, from violence to survival, and from death to life.[21] Latina women theologians continue to

---

engagement with the work of Lugones, see Gonzalez, *Created in God's Image*, 100–101, 136–37, 156–58.

17. Argentine-born feminist philosopher María Lugones, "On the Logic of Pluralist Feminism," quoted in Isasi-Díaz, *En la Lucha*, 197.

18. Isasi-Díaz, *Mujerista Theology*, 62.

19. Rodriguez, *Stories*, 4.

20. For a constructive attempt in response to self-awareness of white privilege in scholarship and the need for intercultural engagement on understandings of the cross, see Reid, *Taking Up the Cross*, 3–8.

21. For further intercultural work, see the contributions of Bingemer, "Masculinity, Femininity, and the Christ"; Aquino, "Jesus Christ: Life and Liberation in a Discipleship of Equals"; and Martell-Otero, "From *Satas* to *Santas*," in Johnson, *The Strength of Her Witness*, part III, "A Symphony of Voices."

offer creative, far-reaching theology that includes contributions on faith, on God, on Scripture, on spirituality, on social justice, on hope in the face of immense suffering, and on strength to survive and flourish. Their commitment to *teología en conjunto* is a commitment to respect voices of women who may not have been considered "theologians." The wisdom of *abuelita* theology exhibits this commitment to honor the lived theology of grandmothers, mothers, godmothers, sisters, aunts, nieces, cousins, and neighbors who sustain life and faith in the ordinary moments of the everyday. Given these diverse voices, each stream of Latina theology will now be outlined in turn.

MUJERISTA THEOLOGY

Beginning with Isasi-Díaz (a Cuban American Catholic) and Yolanda Tarango (a Mexican American Catholic), *mujerista* was the name they chose for their theology.[22] Encouraged by Black womanist theologians, they birthed the term *mujerista* from the word *mujer*, woman. They felt the word "feminist" carried the burden of historical associations with Euro-American hegemony, and they testified to the reality of Latina marginalization which they had experienced at the hands of Anglo feminists.

For Isasi-Díaz *mujerista* theology has three goals. It works to center the voices of Latina grassroots women. It seeks to develop methods that take seriously the understandings and practices of Latinas as sources for theology. It aims at challenging concepts, church teachings, and religious practices that are theologically erroneous because they oppress Latina women.[23] While *mujerista* theology is not exclusively for Latinas, Isasi-Díaz is clear that it is theology articulated from the perspective of Latinas. *Mujerista* theology is not a "disembodied discourse" but is a discourse that arises from the lives and stories of Latina grassroots women.[24] Isasi-Díaz models a careful approach that navigates the ambiguity of "using" others and of "speaking for" others. Her aim is to embody *mujerista* theology as liberative praxis. This is a practice of theological resistance that refuses to withdraw to a "retreat position." She calls for theologians to be accountable,

---

22. For early collaborative work between Isasi-Díaz and Tarango, see Isasi-Díaz and Tarango, *Hispanic Women*. This book also demonstrates *teología en conjunto* by offering a synopsis of each chapter in Spanish.

23. Isasi-Díaz, *Mujerista Theology*, 1.

24. Isasi-Díaz, *Mujerista Theology*, 3.

responsible, open to criticism, and self-aware in terms of context and social location. Writing to Latinas in the United States, who are a marginalized community but may yet enjoy certain privileges, she affirms that their task is "to use those privileges in ways that can contribute to the struggle for liberation. It is a matter of using privileges to undo dominant structures instead of benefitting from them at the expense of others."[25]

During the early development of *mujerista* thought, Isasi-Díaz witnessed to her experience in the world of Euro-American feminism.[26] She recalls initially being welcomed among Euro-American feminists as long as she "toiled in their garden," so to speak. When she began to create her own space in the garden, however, she discovered that "the issue was and is power."[27] In contrast, what is required are "societies in which people can be self-defining and self-determining. To do that power must be transformed and shared."[28] Extending the gardening metaphor, Isasi-Díaz likens the work of *mujerista* theology as putting together a theological bouquet. She would gather the "flowers" of experience and faith inherited from her mother. Yet at the same time, she would find herself struggling against the "weeds" of the discrimination she experienced in both society and academy. Segovia, we recall from chapter 4, names such experience *minoritization*.

Mujerista theologians enable Latinas to both name the oppression they experience and affirm the everyday presence and revelation of God amid family and community.[29] These theologians unveil the realities of sinful structures—societal and religious—that cause Latina women to internalize their own oppression. They empower Latinas to define their preferred future. The characteristics of Latino/a/x theologies more broadly, already discussed in earlier chapters, are present in *mujerista* theology. *Lo cotidiano* as *locus theologicus* is seen as *mestizaje* and *mulatez* situate the histories and identities of Latina women in the United States.[30] *Mujerista* theology is work toward fuller justice for Latinas through its commitment to praxis. Isasi-Díaz defines such praxis as "reflective, liberative action."

---

25. Isasi-Díaz, *En la Lucha*.

26. For further discussion, see Torres, "A Latina Testimonio," 65–75.

27. Isasi-Díaz, *Mujerista Theology*, 18.

28. Isasi-Díaz, *Mujerista Theology*, 19.

29. See Gonzalez, *Embracing*, 16–20, for a discussion on finding meaning in the everyday with particular reference to Sor Juana Inéz de la Cruz.

30. See also Gonzalez, *Embracing*, 10–13.

That *mujerista* theology is praxis means "we cannot separate thinking from acting." It is not reflection on action but "liberative action in and of itself."[31]

Central to *mujerista* theology, for Isasi-Díaz, is a deep understanding of *la lucha*, the struggle, that the majority of Latinas experience simply in order to survive as human beings. Denouncing the erasure of women from the histories of communities, histories of countries of origin, and from the histories of the United States, her repeated articulation of *permítanme hablar* (allow me to speak) insists that Latina women will give voice to their own histories, their own stories, and their own struggles. To speak aloud of such histories, stories, and struggles is, as Gustavo Gutiérrez describes it, subversive memory. Subversive memory strengthens and sustains humanity by resisting compromise and recognizing, through experience, that human beings have the capability to overcome.[32] Isasi-Díaz affirms that this agency to articulate theology for themselves not only gives voice to Latina women but also requires attentive listening on the part of the dominant culture:

> We are asking for a respectful silence from all those who have the power to set up definitions of what it is to be human, a respectful silence so others can indeed hear our cries denouncing oppression and injustice so that others can understand our vision of a just society. . . . For Latinas to speak and to be heard is fundamental . . . for it makes it possible for us to attest to our humanity. . . . To demand that we be listened to is a way for us to assert our own identity, to demand that our understanding of our own humanity has to be taken into consideration in the understanding of all humanity.[33]

Mujerista theology recognizes that Latina women are central in *la familia* and in *la comunidad*. It is within this expansive network of relationships, connections, and resources that justice is to be sought. This orientation of life toward people and persons reflects the emphasis not only on a vision of just society but on an understanding of just relationships. Isasi-Díaz warns that while women may find significance and value in community and family, it may also be the case that community and family are the very location of objectification, negativity, exploitation, abuse, and

---

31. Isasi-Díaz, *Mujerista Theology*, 73.
32. Isasi-Díaz, *Mujerista Theology*, 133.
33. Isasi-Díaz, *Mujerista Theology*, 137.

violence.[34] *Mujerista* theology emphasizes, then, the importance that each person in a family or a community be allowed to play the role of protagonist in their own life. This vision embraces the difference and uniqueness of each person, and yet is established on the interdependence found at the heart of the Latino/a/x meaning of *familia*.[35] Shared times of *fiesta* in families and communities, for example, are celebrations that embody the struggle against suffering, a vision to move beyond suffering, and a commitment to evade suffering. Isasi-Díaz argues that the creativity and joy of *fiestas* are a strategic refusal to be defined by suffering.[36] While she recognizes the need to deepen understandings of embodiment and justice in the family, in the church, and in the community, the celebration of *mujerista* liturgies likewise resource hope. These liturgies create a safe and brave space where pain and suffering can be voiced and lamented yet God's voice and Christian testimony inspire in the struggle.[37]

The cohesiveness that sustains Latina community, for Isasi-Díaz, is centered on five particular elements: the Spanish language, popular religion, social-cultural-psychological survival, economic oppression, and vision for the future.[38] Yet while *mujerista* theology articulates a very particular point of departure for Latina women, and emphasizes their experience and voice, the vision of hope and the pursuit of justice is not limited to Latina women. Rather, *mujerista* theology seeks justice for the whole of humanity. Isasi-Díaz remains attentive to the need to prioritize relationships, within local communities and more broadly, demonstrating mutual concern one for the other. For, she maintains, "individualism is the antithesis of a true sense of community."[39] This concern for wider community is also evident in the contribution of Latina feminists.

---

34. See also León, "Latino Men, Machismo, and Christianity," 279–95.

35. Isasi-Díaz, *Mujerista Theology*, 145.

36. Isasi-Díaz, *Mujerista Theology*, 130.

37. See, for example, the closing ritual in Gonzalez, *Embracing*, 79–82.

38. For further reflection, see Gonzalez, *Embracing*, and Pérez, Coyarrubias, and Foley, *Así Es: Stories of Hispanic Spirituality*.

39. Isasi-Díaz, *La Lucha Continues*, 60.

LATINA FEMINIST AND FEMINIST INTERCULTURAL THEOLOGY

Latina feminist theologians articulate their own particular method and preferred vision of the future. Pineda-Madrid reflects on the liberating social vision advanced by *mujerista* theology and recognizes that this vision has developed the moral agency of women enabling them to flourish and speak their theological wisdom publicly. *Mujerista* theology brings self-awareness of deep and internalized oppression. It sets out to transform structures in society that create this oppression. It is a theology that consistently calls for a turning away from sin and the dismantling of sinful structures. She observes that while *mujerista* theology distances itself from feminist theology it is also indebted to feminist theology. *Mujerista* theology draws upon feminist theory in distinct ways, especially in its use of meta-ethnography, yet it does employ a feminist hermeneutic.[40]

María Pilar Aquino, Daisy Machado, and Jeanette Rodríguez also articulate their appreciation for the contribution of *mujerista* theology. They too, however, defend their use of the term Latina feminists.

> Since the power of self-naming is so crucial to the experience of women, particularly non-white women of grassroots provenance, this decision represents our effort at self-identity in the public sphere . . . what we offer . . . is what Cherríe Moraga has called "a theory in the flesh" which because of the "physical realities of our lives—our skin color, the land or concrete we grew up on, our sexual longings—all fuse to create a politic born of necessity." This theory in the flesh is also plural and multivocal.[41]

Latina feminists articulate the bond they share by living in the physical space of the United States. Each, in some way, experiences racism, sexism, devaluation, and exclusion in a culture and society that "cannot seem to move beyond the white/black focus of its national discourse on race and national identity."[42] They continue to problematize and pluralize examinations of inequalities because a plurality of oppositional expressions rises up from lived experience. They affirm the interconnected realities of colonialism, conquest, and domination (see chapter 2), recognizing that such

---

40. Pineda-Madrid, "Feminist Theory," 350.

41. Aquino, Machado and Rodríguez, *A Reader in Latina Feminist Theology*, xiv.

42. Aquino, Machado and Rodríguez, *A Reader in Latina Feminist Theology*, xv. See also Gonzalez, *Embracing*, 10.

interconnected realities are shared from the expansive southwest of the United States to the Spanish speaking Caribbean. Latina feminists maintain, therefore, that this is both a national and international conversation:

> Latina feminist theologians often work on related topics, but they are not a homogenous, self proclaimed group of scholars. Their commonalities include feminist critical analysis, contextual accent and a liberationist emphasis in their work. Informed by these analyses, these theologians destabilize androcentric and hierarchical theologies, offering an emancipatory vision that promotes the humanity of all.[43]

Pineda-Madrid is careful to challenge the misconception that feminist theory is primarily the domain of Euro-American scholars working at educational institutions in the United States of America or Europe. She seeks to dispel the erroneous assertion that Latina or women scholars of color are simply "borrowing" from the contributions of first-world feminists. While she concedes that "some segments of feminist theory have developed to the benefit of white middle-class women alone," this is not the whole story.[44] De Anda argues that "because of the embodied lived reality of Latinas and the reality of our cultures being suppressed and annihilated, the Latina reality exists as something entirely different from a Western Euro-American and/ or white framework."[45] Latina scholars, then, engage with feminist theory and have resourced a more mature and nuanced discourse for the benefit of all.[46] The work of the feminist postcolonial philosopher and theologian Mayra Rivera, for example, with her focus on Caribbean postcolonial thought takes place at the intersection of the philosophy of religion, literature, and theories of coloniality, race, and gender.[47]

Latina feminists articulate how they experience being partially outside and partially inside the Western frame of reference. They affirm that such "in-betweenness" is an inevitable facet of Latina life.

---

43. Gonzalez, *Embracing*, 8.
44. Pineda-Madrid, "Feminist Theory," 348.
45. De Anda, "Latina Feminist and *Mujerista* Theologies," 272.
46. See chapter 4 on feminist theology in Gonzalez, *Created in God's Image*, 108–32.
47. For an engagement with liberation theology, radical orthodoxy, feminism, and postcolonialism, see Rivera Rivera, *A Touch of Transcendence*. See also Pitts, "Latina/x Feminist Philosophy," in Hall and Ásta, *The Oxford Handbook of Feminist Philosophy*, 120–35.

In this in-between existence we move across racial, cultural, economic, and idiomatic boundaries. We may be citizens but we continue to have outside status. We may be part of the academy, but our research interests continue to be labeled "special topics." We may be members of a parish, but our styles of worship continue to be considered nontraditional and ethnic. The ministries to our communities continue to be underfunded and overlooked in denominational planning. We are daily border-crossers who must learn early on to interpret life on both sides—life in the dominant culture and life in the Latina community—in order to survive.[48]

In a similar vein to *mujerista* theologians, Latina feminists resist the understanding of scholarship as an individualistic, isolated endeavor. Rather they show how their faith grounds not only a corporate struggle of resistance toward survival but also a corporate work of theology, in the academy and in the world. This scholarship is not reticent to focus on religious practice as a source of Latina thought in feminist intellectual history, feminist liberation theology, and feminist interpretation of class, race, and oppression. Such faith, expressed in religious practice, inspires just action. In examining the realities of Latina life in the everyday, these theologians establish critical conversation on far reaching issues from fresh interpretations of Scripture for undocumented women, to a preferential option for the poor that finds expression among Latinas, to ecumenical challenges around understandings of Mary, to significant themes in epistemology. They offer innovative, intercultural, and imaginative theology.[49]

Latina feminist theologians acknowledge the long history of feminist movements in Latin America, and they draw on critical feminist theories rooted there.[50] With Pineda-Madrid, María Pilar Aquino argues that it is a mistake to think that the term *feminista* was transplanted or translated from

---

48. Aquino, Machado, and Rodríguez, *A Reader in Latina Feminist Theology*, xvii.

49. For further examples of intercultural work, see the contributions in part III, "A Symphony of Voices," in Johnson, *The Strength of Her Witness*. For a feminist approach to anthropology, see Gonzalez, *Created in God's Image*. For innovative work on corporeality in biblical theology, political theory, and continental philosophy, see Rivera Rivera, *Poetics of the Flesh*.

50. See, for example, the writings of philosopher and poet Sor Juana Inés de la Cruz (1651–95, Mexico); social activist Flora Tristán (1803–44, France and Peru); political theorist Lola Rodríguez de Tió (1843–1924, Puerto Rico); and the moderately pro-feminist work of philosopher Carlos Vaz Ferreira (1872–1958, Uruguay). Pineda-Madrid notes how these thinkers inform the work of María Pilar Aquino, Michelle Gonzalez, and Mayra Rivera Rivera among others. Pineda-Madrid, "Feminist Theory," 352.

white, first-world contexts. For Latin American feminism has deep historical roots in socio-political and economic analysis that leads to liberative theological vision and practice.[51] This is evident in the life and contribution of Ofelia Ortega, for example, seen in her most recent work *Cuban Feminist Theology: Vision and Praxis*.[52] Also important in this regard is the use of Chicana feminist theory. This theory emerged from the socio-political aspirations of Mexicanos/as, Chicanos/as, and other Latinos/as/xs who sought to dismantle racist and sexist policies in the southwest and west of the United States in response to unjust social structures, civil rights abuses, and police brutality.[53] Again, in this thought, intersecting forms of oppression in cultural constructs and social realities are exposed. Once acknowledged, these interlocking oppressions can be analyzed and critiqued more fully, leading to a reorientation of established categories and the creation of fresh, transformative categories. In this way Latina feminist theologians continue to hold social justice at the heart of their work. Pineda-Madrid affirms that engagement with feminist theory has enabled Latina feminist scholars to focus on a praxis of liberation that not only gives voice to women but also seeks to radically transform unjust social structures. She considers interculturality and intersectionality to be a future development for Latina *feminista* and *mujerista* theology because such work clarifies the complexity of social constructs, and the multidimensional experiences of women in their families, churches, and communities.

In *Latina Explorations for a Just World*, Aquino and Maria José Rosado-Nunes bring together a number of scholars and perspectives that shape an exploration of feminist intercultural theology.[54] They articulate the tensions, attitudes, and emotions experienced as Latin American and Latina scholars seek to work together, modelling how to express pain across difference, how to acknowledge shared experiences, and how to recognize the particularity of contextual concerns. Aquino draws attention to understandings of interculturality that can orient and, for many in the dominant culture, *reorient* theology. First, she explains that interculturality emerges

---

51. See, for example, Bedford, *La porfía de la resurreción*; Azcuy, Bedford, and García B., *Teología feminista a tres voces*; Gonzalez, *Sor Juana: Beauty and Justice in the Americas*; Tamez, *Through Her Eyes*.

52. See Ortega, *Cuban Feminist Theology*.

53. Pineda-Madrid notes this influence particularly in her own work and also in the work of Jeanette Rodríguez, María Pilar Aquino, and Theresa Torres among others, "Feminist Theory and Latina Feminist/Mujerista Theologizing," 352.

54. Aquino and Rosado-Nunes, *Feminist Intercultural Theology*.

from daily life where human interactions take place. This moves beyond tolerance or acknowledgment of cultural diversity and leads to an awareness of interculturality as an opportunity for growth and dialogue. Second, interculturality is a social movement that is dedicated to strengthening relationships so that each person can live together in solidarity and in peace. In this way interculturality is intrinsically connected to the understanding and pursuit of justice. Third, interculturality seeks to transform power relations in contemporary cultures and societies, confronting domination and subordination. Through such transformation, she affirms, women are participating in God's truth. Fourth, she asserts that an intercultural methodology models how diverse methods can interact, so that they "intersect and enrich one another so as to participate more effectively in the project of constructing a new world based on justice."[55] This is a paradigm that she understands to be a "process of critical deliberation" in which theologians are committed to replacing domination with justice, subordination with emancipation, capital with human dignity, a predatory market with an inclusive community, domestication of religion with transformative religion, absolutist Christianity with dialogical Christianity, and a domineering monocultural interpretation with critical ethical-political interpretation.[56]

Nancy Bedford, who was born in Argentina and has spent many years teaching in the United States and Latin America, reflects Methodist and Mennonite influences in recognizing that interculturality is a move beyond tolerance amid diversity toward cultural and political ways for the "mutual transformation and ... flourishing of all."[57] Bedford encourages the exercise of discernment and judgment, exhorting all to be aware of personal positionality in power relations. She calls attention to what she considers to be the tender yet fearless approach of her colleagues:

> It seems to me that theologians, particularly those cognizant of the "colonial difference," are trained to think in such [discerning] ways. Furthermore Latina and Latin American feminist theologians are well-seasoned practitioners of the nonviolent art of "making spaces" for themselves and others. . . . For we know that,

---

55. Aquino, "Feminist Intercultural Theology," in Aquino and Rosado-Nunes, *Feminist Intercultural Theology*, 16.

56. Aquino, "Feminist Intercultural Theology," in Aquino and Rosado-Nunes, *Feminist Intercultural Theology*, 16 and 23.

57. Bedford, "Making Spaces," in Aquino and Rosado-Nunes, *Feminist Intercultural Theology*, 54.

in the matter of finding and making spaces, God's spirit is nearer to us than the air we breathe.[58]

This ability to make space for one another and to allow the Spirit of God to work across difference is a significant aspect of intercultural work modelled by Latina and Latin American feminist theologians. For as Geraldina Céspedes recognizes, this approach is not about setting up a new form of "universal objectivity . . . as the criterion for all forms of knowledge."[59] Rather, an intercultural approach affirms theological depth in diversity. In the academy and in the church, where minoritization is so often experienced, the intercultural approach of Latina feminists and the challenges they identify sets this theology apart.

LATINA *EVANGELICA* THEOLOGY

In creating space for the diversity of voices among Latina women theologians, a third group of scholars are noteworthy. As discussed in earlier chapters, it is often assumed in the United States that Latinas are Roman Catholic. Denominational differences clearly emerge, however, in the work of Latina *evangélicas* who articulate the Latina Protestant experience giving voice to their understanding of womanhood and their recognition of the importance of particularity.[60] As early as 1997, such particularities were being explored and were published in the volume *Teología en Conjunto: A Collaborative Hispanic Protestant Theology*, edited by Loida I. Martell and José David Rodríguez, to which Latina *evangélica* theologians contributed.[61] Martell explains:

> The term "evangélica" does not necessarily translate as "evangelical," which in the United States implies a particular theological and at times political position within Protestantism. Rather,

58. Bedford, "Making Spaces," in Aquino and Rosado-Nunes, *Feminist Intercultural Theology*, 64.

59. Here Céspedes is echoing the words of Ivone Gebara. See Céspedes, "Sources and Processes of the Production of Wisdom," in Aquino and Rosado-Nunes, *Feminist Intercultural Theology*, 39.

60. See Martell-Otero, Maldonado Pérez, and Conde-Frazier, *Latina Evangélicas*.

61. See the constructive series of essays in Rodriguez and Martell-Otero, *Teología en Conjunto*, in particular Chavez Sauceda, "Love in the Crossroads: Stepping-Stones to a Doctrine of God in Hispanic/Latino Theology," 22–32; Conde-Frazier, "Hispanic Protestant Spirituality," 125–45; and Martell-Otero, "The Ongoing Challenge of Hispanic Theology," 146–66.

"evangélica" in Spanish simply denotes one as a Protestant. In Puerto Rico, few Protestants call themselves "Protestantes," with its implications about protest. Most call themselves evangelic@s. because they see themselves as a people of "The Book"—*el evangelio* or "good news." Thus, the Bible holds a preeminent place in evangélica theology.[62]

Martell emphasizes the constructive engagement with Scripture undertaken by *evangélicas* that she describes as "reading against the grain." Authority is ascribed to the Bible and at the grassroots women take the Bible seriously because it is a space in which they encounter God in daily life. "Reading against the grain," maintains Martell, "honors the communal narratives that arise when evangélicas interweave biblical interpretation with *testimonios* (witness) and *coritos* (short refrains). . . . [R]eading against the grain is a salvific process in which evangélicas experience empowerment, healing and transformation."[63] Scripture is read by *evangélicas* through the particularities of their lived experience. Martell notes that these particularities are often shaped by neglect, violence, abuse, and poverty as they are shaped by hope, life, family, and faith. Elizabeth Conde-Frazier calls such reading the "hermeneutic of the reality of life." In this interpretive approach women "establish a dialogue between the sacred text and the text of their lives."[64] In explication of such readings by *evangélicas*, Conde-Frazier cites the work of Aida Besançon-Spencer on women in ministry; Leticia Guardiola-Saenz on historical change and transformation; and Daisy Machado on justice, feminists, and the undocumented woman.[65] She explains that for *evangélicas* there is liberation not only in the reading of the text but in the commitment to action that will take place in light of the reading of the text. "In this way the hermeneutical space births a word that becomes a liberating event in the community. Thus it becomes an enfleshed or incarnated word."[66]

Latina *evangélicas* expect such readings of Scripture to take seriously an anticolonial reading of Scripture that listens to the voices of the absent, the silenced, and the colonized. At the same time, it should be a reading that is critically aware of how Scripture has been "complicit" in the colonizing

62. Martell, "Reading against the Grain," 104.
63. Martell, "Reading against the Grain," 105.
64. Conde-Frazier, "*Evangélicas* Reading Scriptures: Readings from within and beyond the Tradition," in *Evangélicas*, 85 and 89.
65. Conde-Frazier, "*Evangélicas* Reading Scriptures," 80–83.
66. Conde-Frazier, "*Evangélicas* Reading Scriptures," 89. See also Conde-Frazier, "Participatory Active Research," 234–44.

process in the past. Martell recognizes the need for nuanced readings that acknowledge complexity, attend carefully to work undertaken in biblical studies, and discern the Spirit at work in holistic responses to Scripture. Martell is attentive to "minority voices" in the biblical text. She argues that they bear constant witness to survival and counter-narratives of resistance that must never be overlooked or silenced.

> If we learn to read Scripture in this way, it becomes a way of life. We learn to hear the non-voices around us—the stories never passed down of slaves, of native peoples destroyed, of comfort women abused and thrown aside as refuse, of slaves trafficked who have become the engine of nations' economic booms, and countless others. We learn to read against the grain and so acknowledge our complicity in the world's injustice. We learn not to take comfort in a false Christianity of unholy sanctity that allows us to pretend to be religious, while we grow deaf to the cries of the suffering and exploited around us.[67]

In her foreword to the foundational text *Latina Evangélicas: A Theological Survey from the Margins*, Serene Jones comments, "Rarely do I come across a book in the field of systematic theology that by the end of the first page has stirred in me three very different reactions. It made me think very, very hard. It surprised me with the newness of its idea. And best of all, it caused me to smile."[68] There is much wisdom to be gathered here regarding Latina Protestant experience and theology. This theology leans into the postcolonial and the feminist in a way that invites all to reflect on God, Scripture, ecclesiology, eschatology, and daily life afresh. As Latina *evangélicas*, they demonstrate how to move beyond both Catholic theological approaches and received Protestant interpretations. Interaction with the Holy Spirit, for example, is depicted as dancing with the "Wild Child" of the Trinity. The doctrine of the Trinity is explored through the concept that God *"es y son familia,"* is and are family. The worth of the human family is deepened through the conviction that because of salvation, Latina women are no longer despised *satas* but beloved *santas*—a powerful reminder of being excluded *sobrajas* no more.[69] Latina *evangélicas* read and reflect

---

67. Martell, "Reading against the Grain," 120.
68. Jones, "Foreword," in *Latina Evangélicas*, xi.
69. Martell draws on Puerto Rican vocabulary here to assert that women are no longer despised *satas* or "mongrels" but beloved saints. They are no longer excluded or discarded as *sobrajas* or "leftovers."

from within the Protestant tradition in a way that confronts the tradition as needed but does so with a life-giving efficacy that leads well beyond the tradition itself. They pursue an ecumenical approach that is appreciative of other theologies and yet offers a distinct *evangélica* perspective. Martell states:

> [O]ur theology transcends the theologies we inherited. Those wise women taught us about the power of prophetic words and the responsibility we have to seek and hear them. They did not simply pass on *el evangelio* (the gospel) as a set of accepted dogmatic statements. They nurtured us with a keen sense of the Spirit's ability to create anew. While their teachings were our starting point, an ongoing communal collaborative effort to constructively expound upon various themes from the perspective of *evangélicas*— a *teología en conjunto*—leads us to critically discern aspects of our inherited traditions that have been colonized. Thus, this book also represents a post-colonial reinterpretation of our theologies.[70]

Gathered in one volume, Jones notes that this theological work provides an "abiding wisdom . . . offered for all, that cannot help but enrich the faith of those who engage it."[71]

ABUELITA THEOLOGY

The wisdom highlighted by Latina *evangélicas* through testimonies of grandmothers, mothers, godmothers, aunts, sisters, nieces, and cousins conveys a faith that is lived in dedication to religious practices and tradition, and in service to family. Given that the private space of home and family is seen as the feminine domain, some refer to this wisdom as theology and philosophy "of the kitchen."[72] This is an approach rooted in reality "as it is" looking toward realities that might yet be. Jeanette Rodriguez explains:

> If theology is faith reflecting upon life then there is a whole theology here in these stories. In these are "organic" theologians telling us: who this God is, how this God works, what this God does, how dependent they are upon this God and how their life and this God represent the same thing. They are doing theology. But they are not using the scholarly language of the tradition of theology. What

---

70. Martell-Otero, *Latina Evangélicas*, 2.
71. Jones, foreword to *Latina Evangélicas*, xii.
72. Gonzalez, *Embracing*, 19.

emerges is a spirituality that is rooted in reality *as it is* challenging us not to sanitize God but to "see" beyond seeing.[73]

This wisdom continues to find expression in what is now becoming known as *abuelita* theology, theology of our grandmothers.[74] In *Abuelita Faith: What Women on the Margins Teach Us about Wisdom, Perseverance, and Strength*, Cuban American writer Kat Armas weaves personal story with biblical reflection as she draws on the theological insight of nameless, marginalized women. Such an approach is "the practice of uncovering and naming our abuelas who have inspired, taught, and guided us in our process of belonging and becoming." She recognizes that these stories and reflections hold both beauty and pain, inhabiting a "complicated, interstitial space."[75] Reflecting the tradition of the New Testament figures Lois and Eunice (2 Timothy 1:5) in Latino/a/x religious cultures, it is most often the matriarchal figures who preserve spirituality within families. They pass on religious traditions and practices from one generation to the next.[76] Armas notes that the role of *abuela* might be considered that of the "live-in minister," as women often function like priestesses and theologians in their homes and in their communities.[77] As discussed in chapter 3, such women survive as witnesses and bear distinct testimonies to distinct understandings of God and faith. Armas argues that *abuelita* theology helps women articulate how it is possible for marginalized, impoverished, and subjugated people to continue to have faith in the God of liberation. *Abuelita* theology is testimony to the endurance of faith across centuries in the face of great trial and exploitation.[78] Theresa Torres too points to such resilience and strength passed from one generation of women to the next:

> As I reflected on the various types of prayer I rely on to give me strength and support on a daily basis and to carry me through the

---

73. Rodriguez, *Stories*, 31.

74. In Spanish *abuela* and *abuelita* mean grandmother. *Abuelita* conveys a sense of affection, warmth, or endearment and is often used by grandchildren and close family members.

75. Armas, *Abuelita Faith*, 156–58.

76. See 2 Timothy 1:3–5 NRSV, "I am reminded of your sincere faith, a faith that lived first in your grandmother Lois and your mother Eunice and now, I am sure, lives in you."

77. For further discussion, see Medina and Gonzalez, *Voices from the Ancestors*; see also the section entitled "A New Liturgy—La Teología de las Abuelas," in Salvatierra and Wrencher, *Buried Seeds*, 140–42.

78. Armas, "The Liberating Theology of Our Abuelitas," *Sojourners*, July 7, 2021, accessed March 18, 2023, https://sojo.net/articles/liberating-theology-our-abuelitas.

dark times, I had to return to my childhood. It was my *abuelita*....
I keep these nuggets of wisdom, knowledge, and strength close to
my heart and soul. Because what she taught me was that prayer is
about life—there is no division between daily life and daily prayer,
they are one and the same. She taught me that the great Good that
we call God is present all around us and we are one in the great
Good.[79]

TOWARD JUSTICE IN COMMUNITY

The theologians discussed in this chapter push traditional theology by "presenting a historically conditioned vision of the human that is not an abstract, universal theoretical category."[80] Women, created in the image of God, across difference, speak from within relational networks of families and communities. Gonzalez argues:

> The image in which we are created is a relational Trinity that exists in community. Thus the image of God in us represents the communal dimension of humanity. Christians believe that God is monotheistic yet at the same time Triune. God exists as Creator, Sustainer and Redeemer, as a community of three in one. Therefore, the image of God within us must be communal and social. We must understand our salvation as social. Our lives are intimately connected to the rest of humanity. Harmony, order, balance and solidarity mark the common good. The communion that is humanity mirrors the communion of the Trinity that must be enacted through solidarity.[81]

Despite the fact that a communal anthropology is grounded in the understanding of the human being as relational, she also warns against sentimentality and naivety. For there can be division, marginalization, and exploitation within community and therefore not every community can or should be celebrated. Nonetheless, Gonzalez affirms that relationships "define who we are. It is through our relationships with others, and our relationships with the divine, that our identity is formed.... The human person is not solely constituted by human relationships; one's relationship

---

79. Torres, "What My Abuelita Taught Me about Prayer and Memory," in Medina and Gonzalez, *Voices from the Ancestors*, 142–43.
80. Gonzalez, "Who We Are," 78.
81. Gonzalez, *Embracing*, 15.

with the divine as giver of life is foundational."[82] This relationship with the God of justice, then, is the foundation of all other relationships.

In recent decades Latina theologians have moved far beyond what may be considered solely *mujerista*, Latina feminist, Latina feminist intercultural, or Latina *evangélica* concerns. But the pursuit of justice remains central. Latina scholars offer a breadth of research across disciplines, as seen throughout this book. This includes work in church history, religious history, biblical studies, doctrine, systematics, social justice, spiritualities, Afro-Caribbean religions, education and pedagogies, race, suffering, salvation, and eco-theology.[83] As women in the church and in the academy, who exist across borders of languages and cultures, and who recognize the insufficiencies and inconsistencies of much traditional theology, these scholars look unflinchingly at brutality and violence, recognizing the urgency to reexamine theological categories and assumptions. They name themselves. They name realities for women. They call out the church and the academy. In doing so they bear testimony to the God of justice.[84] These theologians remind all theologians to look beyond themselves and their own immediate issues to the realities of the everyday world:

> Because Latina feminist and *mujerista* theologies take *lo cotidiano* and *lo popular* . . . as their theologically rooted places and because women from these places have cried out against injustices suffered, these theologies struggle for justice by demanding better social relationships and fuller flourishing of life. . . . Justice is

---

82. Gonzalez, "Who We Are," 79.

83. See, for example, Gonzalez, *Afro-Cuban Theology*; Gonzalez, *A Critical Introduction to Religion in the Americas*; Gonzalez and Edmonds, *Caribbean Religious History*; Ress, *Ecofeminism in Latin America*; Gebara, *Longing for Running Water: Ecofeminism and Liberation*; Conde-Frazier, Kang, and Parrett, *A Many Colored Kingdom*; González-Andrieu, "The Good of Education: Accessibility, Economy, Class and Power," and Martell-Otero, "*Hablando Se Entiende la Gente*: Tower of Babble or Gift of Tongues?," in *Teaching Global Theologies: Power and Praxis*, 54–74 and 143–62; Martell-Otero, "From Foreign Bodies in Teacher Space to Embodied Spirit in *Personas Educadas*: or, How to Prevent 'Tourists of Diversity' in Education," and Conde-Frazier, "Thoughts on Curriculum as Formational Praxis for Faculty, Students and Their Communities," in *Teaching for a Culturally Diverse and Racially Just World*, 52–68, 126–46; and Conde-Frazier, *Atando Cabos*.

84. See, for example, Pineda-Madrid, *Suffering and Salvation*; Pineda-Madrid, foreword to Teuring, *Fragile Resurrection*; Gebara, *Out of the Depths*; Pilar Aquino and Schüssler Fiorenza, *In the Power of Wisdom*; Machado, "The Unnamed Woman: Justice, Feminists and the Undocumented Woman," in *A Reader in Latina Feminist Theology*, 161–76.

not measured in huge outcomes or massive amounts of social and structural change. For *mujerista* theologies, justice is measured in small bits gleaned in our daily existence. For this reason, the theological category is *"un poquito de justicia"* because just a little bit of justice continues the momentum in the cry and struggle for life.[85]

There is no doubt that the pursuit of justice permeates the work of Latina theologians. This is also a key feature of Latino/a/x theologies more broadly. In the closing chapter we will examine further the ways in which Latino/a/x theologies look for the Spirit of God at work in the world and how they bear witness to the need for faith and justice in the contemporary public square in the United States.

IN CONVERSATION

Maria Teresa Bautista-Berrios

Llévame donde la gente
Necesiten tus palabras
Necesiten tus ganas de vivir
Donde falte la esperanza
Donde falte la alegría
Simplemente
Por no saber de ti.[86]

I am currently a seminarian at Virginia Theological Seminary working toward my MDiv on my journey toward ordained ministry. Before moving to the East Coast, I was a missioner/church planter at Episcopal Church in Northshore, with the focus of developing an Episcopal presence between Hwy 610 and 8 in the East Harris Convocation of the Diocese of Texas. Previously I was the missioner associate for Houston Canterbury, an Episcopal campus ministry at

---

85. De Anda, "Latina Feminist and *Mujerista* Theologies as Political Theologies?," 274. See also Isasi-Díaz, *Mujerista Theology*, 105–8. For more discussion on *lo popular*, the popular, often used in reference to religious practices, see Espín and Díaz, *From the Heart of Our People*, 263.

86. Lyrics from the much loved hymn "Alma Misionera." Lyrics and Music Anon. "Lord, Lead me where people need your words, where people have lost the will to live, where there is no hope, where there is no joy, only because they do not know you." Translation by Sharon E. Heaney.

Texas Southern University, University of Houston, San Jacinto and Houston Community College. I graduated from the University of Houston-Downtown with a BS in Psychology in 2018. Prior to work in the Diocese, I was a community organizer with The Metropolitan Organization (TMO) and youth group coordinator for Epiphany Episcopal Church. I also served as the chair for the Commission on Black Ministry. I grew up within the Episcopal Diocese of Washington D.C. and moved to Houston in 2014, along with my parents, The Rev. Simon and Amarilis Bautista, and my siblings, Tito, Leaquina, and Lily. As an Afro-Latina with two parents from the Dominican Republic, I am bilingual in Spanish and English. I enjoy life with my husband Fabian our baby girl Camila, and our puppy Noelani.

The voices of women in this chapter are important to me because I am seen. My experience in the United States as a young woman of Dominican descent is named. I am named. The stories of my family are named. The wisdom of those we love is named. My parents are who they are, and I am who I am because of our grandmothers. These women were never called theologians and they still are not called theologians, but they are the wisdom, and the understanding of what faith means in our home.

My family background is mostly Roman Catholic and so for me the *mujerista* and *abuelita* theologies speak to much of what I have known. In my family, our mothers and grandmothers taught us that faith and the church family are central. In conflict, we pray. If there is no food, we pray. We pray in the midst of struggle. This is the hope and faithful testimony they taught us. I have survived many things in life because of the prayers of my grandmother. Faithful prayers and struggle are my heritage. And so this chapter encapsulates the women who carry my family, my school, my church. It has been so helpful for me also to read more about Latina *evangélicas* in the context of the United States. It reminded me of the women I know who take Scripture seriously.

I need others I study and work with to learn that this conversation exists in theology and that it is ongoing. This is so important for our ministries and for our vocations. I want my white Anglo friends to learn from this theology. I want them to know that when they come into a Spanish-language space in their community that they will find real faith there among the women. I want my male Latino colleagues to hear these voices of women in theology too. For toxic masculinity and *machismo* are alive and well in our families and our churches. I long for these women to be respected. So often they are laughed at in church—"What would you know about liturgy? What would you know about anything?" Their dignity is undermined. Their experience is dismissed. Their contribution in the community is diminished. Their well-being is overlooked. Yet, this kind of woman is the pillar of her family, and she is a pillar of faith.

I need my dominant culture colleagues to be attentive to this emphasis on family and faith. Sometimes I hear my notions of family mocked. I just wish we could have priorities that are not driven by the dominant culture. For me, family and relationships are everything. We are not individual people. Family and relationships shape our identities and are our identity. My family are the air that I breath. Brokenness in family, and brokenness in relationships means brokenness in trust. This kind of brokenness can shatter our whole identity. This is why the pursuit of justice for families has such deep pastoral implications. Separation of families, separation from families, and other such challenges associated with immigration, are so devastating in our Latino/a/x cultures. Given serious social concerns, we need colleagues to be strong leaders who make a way for justice and who harness energy for justice. Have a compassionate, understanding heart in your ministry and in your pastoral care. For like family, justice is also the air that we breath.

The voices of women in this theology bridges the in-betweenness that is so hard to navigate in the United States. Their stories and wisdom connect us across generations, across languages, across cultures, and across identities. I especially love to learn about women in Caribbean theologies and I look forward to hearing more from emerging Afro-Latina voices. They speak directly to my experience of feeling like there is no real home in the United States. They encourage me to hope for a more expansive identity. For to be Afro-Latina is a very particular experience of in-betweenness and colorism here. There is nothing more difficult than walking into a Spanish-language congregation and they refuse to speak to you in Spanish because they think you are African American. They simply cannot fathom that someone of my skin color would be Latina. I remember too my Dad once wrote about other spaces he would walk into. He would recall "I'm black until I start talking." It is so complex—the unknown, the unsaid, the being misunderstood. What does it really mean to be Afro-Latina here in the United States and what are the possibilities in the future?

It is beautiful to me that despite everything, even in the midst of the in-betweenness, testimonies of women are being heard. The testimonies of women point to sacred spaces. In these spaces for women beautiful conversations can take place. Of course, I recognize that such sacred spaces can be, simultaneously, spaces where oppression can take place. I do not love to cook but I do love to be in the kitchen. It is a sacred space. There can be such beauty in that spot. No matter our differences, we all meet in the kitchen. In my family, women from the Dominican Republic, El Salvador, Mexico, and the United States gather there. This is where we get things done. This is where we can talk. Everything is as one language here. Christian theologians need to take more heed of this voice.

FOUNDATIONAL READING

Armas, Kat. *Abuelita Faith: What Women on the Margins Teach Us about Wisdom, Persistence, and Strength.* Grand Rapids: Brazos, 2021.
De Anda, Neomi. "Latina Feminist and *Mujerista* Theologies as Political Theologies?" In *T. & T. Clark Handbook of Political Theology*, edited by Rubén Rosario Rodríguez, 271–84. London: T. & T. Clark, 2020.
Gonzalez, Michelle A. *Embracing Latina Spirituality: A Woman's Perspective.* Cincinnati: St. Anthony Messenger, 2009.
Isasi-Díaz, Ada María. *En la Lucha / In the Struggle: Elaborating a Mujerista Theology.* Minneapolis: Fortress, 1993.
Martell-Otero, Loida, Zaida Maldonado Pérez, and Elizabeth Conde-Frazier. *Latina Evangélicas: A Theological Survey from the Margins.* Eugene, OR: Cascade, 2013.
Pineda-Madrid, Nancy. "Feminist Theory and Latina Feminist/Mujerista Theologizing." In *The Wiley-Blackwell Companion to Latino/a Theology*, edited by Orlando Espín, 347–64. Chichester, UK: Wiley, 2015.

FURTHER READING

Aquino, María Pilar, Daisy L. Machado, and Jeanette Rodríguez, eds. *A Reader in Latina Feminist Theology: Religion and Justice.* Austin: University of Texas Press, 2002.
Aquino, María Pilar, and Maria José Rosado-Nunes, eds. *Feminist Intercultural Theology: Latina Explorations for a Just World.* Maryknoll, NY: Orbis, 2007.
León, Luis. "Latino Men, Machismo, and Christianity." In *The Oxford Handbook of Latinx Christianities in the United States*, edited by Kristy Nabhan-Warren, 279–95. Oxford: Oxford University Press, 2022.
Pineda-Madrid, Nancy. *Suffering and Salvation in Ciudad Juárez.* Minneapolis: Fortress, 2011.
Pitts, Andrea. "Latina/x Feminist Philosophy." In *The Oxford Handbook of Feminist Philosophy*, edited by Kim Q. Hall and Ásta, 120–35. Oxford: Oxford University Press, 2021.
Sanchez, Delida, Hector Y. Adames, and Silvia L. Mazzul, eds. "AfroLatinidad: Theory, Research, and Practice." *Journal of Latinx Psychology* 9.1, special edition (2021).
Zamora, Omaris Zunilda. "Let the Waters Flow: (Trans)locating Afro-Latina Feminist Thought." PhD thesis, University of Texas, 2013.

6

La Justicia

The Spirit at Work in the Public Square

> The gospel has been committed to a community, is transmitted by that community, and demands a community experience. Without community there cannot be a living representation of the gospel. It is the community of believers that announces the kingdom of God as a reality, which proclaims a new order of life under the sovereign action of God. . . . The witness has no meaning, however, if it is not backed by a community whose love is translated into works of mercy, a community whose faith is manifested in a commitment to social justice and whose hope is reflected in the struggle for a just peace.[1]
>
> —Orlando E. Costas

IN CHAPTER 1, TEOLOGÍA *en conjunto* focuses the task of theology on community, collaboration, and commitment. In chapter 2, the concept of *mestizaje* is introduced as naming the complexities of community in the face of the pluralities of history, story, culture, and identity. Among such complexities, chapter 3 identifies the importance of *lo cotidiano* as *locus theologicus*. Here the presence of God and the power of the living Christ are discerned amid the ever-present struggle of hope and hopelessness

---

1. Costas, *Liberating News*, 135.

in Latino/a theologies. Such discernment is done in conversation with Scripture. Thus, chapter 4 outlines the significance of interpreting and proclaiming Scripture *latinamente*. In this approach, interpreters read and are read by the biblical text. Chapter 5 acknowledges that received readings of Scripture and theology do not always serve the liberation of all. While the contribution of women theologians permeates every chapter in this book, particular attention is given in chapter 5 to the theology of Latinas. They face interwoven and multilayered oppressions *en la lucha*. Consequently, in Latino/a theologies justice can never be an abstract concept or an acontextual theological theme. Always there is the need to discern the Spirit at work in the world for the sake of life and life-giving practice. Therefore, in this final chapter, discerning the Spirit at work in the public square and discerning the frontiers the Spirit might be calling Latino/a/x theologians toward will be considered. The topics in this chapter are not a definitive or exhaustive list. Rather, they are present and pertinent concerns in the current conversation in Latino/a/x theologies and are identified by Latino/a/x theologians as noteworthy and necessary. No doubt these topics will change. New issues will arise. Fresh theology will emerge. But for now, grounded in the conviction that the Spirit of God is at work, we look to the themes of *fronteras*, exile, and diaspora; the focus on movement, migration, and immigration; and the need for further development in queer theologies from Latino/a/x perspectives.

THE SPIRIT OF GOD AT WORK IN THE WORLD

Latino/a/x theologies in the United States take seriously that the Spirit of God is at work in the world.[2] Published in 2015, *Pentecostals and Charismatics in Latin America and Latino Communities*, edited by Néstor Medina and Sammy Alfaro, examines the contours, challenges, and prospects of

---

2. See Barba, "Latina/o Pentecostalism," 130–50; Schnieder, "Pentecostals/Charismatics," 322–36; García-Johnson, *Spirit outside the Gate*; Smith, *Pentecostal Power*, in particular chapter 3, Carmelo Alvarez, "Hispanic Pentecostals in the United States," 63–84; Ramirez, *Migrating Faith*; Garrard and Dorran, "Pentecostalism and Neo-Pentecostalism in Latin America: Two Case Studies," 291–308; Cleary, *The Rise of Charismatic Catholicism in Latin America*; and Miller and Yamamori, *Global Pentecostalism*. For a thoughtful analysis that draws from ethnographic research at the intersection of Pentecostalism, Latinx Protestantism, and assimilation theories, see Tian-Ren Lin, *Prosperity Gospel Latinos and Their American Dream*. For insight into the Afro-Latino Pentecostal tradition, see Alvarez, *Pentecostal Orthodoxy: Toward an Ecumenism of the Spirit*.

renewal movements across the Americas.³ Medina and Alfaro affirm that scholars are crossing interdisciplinary boundaries to correct previous misconceptions and develop a greater understanding of the social, political, economic, and cultural factors that contribute to the expansion of Pentecostalism and charismatic renewal movements. They caution against reductionist or simplistic readings to explain Pentecostalism and its phenomenal growth in Latin America and the Caribbean.⁴ These diverse renewal movements take on a life of their own among Latino/a/x communities in the United States.⁵ They recognize that "the way Pentecostals-charismatics view themselves and the world, the way they understand the connection between church and social contexts, and the way they think theologically about their faith is *blaringly* absent" from earlier studies.⁶ In contrast, the selection of contributions in their volume range from discussions on the indigenization of the church in Latin America; transformative social ethics in Argentina; social engagement as a new and contested ritual in El Salvador; theological reflections on violence in the context of Honduras; revivalism as revolutionary, reactionary, or remote in Sandinista Nicaragua; the experience of existing between two worlds in youth ministry in the United States; the social impact of Pentecostal revival in Puerto Rico; renewal and *El Camino de la Leche*; and a Latina/o Pentecostal response to the McDonaldization of the church in the United States.⁷ Medina and Alfaro argue that

---

3. Medina and Alfaro, *Pentecostals and Charismatics*.

4. See Rivera-Pagán, "A New Pentecost: Conversion in the Caribbean," 329–46.

5. See Cruz, "A Rereading of Latino(a) Pentecostalism," in Valentín, *New Horizons in Hispanic/Latino(a) Theology*, 201–16; Medina, "*Nepantla* Spirituality: Negotiating Multiple Religious Identities among U.S. Latinas," in De La Torre and Espinosa, *Rethinking Latino(a) Religion and Identity*, 248–66; Villafañe, "An Evangelical Call to a Social Spirituality: Confronting Evil in Urban Society," in Bañuelos, *Mestizo Christianity*, 209–23.

6. Medina and Alfaro, *Pentecostals and Charismatics*, 2.

7. See the variety of chapters in Medina and Alfaro, *Pentecostals and Charismatics*, including Sepúlveda, "The Power of the Spirit and the Indigenization of the Church: A Latin American Perspective," 17–34; Gladwin, "Toward a Transformative Latin American Pentecostal-Charismatic Social Ethics: An Argentine Perspective" 49–66; Bueno, "Translating Pentecost into Transformed Communities in El Salvador: Social Engagement as a New and Contested Ritual," 67–80; Alvarez, "No More Violence! Renewal Theological Reflections on Violence in the Context of Honduras and Its Immigrants to the United States" 81–96; Smith, "Revivalism as Revolutionary, Reactionary, or Remote? Pentecostal Political Heterogeneity in Sandinista Nicaragua," 97–110; Rodríguez, "Between Two Worlds: Hispanic Youth Ministry in the United States," 127–40; DeAnda, "History, Renewal and El Camino de la Leche," 141–56; Contreras-Flores, "The Social Impact of the 1916 Pentecostal Revival in Puerto Rico," 157–68; and Estrada-Carrasquillo, "A

one can no longer speak (as if one ever could) of *a* pentecostal, *a* charismatic, or *a* renewal theology. The realization of the movement's multicultural and multiethnic diversity forces us to reconsider the role of contextual particularity in the way people worship and think theologically.... Significantly, socially conscious, praxis-oriented theologies are emerging from within these communities, theologies that seek to engage the distinctive themes of pentecostal theology from within the purview of poor, marginalized, and oppressed communities, and that aim to thrust the pentecostal church into authentic social engagement and political action.[8]

As with other Latino/a/x theologies in the United States of America social engagement and political action remain at the heart of communities seeking renewal in the power of the Spirit. Despite this, Medina notes that "one would be hard pressed to find any substantial work dealing explicitly with the work and nature of the Spirit in Latina/o theology." This "apparent dearth" of writing on the work of the Spirit does not mean that the Spirit is entirely absent in Latina/o theology. Rather, "a strict pneumatology is yet to be elaborated."[9]

In 1993 Eldin Villafañe published his now classic work *The Liberating Spirit: Towards an Hispanic American Pentecostal Social Ethic*.[10] For Villafañe, it is in the power of the Spirit that the community of faith demonstrates the love of God in Christ through embodying characteristics of the reign of God.[11] This is a spirituality grounded in a commitment to holistic transformation that is both personal and societal for the "spiritual pilgrimage of the believer is a pilgrimage of love. Any true spirituality is ultimately the loving of God and the neighbor as oneself (Matthew 19:19)—the integration of the spiritual and the ethical, of worship and service, of identity and vocation."[12]

Latina/o Pentecostal Response to the McDonaldization of the Church in the United States," 211–27.

8. Medina and Alfaro, *Pentecostals and Charismatics*, 228–29. See also Robeck, *Towards a Pentecostal Theology of Praxis*.

9. Medina, "Theological Musings toward a Latina/o Pneumatology," 173–89, at 173 and 180. Helpful essays include García-Johnson, "The Spirit in the Colonial Difference," 301–10, and Castelo, "Latinx Perspectives," 319–26, in *T. & T. Clark Handbook of Pneumatology*, and also García-Johnson, "In Search of Indigenous Pneumatologies in the Americas," 142–64.

10. Villafañe, *The Liberating Spirit*. See also Villafañe, *Introducción al Pentecostalismo*.

11. See also Cavazos-González, *Beyond Piety*, available in Spanish as *Más allá de la devoción*, and Isasi-Díaz, "Kin-dom of God: A Mujerista Proposal," 171–90.

12. Villafañe, *The Liberating Spirit*, 169. See also the foundational work of Ismael

Villafañe draws on Galatians 5:25 to emphasize both a spirituality that follows Jesus Christ in obedience to God and an ethic of the Spirit: if we live in the Spirit (theological self-understanding), let us also walk in the Spirit (ethical self-understanding). To take the call of God seriously, argues Villafañe, means that the church will be "a community of the Spirit *in* the world and a community of Spirit *for* the world."[13] In this way he imagines how the church can bear witness to the Spirit of God as a place of cultural *survival*, a *signpost* of protest and resistance, a liberated and liberating community of *salvation*, an agent of *shalom* through reconciliation, a *seedbed* for community leadership and a source of social *service*, strength, and support.[14] Roberto Goizueta warns against abstract understandings of church living in the power of the Spirit. He speaks to the importance of being "grounded in the lived ecclesiologies of the majority of the world's Christians who live not in Jerusalem but in Galilee, on the margins of society."[15]

Writing in 1997, Samuel Solivan addresses what he considers to be the depersonalization of the Spirit in much North America Christianity. Such depersonalization is evident in appeals made to the Spirit as a force or an energy or an influence rather than the third person of the Trinity:[16]

> The personalization of the Holy Spirit is important to Hispanic American pneumatology because the relationship of the Spirit to persons, in this case Latinas and Latinos who daily experience treatment as nonpersons, can provide a transformative model of personhood and self-esteem.... The restoration of our full humanity as children of God and beloved of Christ is made possible through the transforming power and presence of the third person of the Trinity, who is the bearer of all the gifts of wholeness, faith,

---

García in *Dignidad: Ethics through Hispanic Eyes*. It is also important to note the contribution of Orlando E. Costas (1942–87), the Puerto Rican-born theologian and missiologist, to the understanding of such holistic transformation. See, for example, Orlando Costas, *The Integrity of Mission: The Inner Life and Outreach of the Church* and *Liberating News*.

13. Villafañe, *The Liberating Spirit*, 194, 196. See also García-Johnson, "The Politics of the *Espiritu*," 355–72, at 360–63.

14. Villafañe, *The Liberating Spirit*, 199. For further discussion on how Mexican American Pentecostal churches have developed and established for themselves a particular religious space, see Sánchez-Walsh, *Latino Pentecostal Identity*.

15. Goizueta, "The Church: A Latino Catholic Perspective," 133–52, at 152.

16. See also Maldonado Pérez, Martell-Ortero, and Conde-Frazier, "Dancing with the Wild Child: Evangélicas *and the Holy Spirit*," in *Evangélicas*, 14–32, at 17–20.

La Justicia

hope, and love. No lesser being is able to overcome the forces and powers of the evil one.[17]

In his exposition of Acts 2, and in his examination of the life and ministry of Jesus in the Gospels, Soliván emphasizes the divine intent of diversity and inclusion in creation and in salvation. This divine intent, also present elsewhere in the New Testament and in the Old, is the restoration of full personhood. To walk in the Spirit, Soliván affirms, demands a commitment to live in harmony with the reign of God and thus live in harmony with one another. This means the church should embody love and justice in *lo cotidiano* through care for the unlovely, the stranger, the foreigner, the sojourner, and the sinner (James 2:1–8): "To be led by the Spirit is no easy task; it is a call, a vocation to incarnate the kingdom of God, to incarnate in our daily lives, collectively and individually, the ethic of love...."[18]

Soliván argues that all people, from every race, tribe, and nation, are created in God's image and are expressions of God's grace. Justice and love in diversity and across difference stand against structures of dominance and denial of humanity.[19] For "as long as the diversity God has intended and the Spirit has empowered is disallowed intentionally or unintentionally, we all fall short of the Holy Spirit's fullness we claim to have or at least seek."[20] For Soliván, such falling short is present in the very terms that Christians do theology. This is seen particularly in the unhelpful binary of orthodoxy versus orthopraxis.[21] Communities that experience oppression and suffering are often forgotten in orthodoxy's preoccupation with propositional truths or orthopraxis' academic theological reflection on praxis that can remain distant from the realities of struggle and suffering. In light of the divine work of the Spirit, Soliván proposes an understanding of *orthopathy* that recognizes the power of the Holy Spirit at work to unveil injustice, to empower believers to transform despair into hope, and to bring wholeness.[22] In the words of Yara González-Justiniano, "Hope is knowing that reality is not the exhaustion of all possibilities. The Spirit weaves together the

---

17. Soliván, "The Holy Spirit," 50–65, at 53 and 55.
18. Soliván, "The Holy Spirit," 63.
19. See also Espín, "Immigration and Some of Its Implications," 28–29.
20. Soliván, "The Holy Spirit," 62.
21. See Soliván, *The Spirit, Pathos and Liberation*.
22. See Medina, "Theological Musings toward a Latina/o Pneumatology," 175.

intentions of the people who lend themselves to be met by her."²³ Conde-Frazier too recognizes this work of the Spirit for *la justicia* when she writes:

> These theologians [liberation theologians in the United States] have emphasized the Spirit's work of bringing one into truth and into connectedness and mutuality for the purpose of creating communion and building community. This is important for transforming domination, marginalization, and dehumanization into freedom and life. The Spirit also empowers the oppressed so that agency, speech, and political action become part of their daily experiences. Her work is seen in the bringing forth from innocence to awareness (conscientization) and in the dialectic between theory and practice.²⁴

In his "constructive theological musings," Medina offers three reflections toward articulating a Latino/a/x pneumatology. Firstly, he recognizes the need to include the unique experiences of women in pneumatological discussions such as conceiving, giving birth, breast-feeding, praying, accompanying the sick and dying, sharing hope. For Medina, the embodied experiences of Latinas help to "speak about the divine Spirit as present/active/enfleshed in the material world, and not detached or disembodied as often appears among traditional pneumatologies."²⁵ Maldonado Pérez captures the essence of this:

> "Wholly present in each and being wholly everywhere," this "Supplier of life" is God with us. She is the passion in the Word-become-Verbo for us. She is God's animator, the "verb" in the Word, if you will. As our Advocate (Helper, Comforter, Counselor), the Holy Spirit is not only God with us; She is God for us. And, for *evangélicas*, the Holy Spirit especially is God in us, the one in and through whom we commune with the divine. Filled, inspired, and moved by the Holy Spirit, *evangélicas* engage life from the perspective of

---

23. González-Justiniano, *Centering Hope as a Sustainable Decolonial Practice*, xiii. See also González-Justiniano, "Practices of Hope."

24. Conde-Frazier, "The Holy Spirit," 31–45, at 45. See also Segura, "Liberation Theology's Spiritual Legacy for the Latin American Church," 377–92.

25. Medina, "Theological Musings toward a Latina/o Pneumatology," 181. For further reflection on cultural expressions as devotion to the Holy Spirit in Mariology and women's experiences, see Medina, "Theological Musings toward a Latina/o Pneumatology," 178–80; De Anda, "Images of God"; Espín, "Mary in Latino/a Catholicism: Four Types of Devotion," 16–25; Nanko-Fernández, "From *Pájaro* to Paraclete," in Espín, *Building Bridges*, 13–28; and Rivera Rivera, "Thinking Bodies: The Spirit of a Latina Incarnational Imagination," 207–25.

the One who is able to move over chaos, nothingness and death, speaking life into death-bearing situations and being midwives to hope. The Holy Spirit emboldens us, even through the shadow of death, to fight the good fight on behalf of those gripped by despair. And it reminds us all, even those who would confuse patriarchy for orthodoxy, that we do all of this as nothing other than *hijas de Dios*—women, mothers, daughters, leaders, pastors, bishops, apostles, vessels and instruments of God's will and glory.[26]

Secondly, Medina proposes that the Latino/a/x principal of *convivencia*, the act of living and sharing life in community together, can shape how the relational characteristics of the Spirit of God might be understood.[27] Living with and sharing life together in celebration amid suffering and despair, and through relational interconnectedness, allows for a reimagining of the human interconnectedness with the divine. As human beings in Latino/a/x communities are formed in relationship with one another, this relational characteristic is not only culturally foundational but also spiritually foundational. Medina observes that not only do human beings encounter one another in the moments and experiences of *lo cotidiano* but they find the empowerment and the strength of the Spirit present with them in those moments to continue in the struggle. Thirdly, therefore, echoing the Christological contribution of Goizueta, Medina offers the Latino/a/x notion of *acompañamiento* or accompaniment, to be a theological category for speaking pneumatologically about walking with and alongside "specific concrete people in their concrete lives."[28] Medina explains that a pneumatology of *acompañamiento* emphasizes that human beings are strengthened and empowered to accompany one another in contexts of discrimination and injustice, following the example of Jesus, because of the work of the Spirit. Discrimination, abuse, exploitation, and marginalization deny life. A relationship with God can reclaim it. Medina argues that in this reclamation the Spirit is not only fulfilling the work of Jesus but is also completing "the divine Triune God's original created intent to be in communion with humanity and the rest of creation."[29]

---

26. Maldonado Pérez, "Dancing with the Wild Child," in *Latina Evangélicas*, 14.

27. See also Benavides, "The Spirit," 25–32, at 25 and 29; see also chapter 3, "Liberating Faith: Popular Religiosity and Power among Latinx Migrants in the United States," in Tulud Cruz, *Christianity across Borders*, 49–64.

28. Medina, "Theological Musings toward a Latina/o Pneumatology," 184. See also García-Johnson, *Mestizo/a Community of the Spirit*, 110–20.

29. Medina, "Theological Musings toward a Latina/o Pneumatology," 185.

For García-Johnson, because the church is the community of the Spirit, the church symbolizes the intersection between the Spirit of God and humanity, evident in a renewing of culture and society. He offers a practical pneumatology that speaks to Christian identity and Christian ethical responsibility, weaving together the significance of the death of Christ on the cross and the implications of the empowering work of the Spirit expressed in the life of the church.[30] Conde-Frazier explores the charisms of the Spirit that empower disciples to carry out the *trabajo personal* (one-on-one ministry) needed to transform suffering communities. The Spirit may grant charisms of prophecy, wisdom, healing, tongues, and discernment.[31] Such testimony to the work of Christ, and expressions of experiencing the Spirit, are explored further by Alfaro. He writes, "What becomes significant in the Pentecostal reflection of Jesus . . . is the importance of the working of the Spirit both in the life of Jesus (as recorded in the biblical text) and also in our experiential understanding of Jesus' continued work in our lives today through his Spirit."[32] The kingdom that Jesus envisioned, argues Alfaro, is one of radical social, political, and economic transformation. Where the reign of God is established justice triumphs over injustice.

> For Jesus is not just our personal Savior; he is the Redeemer of the world. Jesus is not just our personal Sanctifier; he yearns to bring corporate sanctification to the church and society. He is not just our personal Healer, but also the One who can deliver all people from every social evil. He does not baptize us with his Spirit for our own personal enjoyment; he does so to send us out on a Spirit-led mission to the poor and the oppressed. Lastly, Christ is not just our Coming King; but the Proclaimer of God's reign among us—a reign that does not operate only in the spiritual dimension, but that denounces injustice and demands a praxis of love and justice. I believe that such a vision can be undertaken and put to practice as we wrestle with the meaning of the life and mission of Jesus in the power of the Spirit.[33]

García-Johnson expands and extends these theological and missiological reflections in his 2019 contribution *Spirit outside the Gate: Decolonial Pneumatologies of the American Global South*. In this work he examines

---

30. See García-Johnson, *Mestizo/a Community of the Spirit*.
31. Conde-Frazier, "Dancing with the Wild Child," in *Latina Evangélicas*, 21–28.
32. Alfaro, *Divino Compañero*, 29.
33. Alfaro, *Divino Compañero*, 127 and 148.

how the Spirit of God is at work as the church unlearns and relearns what it means to become "the Church without Borders."[34] Zaida Maldonado Pérez affirms this: "For, at the beginning, in the middle, and in the end, the Holy Spirit is about God's mission and the benefits of God's grace are for *all* of God's children, indeed, for all creation."[35]

If a community, inspired by the Spirit, is to see the deeper realities of church without borders, it inevitably must deal with the realities of *fronteras*, exile and diaspora, and the implications of movement, migration, and immigration. For, as Harold Recinos argues, "Public theology is in the position of projecting a religious witness that aims to transform the reality out of which economic and political are shaped in light of a more compassionate view of the public realm."[36]

FRONTERAS, EXILE, AND DIASPORA

In the United States today, faith articulated in the public square inevitably leads to issues surrounding national identities and belonging.[37] Daisy Machado, as seen in chapter 2, clearly expresses concerns about the holding of power and employing that power to name and to exclude in national dialogue.[38] With other Latina theologians (see chapter 5), she offers a different paradigm in which the need to examine the power of names is acknowledged, and the significance of self-naming is primary. Matilde Moros, too, affirms that naming a community is, in fact, an issue of social and economic justice. She explores the connotations of the names used to describe communities which we have touched on already in this study: Hispanic, Latin, Latino, Latina, Latinx, and Latine, among others. Moros also points out complexities of language given that Brazil was colonized by the Portuguese and given that there are other non-Spanish-speaking territories such as Suriname, Belize, parts of Nicaragua, Panama, and Colombia where English is dominant. Yet they too are "Latin American." She explains that "this debate of whether the community is Hispanic or Latino/a has not always been generated from within the community itself; it is in large

---

34. García-Johnson, *Spirit outside the Gate*, 276. See also Brazal and Dávila, *Living With(out) Borders*.
35. Maldonado Pérez, "Dancing with the Wild Child," in *Latina Evangélicas*, 31.
36. Recinos, *Wading through Many Waters*, 4.
37. See Espín, "Immigration and Some of Its Implications," 19–32.
38. Machado, *Of Borders and Margins*, xiii.

part a response to US history, census categories, and broad ignorance of the complexity that makes this larger community one."[39] For theologians seeking to be alert to power dynamics, it is necessary to be aware not only of the complex historical narratives of nations and nationalisms, but also the complex socio-linguistic factors that shape and influence identities.

Latina theologians and Latino/a/x theologies, more widely, assert that naming makes meaning. How communities name themselves and how others name them is telling. Moros recognizes that when close attention is paid to conversations on national identities and naming it inevitably leads to conversations about borders, borderlands, and border crossings:

> [O]ver the last five generations there are families that have resided on what is now US territory since before there was officially a country named the United States of America, and there are families that continue to migrate back and forth over geographic borders. There are as well families that reside in the US but whose members are a mixture of citizens from multiple lands, and whose children are born and/or raised in the US, and who know no other home. This history makes for a very great wealth of social and economic justice issues, but much of this identity voyage is economic in nature, and as such, doing theology from a particular place becomes a social justice statement.[40]

Carmen Nanko-Fernández brings such borderland reflections into focus in her chapter "Alternately Documented Theologies: Mapping Border, Exile and Diaspora."[41] She encapsulates the experience of theologians from racially and ethnically underrepresented communities. Nanko-Fernández argues that diasporic theologians and biblical scholars—including those who are Latino@, Asian American, and African American—"remain academia's undocumented scholars."[42] For Nanko-Fernández, failure to acknowledge the theologizing around migration, so often formed by diasporic experience, in the academy is a replication of the marginalization experienced by communities these theologians are from. She echoes the words of Fumitaka Matsuoka who names this as "racism of omission."[43]

---

39. Moros, "Theologizing Social and Economic Justice," 313–27, at 319.
40. Moros, "Theologizing Social and Economic Justice," 318.
41. Nanko-Fernández, "Alternately Documented Theologies," 33–56.
42. Nanko-Fernández. "Alternately Documented Theologies," 33–56, at 33.
43. For further reflection, see Matsuoka and Fernandez, *Realizing the America of our Hearts*, and Matsuoka, *Out of Silence: Emerging Themes in Asian American Churches*.

Diasporic theologians model how to do theology in multiple directions. They do not merely theologize either from the home they left behind or from the place in which they now find themselves, though they certainly do both of these things. However, in addition, they also theologize *from* the home they left behind *to* the place in which they now find themselves, *and vice versa*, navigating through and across the spaces in between. It becomes clear, again, that the Spirit of justice is not only at work in the public square in the United States but is also at work in making porous the borders of academy, library, and classroom. For Nanko-Fernández the importance of both place and movement is expressed as *via theologica*. This may be, in the words of Nancy Bedford, "a possible variation on a *locus theologicus*."[44]

Nanko-Fernández honors the diversity of experiences and perspectives of movement or migration in the Americas. She warns against any attempt to create a universal theology of migration. Rather, she is attentive to a plurality of migration stories that include—Latino/a/x migratory experiences, Asian North American experiences, and African American experiences. She notes, for example, that African American theology can "introduce a range of lenses from liberation to forced displacement all shrouded in the sin of racism."[45] Given such work, she calls for a more nuanced discourse on migration that is especially necessary in pastoral care and in the formation of public policy. Nanko-Fernández identifies three "coordinates" that can help orientate theologians. She highlights *frontera* (border), exile, and diaspora. Such orientation helps theologians face the substantial theological and biblical material on migratory experiences arising from voluntary migration, forced movement, and settlement.

For some, explorations of the meanings and histories of border or *frontera* can be provocative. Borderland spaces, border crossings, and contested borders bring into view both notions of national fixity and Mexican American, Tejano, and Chicano fluidity. Life along such borders in the west and southwestern regions of the United States of America is often characterized by complex dynamics of communities "on the move" and communities "moved in on."[46] They are places that experienced the intensity of Spanish exploration. They are places that witnessed the far-reaching implications

---

44. See Nanko-Fernández, "Alternately Documented Theologies," 34.

45. Nanko-Fernández, "Alternately Documented Theologies," 35.

46. Nanko-Fernández, "Alternately Documented Theologies," 36. See also Goizueta, "Resisting the Frontier, Meeting at the Border," 98–117. Also helpful in understanding the issues is chapter 1, "The Indian Question in the United States," in Mamdani, *Neither Settler nor Native*, 37–100.

of Catholic evangelization. They are places that know the horrors of violence against indigenous peoples. The borderlands hold the memories and consequences of English-speaking migrations and US imperial aspirations. Nanko-Fernández reminds her readers that the first "illegal aliens" and "undocumented" incursions were, in fact, carried out by white US citizens who migrated, for example, into what now is known as Texas, between 1821 and 1835. It was the presence and settlement of these strangers in the land that led to the invasion and the seizure of Mexican lands. This disenfranchisement of former Mexican citizens, whose descendants had lived on the land for generations, meant they would be labelled "strangers" in their own homeland. Such histories around this contested border have led to Mexican Americans, even today, being victimized as "outsiders."[47] The issue of political citizenship has become deeply racialized.

Understandings of *frontera* can become "lens and locus" in theology. Nanko-Fernández draws on Chicano scholarship and postcolonial culture studies observing that "La frontera is perceived as liminal space, with all the ambiguities, possibilities and violence con-tested places of intersections, encounters and clashes hold."[48] We have already seen, in chapter 2, the potential for *frontera* in Christian hermeneutics and theology in the work of Virgilio Elizondo. He frames his Christology with the notion that Jerusalem is "borderland." As we have seen, this move would be later critiqued by Néstor Medina and Jean-Pierre Ruiz in their deepening reflection on *mestizaje* and borderlands. Representing theology from traditionally underrepresented communities in the academic world on racial, ethnic, cultural, and diasporic diversity, they will not allow any romanticization of borderlands. In the same way that theologians warn against the romanticization of *mestizaje*, Nanko-Fernández cautions against "fetishizing" or "romanticizing" the southern border of the United States. She argues that "spiritualizing interpretations of others' real life dangers has a voyeuristic quality and camouflages the ugliness of socio-economic injustices and violence that characterizes life on the edge."[49] Goizueta too unveils the dehumanizing realities of border crossings and exile. In his theology of accompaniment, he calls the church to testify to its nature as a community across boundaries.[50]

---

47. For further discussion, see Haynes and Wintz, *Major Problems in Texas History*.
48. Nanko-Fernández, "Alternately Documented Theologies," 37.
49. Nanko-Fernández, "Alternately Documented Theologies," 38.
50. See Goizueta, *Caminemos con Jesús*. See also Goizueta, "Christ of the Borderlands,"

La Justicia

In naming the brutality and horrors often experienced by women during migration, and in serious academic work on suffering and violence against women in the borderlands, Latina theologians evidence robust and justice-oriented responses to the realities of the *frontera*.[51] While borders are contested spaces, they are rarely the final destination of migrants. Thus, complex, failed, misguided public policies and public conversations surround this issue. Nanko-Fernández asserts that "theological contributions to the public conversation will remain limited if we stay fixated on the crossing but neglect to attend to the living, to the mundane perils and anxieties associated with going to school, earning a just wage in a safe workplace, renting an apartment, opening a bank account, getting married, driving a car."[52] Theologians need to attend not only to the notion of *frontera* and crossing borders. They also need to attend to the implications of life in exile beyond such borders.[53]

An examination of the theme of exile in Latino/a/x theologies reveals a powerful autobiographical thread.[54] Collective and shared experiences, that avoid the depreciation of distinct differences, are present in Latino/a/x theologies. For insight drawn from Cuban American stories, Nanko-Fernández points to the biblical scholarship of Segovia, the historical contributions of Justo González, and the *mujerista* contribution of Isasi-Díaz (see chapters 4 and 5 in the current study). In their scholarship, historical waves of immigration are evident. It becomes clear that the Babylonian exile serves as a hermeneutical lens to understand vocation, create paradigms, and clarify method. For many, while this journey from Cuba created an improvement in economic conditions, it also created deep loss and "poverty" in terms of identity, roots, dignity, and family. There is a shared testimony of expulsion and loss, with a deep longing for home and an endurance demanded to flourish in the everyday bilingual reality of the United States of America. Segovia models deep biblical work in this "contested experience and embrace of otherness" as he develops a reading strategy and employs his experience of exile to engage difference. Such a

---

177–95. See also Goizueta, "*Corpus Verum*," 143–66.

51. See Pineda-Madrid, *Suffering and Salvation*, and Luévano, *Woman-Killing in Juárez*.

52. Nanko-Fernández, "Alternately Documented Theologies," 39.

53. See also Carroll R., *Christians at the Border*, and Carroll R., *The Bible and Borders*.

54. It is helpful to learn from the discussion and model of *ejercicios de reflexión creativa* in chapter 1, "Soy americano/a/x," in García-Johnson, *Introducción a la teología del nuevo mundo*, 23–32.

strategy brings to the fore themes of immigration, assimilation, and minority formation. For Francisco García-Treto, reading the Hebrew Bible through an exilic lens provides a testimony to survival.[55] González too uses exile as a paradigm to interpret Scripture. He considers the implications of exile and the experience of being "alien" (even in one's own land) as realities shared across diverse Latino/a/x communities:

> We have come to the center, yet we remain at the periphery.... [W]e no longer know where the center is—for that is the very nature of exile, a life in which one is forced to revolve around a center that is not one's own, and that in many ways one does not wish to own.[56]

For Isasi-Díaz, the experience of exile takes on a vocational character and permeates her work.[57] Nanko-Fernández integrates shared exilic experience and displacement within a framework that recognizes difference. In the United States, it is evident that all exiles, and indeed all exiled theologians, have not been received or treated in the same manner. Such disparities and particularities have very often been ignored in forming equitable public policy, appropriate pastoral care, and informing social conscience.[58] These scholars, in theological discourse, seek to center such inequality, provide just pastoral care, and resource Christian formation with social conscience.

The presence of communities who share the experience of exile and displacement centers the theme of diaspora. Some theologians did not experience a perilous journey, or a border crossing, nor were they, strictly speaking, exiled. Their experience of movement has been a different one. Nanko-Fernández notes that the significance of internal migration, for example, can be perceived in the work of Boricuas, Nuyoricans, and other dispersed Puerto Ricans, such as Samuel Solivan, Edwin Aponte, Luis Rivera-Rodríguez, and Jean-Pierre Ruiz.[59] She recognizes that the particularity of this experience can lead to a "complex relationship" between

---

55. See, for example, García-Treto, *Salmos* and García-Treto, *Job, Proverbios, Eclesiastés y Cantar de los Cantares*.

56. Nanko-Fernández, "Alternately Documented Theologies," 42, quotes González, *Santa Biblia*, 92.

57. See Isasi-Díaz, "By the Rivers of Babylon," 149–64.

58. Nanko-Fernández, "Alternately Documented Theologies," 43.

59. *Boricua* is a person born in Puerto Rico or a person of Puerto Rican descent. *Nuyorican* describes a person of Puerto Rican descent born or living in New York.

being colonized and being an imperial citizen.⁶⁰ She observes that there is often less nostalgia and remembering in Puerto Rican reflection because it is compounded with such layers of complication. Nanko-Fernández points to the work of Ruiz, as a New York born theologian with a Puerto Rican father and a Belgium mother, who proposes that it is necessary to be "reading about immigrants but also reading as immigrants and reading with immigrants." This kind of strategy exposes the multidimensionality not only of Scripture but of the contexts of migration and the implications of migration. Ruiz models attentiveness to multiple perspectives with "complex harmonies and sometimes with harsh dissonances."⁶¹ Likewise, Nanko-Fernández points to the work of Rivera-Rodríguez who urges caution and constructive criticism in the retrieval of biblical texts. Such contextual themes from Latino/a/x histories and experiences must not fund naïve interpretations but must rather counteract naïve interpretations. The politics of hermeneutics in ministerial, pastoral, and ethical work must be acknowledged. For this reason, M. T. Dávila highlights the interaction of social mobility, class, immigration, race, militarism, and social justice in the Puerto Rican experience. Migration, in other words, cannot be treated in isolation nor can it be treated simply as hermeneutical lens.

MOVEMENT, MIGRATION, AND IMMIGRATION

Victor Carmona, a Mexican American with experience of the US immigration system, observes that the mature body of US Hispanic/Latino/a/x theology *and* the nascent literature on immigration theology and ethics means that Latino/a/x theologians have a "unique ability to engage the breadth of the migratory process."⁶² He provides a literature review on the scholarship of migration in the Anglophone world. Reflecting on the contextual experiences of those living in the US whose roots through birth or heritage lie in Spanish-speaking Latin America, Carmona notes that the context is significantly marked by migration even if someone is not personally part of the first phase of migration. He reminds his readers that the majority of Latinos/as/xs in the United States, who often experience discrimination, were born in the United States. Such struggle becomes a source for

60. Nanko-Fernández, "Alternately Documented Theologies" 36.
61. Ruiz, *Readings from the Edges*, quoted by Nanko-Fernández, "Alternately Documented Theologies," 45.
62. Carmona, "Theologizing Immigration," 365–85, at 365.

theological work for Carmona. Jorge Castillo Guerra, for example, considers this "inter space" between native culture and resident culture, to be the very reason that theology on hybridity, *mestizaje*, and *mulatez* has emerged. Castillo Guerra describes such "inter space" experiences as akin to "being in-between and in-both," or to suffering the "double denial" that is the reality of "belonging neither to the territory of origin nor to the territory of destination."[63]

Carmona provides a careful history of the United States immigration system in conversation with the order of love and charity in Aquinas. He recognizes the ways in which immigration preference is offered to some nationalities. He notes how US American business creates a status of permanently segregated non-citizen worker. He acknowledges the realities of mixed-status families and the subsequent creation of a "permanent underclass." In conversation with Aquinas, Carmona is concerned with discerning ethical immigration policy and practice. He explores pertinent features of human connection by natural origin in families, the "friendship of kindred" and depth of just love that may arise through the friendship of fellow citizens. He argues that just decisions regarding immigration and documentation should be made from a sense of beneficence that affirms the principle of family unity and the common good. Human beings owe one another the duty of seeking the common good as a basic response to the call of the gospel to love God and neighbor.[64]

> We tend to presume that undocumented immigrants are strangers who lead isolated lives, but the majority of them are husbands and wives, mothers and fathers, of US citizens and permanent residents. The immigration debate centers on the punishment that adult undocumented immigrants should suffer for breaking immigration law, including deportation. Yet the future looks bleak for a society that purposefully breaks apart millions of immigrant and mixed status families in the name of justice and fairness. Such a society will be unable to nourish—or be nourished by—a love that is rational, ordered, and just.[65]

As Carmona grapples with the intricacies of the immigration system, Moros addresses the question of how to theologize social and economic justice. She maintains that it is important to examine not only current affairs

---

63. Castillo Guerra, quoted in Carmona, "Theologizing Immigration," 367.
64. Carmona, "Theologizing Immigration," 373.
65. Carmona, "Theologizing Immigration," 382.

but also the broader system and ethos of injustice that damage Latino/a/x communities in the United States. She recognizes that being Latino/a/x in the United States is to be "a person of ambiguous 'othered' ethnic status."[66] It is this "othered" reality, then, that is the context for much Latino/a/x theologies: "Latino/a theologians speak of borders, margins, diaspora, and barrios. All of these are a way to speak of territories, but also about bodies, and about economies; they are as well a way to distance oneself from dominant theology."[67] For Moros, given the implications of migration and immigration in the United States for human lives, Latino/a/x theology on social and economic justice should further transnational engagement and situate this theology in the ongoing realities and dialogues about the nature and implications of globalization more widely.[68]

> The systematization of Latino/a Catholic, Protestant, or any other form of theology is problematic when the story is not complete in any one phase of waves of immigration. Other communities, from other parts of the world, have a clearer vision of waves of immigration to the US, voluntary or involuntary, and the history itself of when their families or cultural groups immigrated or migrated or were brought to the Americas clarifies the history of who these communities are within US culture. Latino(a) communities instead continue to have a flow of new people arrive on US soil daily, while also laying claim to a historic relation to original peoples from the Americas, and to national identities that vary widely from region to region, from country to country, and across histories within the very complex American nations.[69]

Luis Rivera-Pagán seeks to do the kind of work that Moros calls for in "Xenophilia or Xenophobia: Toward a Theology of Migration."[70] Framed as love of the other or fear of the other, Rivera-Pagán identifies five key elements of rising xenophobia in the contemporary United States of America. First, he observes narratives that are spreading fear of "broken borders,"

---

66. Moros, "Theologizing Social and Economic Justice," 313–27, at 313.

67. Moros, "Theologizing Social and Economic Justice," 316.

68. Moros, "Theologizing Social and Economic Justice," 322. See also Aquino, "Theology and Identity in the Context of Globalization," 418–40.

69. Moros, "Theologizing Social and Economic Justice," 324.

70. Rivera-Pagán, "Xenophilia or Xenophobia: Toward a Theology of Migration," in *Essays from the Margins*, 84–103. See also Padilla and Phan, *Contemporary Issues of Migration and Theology*, and Groody, *A Theology of Migration: The Bodies of Refugees and the Body of Christ*.

criminal activities, intruders, and the threat of "others." Second, he identifies discourse that intentionally connects the threat of terrorist activities with unauthorized migration since 9/11. Third, he sees historical racism and xenophobia—especially directed toward people with African ancestry, foreign-born immigrants who do not speak English, and people from non-European cultures—converging on Latino/a/x and Hispanic peoples. Fourth, he highlights the dramatic increase in aggressive anti-immigrant groups. Fifth, he names the excessively punitive responses from the federal government and from individual states on immigration issues.

> The xenophobia and scapegoating of the "stranger in our midst" has resulted in the chaotic condition that now plagues the immigration system in the United States, judicially, politically, and socially. All recent attempts to enact a comprehensive immigration reform have floundered thanks to the resistance of influential sectors that have been able to propagate efficaciously the fear of the "alien."[71]

Rivera-Pagán is not naïve. He recognizes that migration and xenophobia are serious social quandaries. He acknowledges that there are significant concerns to be addressed in the face of the growth of unauthorized migration. He also asks what cultural and linguistic impact the dramatic increase in the Latino/a/x or Hispanic population in the United States will have on the ways in which people collectively self-identify in the future. He then explores the "sinister" narratives that specifically accompany the Latin American migration to the United States. This discourse is propagated not only in the media but also in academia when immigration is conveyed as "a major potential threat to the cultural and possibly political integrity of the United States." In this way, Rivera-Pagán argues, the Latin American migrant has been named as the newest "perfect enemy" in the United States.[72]

In the face of such sinister discourse, Rivera-Pagán proposes a biblical theology of migration that centers on love of the other and xenophilia rather than fear or hatred of the other. He calls theologians to pay attention to authentic stories of suffering, hope, courage, resistance, ingenuity, and death that unfold daily in the wildernesses of the Southwest. People are facing the excruciating reality of misery in their homelands or marginalization in the rich West/North. So often treated as "nobodies," "disposable," or "wasted lives," Rivera-Pagán speaks to the ethical challenge presented in

71. Rivera-Pagán, "Xenophilia or Xenophobia: Toward a Theology of Migration," 89.
72. Rivera-Pagán, "Xenophilia or Xenophobia: Toward a Theology of Migration," 91.

La Justicia

Scripture—to care for the stranger in the Torah, to confront social injustice in the Prophets, to practice the hospitality of Job, to remember the experience of the people of Israel exploited in the midst of empire, to protect the sojourner, and to respect the foreigner.[73] This, argues Rivera-Pagán, should be the very essence and nature of the people of God. For such ethics reflect God's nature and God's care of God's people in Scripture. At the very same time, he recognizes the complexity of such an appeal:

> How comforting it would be to stop right here, with these fine biblical texts of xenophilia, of love for the stranger. But the Bible happens to be a disconcerting book. It contains a disturbing multiplicity of voices, a perplexing polyphony that frequently complicates our theological hermeneutics. Regarding many key ethical dilemmas, we find in the Bible often times not only different, but also conflicting, even contradictory perspectives. Too frequently we jump from our contemporary labyrinths into a darker and sinister scriptural maze.[74]

While xenophilia is present in the witness of Scripture, so too are "statements with a distinct and distasteful flavor of nationalist xenophobia."[75] In Ezra and Nehemiah, for example, readers must grapple with concerns around slavery, treatment of aliens, and people understood as property. Traditionalism, conservatism, exclusivity, and xenophobia exist in the text. Scripture includes rules of warfare and annihilation, and recounts horrific violence against women. Rivera-Pagán argues that such texts of terror cannot and should not be evaded. He draws on the disruption to received ethical values and religious worthiness brought by Jesus as he preached and lived the kingdom of God. The poor, the marginalized, the hungry, the naked, the stranger, the "least of these" are "in their powerlessness and vulnerability, the sacramental presence of Christ."[76]

> When, in a powerful and imperial nation, like the United States of America, its citizens welcome and embrace the immigrant, who reside and work with or without some documents required by the powers that be, they are blessed, for they are welcoming and embracing Jesus Christ.[77]

---

73. See also González, *The God Who Sees*.
74. Rivera-Pagán, "Xenophilia or Xenophobia: Toward a Theology of Migration," 96.
75. Rivera-Pagán, "Xenophilia or Xenophobia: Toward a Theology of Migration," 96.
76. Rivera-Pagán, "Xenophilia or Xenophobia: Toward a Theology of Migration," 98.
77. Rivera-Pagán, "Xenophilia or Xenophobia: Toward a Theology of Migration," 98.

Xenophilia, for Rivera-Pagán, is an embracing, exclusion-rejecting practice toward the stranger, the alien, or the "other." It is the local offer of hospitality, love, and care. Yet, xenophilia cannot ignore the transnational complexities and the intensification of global inequalities. Such complexities call for international, ecumenical, and intercultural theological perspectives, policies, and practices.

The theological and methodological contributions of Elizabeth Conde-Frazier and Miguel De La Torre to an ecumenical, international, and intercultural perspective are important. Respectful, responsible, compassionate narratives are woven together in their work in a way that neither fetishizes nor romanticizes the issues. In "Latina Women and Immigration," for example, Conde-Frazier privileges the voices of women as they relate the realities of their immigrant journeys and experiences. In the same spirit as Bedford, Conde-Frazier does not shy away from painful testimonies of violence, sexual abuse, and exploitation. She gives voice to the poignant theologizing of these women in response to the Gospel narrative of, for example, the woman who had been bleeding for twelve years and who was healed when she touched the cloak of Jesus (Matthew 9:20–22). Deep spiritual understandings emerge and are expressed despite great pain. Such women demonstrate how to create safe and brave space, hospitality, and protection for one another amid lament and protest.[78]

In *Listen to the Children/Escuchemos a los niños*, Conde-Frazier navigates the stories of immigrant children who are often the very definition of "the least of these" as articulated by Rivera-Pagán.[79] Voices that are usually dismissed, disregarded, and silenced are privileged. The knowledge and dominance of the "educated" expert is resisted, and instead *teología en conjunto* allows children to name themselves and to tell their own stories. De La Torre, too, narrates the pain and suffering of immigrant journeys in *Trails of Terror and Hope: Testimonies on Immigration*.[80] A scholar and pastor, De La Torre is unafraid to speak out on controversial issues: "One reason the churches have fallen short is undoubtedly because many Christians have fallen into the trap of anti-immigration rhetoric, rhetoric that

---

See also Adams, Carcaño, Kicanas, Smith, and Talmage, *Bishops on the Border*.

78. Conde-Frazier. "Latina Women and Immigration," 54–75. See also González, *Beyond Welcome: Centering Immigrants in Our Christian Response to Immigration*.

79. Conde-Frazier, *Listen to the Children: Conversations with Immigrant Families*.

80. De La Torre, *Trails of Terror and Hope*.

reduces immigrants to objects or the unknown and threatening other."[81] In *Introducing Latinx Theologies*, with Aponte, De La Torre argues:

> In such a time as this, knowing our contexts is desperately needed and understanding Latinx theologies is more relevant than ever. . . . Included are marginalized, so-called chicken bone, vibrant theologies that confound stereotypes, but at the same time provide their adherents with resources as they fight in the struggle for life, contending with both hope and hopelessness, confident in the presence of the Divine who accompanies them on the journey.[82]

QUEER THEOLOGIES

Discerning the Spirit at work on *la frontera* and in exile and diaspora alongside concerns of movement, migration, and immigration center on the foundational Christian belief that human beings are created in the image of God. In *Grace and Humanness*, Orlando Espín argues that mutual respect and appreciation for one another is the foundation of a constructive anthropology. Writing in 2007, he proposed that theologians should reframe the question *what* is a human person? Instead, he suggests theologians should ask, *who* is a human person? If this move were to be made, he argues that Latino/a/x and Black Catholic theologies and theologians could no longer ignore broader issues in human and civil rights.[83]

> The moment we ask Who are human persons? in historical reality, which is the only reality that exists, then we have to deal with and squarely face issues of power and of power asymmetries, issues of domination and hegemony, issues of manipulation and alienation, and issues of sin and grace as these exist, are dynamically intertwined, and as they are contextualized in the real human world. To ask Who are human persons? necessarily leads to unmasking all sorts of unethical options and perspectives that often underlie theological reflection and suck the prophetic and ethical from its constructs.[84]

---

81. De La Torre, *Trails of Terror*, 7.
82. Aponte and De La Torre, *Introducing Latinx*, xliii.
83. Espín, *Grace and Humanness*, 52.
84. Espín, *Grace and Humanness*, 55.

Espín demonstrates how understandings of humanity and understandings of identity need to be contextualized. He argues that contextualization is always complex, intersecting, multiple, and plurichrome. This complexity creates difference, and he notes, therefore, that "we *are* our diverse, living contextualizations."[85] The Spirit of justice creates a shared passion for justice and a shared commitment to justice, equality, and liberation. The Spirit calls theologians to be present and vocal on understandings of humanity and human identity. All persons are bearers of human dignity given by the Creator. Black and Latino/a/x theologians know, observes Espín, what it is to be denied human dignity and to experience oppression, dominance, exclusion, and violence. Therefore, they are called to discern afresh what it means to pursue justice for all persons. They are called to admit the complexity of identities, to strive to move beyond insufficient descriptions of one another related not only to race and culture but related also to sexuality and gender.[86]

De La Torre and Aponte concur. They recognize that in regard to LGBTQI+ issues, no one position is held collectively by Latinx scholars.[87] They perceive nuanced differences in attitudes toward LGBTQI+ persons located within Latinx communities, compared to the homophobia they perceive in the dominant culture in the United States. From a Latinx perspective, homosexuals may be held in contempt because they have chosen not to prove their manhood or dominance in the sexual act. They also note that the experience of lesbians in Latinx contexts deserves analysis.[88] For they argue that lesbianism is often ignored or tolerated because of the emphasis on a macho construction of sexuality in Latinx societies. They recognize, therefore, that space needs to be created for the voice of lesbian Christians. They also acknowledge too the limited discussion around issues for bisexual and transgendered people, maintaining that "the adage 'Se dice nada, se hace todo' (Say nothing, do everything) has remained the accepted norm of the

---

85. Espín, *Grace and Humanness*, 54.

86. For broader discussion, see Ruiz, Bartkowski, Ellison, Acevedo, and Xu, "Religious and Gender Ideologies among Working-Age U.S. Latinas/os," 1–17, and Acosta, "How Could You Do This to Me?": How Lesbian, Bisexual, and Queer Latinas Negotiate Sexual Identity with Their Families, 63–85.

87. De La Torres and Aponte, *Introducing Latinx*, 184.

88. See also Fountain-Stokes, "De sexilio(s) y diáspora(s) homosexual(es) latina(s): cultura puertorriqueña y lo nuyorican queer," 138–57; García, "Now Why Do You Want to Know about That?," 520–41.

La Justicia

Latinx theological community."[89] Aponte and De La Torre also acknowledge that many Latinx scholars serve in more socially and theologically conservative denominations, congregations, or seminaries. In such settings, homosexuality is viewed as a sin and to come out as gay would most probably end a career. Despite this, Aponte and De La Torre look toward change:

> As a newer Latinx generation obtains PhDs in religion and enter the academy, many are more versed in queer theory. Among these newer Latinx scholars, many are openly identifying with their sexual identity, some because they see themselves as scholars rather than practitioners of a faith tradition, while others reject the dichotomy that one cannot be religious and openly gay, lesbian, bisexual, or transgendered. The degree to which this openness is a result of the generational shifts occurring among Latinx religious scholars awaits further study.[90]

Scholar-activist R. Henderson-Espinoza names a "queer omission" in Latino/a/x theologies and makes a foundational contribution to the discussion in "Queer Theory and Latina/o Theologizing."[91] It is at the intersection of multiplicity and difference that Henderson-Espinoza situates Latin@ theology:

> Both Latin@ theology and queer theory help reimagine the borders of thinking, creating paradigms that leave traces of intellectual transgressions that . . . are seen in the intellectual work of *retorcer* (twisting/turning) and *volverse* (a becoming process). These transgressive paths create critical and creative openings for new theological discourse to emerge as radically different from the dominant strands of normative theologies (and ideologies), and one such opening is a queer opening whereby a robust critique of

---

89. De La Torres and Aponte, *Introducing Latinx*, 184. For further discussion, see De La Torre, *Out of the Shadows into the Light*, in particular Luis León, "Cesar Chavez, Christian Love, and the Myth of (Anti) Machismo," 59–75, and De La Torre, "Confession of a Latino Macho," 88–103. For a contribution written for the local church, see De La Torre, *A La Familia*.

90. De La Torres and Aponte, *Introducing Latinx*, 185.

91. Henderson-Espinoza, "Queer Theory and Latina/o Theologizing," 329–46, at 330. For further work at the intersection of ethics and transqueer Latinx scholarship with liberationist activism and social healing, see also Henderson-Espinoza, *Activist Theology*, and Henderson-Espinoza, *Body Becoming: A Path to Our Liberation*.

the standpoint of difference and destabilized identities can intersect with new contours of Latin@ theologizing.[92]

Henderson-Espinoza identifies the need to be attentive to marginalized bodies who experience oppression as members of a sexualized minority. They explain that queer production of theology commits to displacing and disrupting traditional theological expressions and normative doctrines of the church. While progressive thought at work in Latina feminist and *mujerista* theologies uncovers a heteronormative theology, they argue that the particularities of difference in the lives of queer persons are nonetheless eclipsed. They propose that the process of queering *mestizaje*, for example, and looking in the direction of "MezQueerTaje" allows for creative, critical engagement that acknowledges difference, multiplicity, and the significance of space in/between.[93] A robust framework of sex, gender, and sexuality that examines the effects of such realities on Latino/a/x bodies is much needed. This would be a "relational theology in conversation with a relational queer theology, displacing the white norms of both domains."[94]

The Spirit of justice at work in such relational theology and in the public square is not limited to the witness of the church. Nonetheless, as the community of the Spirit, the church seeks to discern how and where the Spirit moves.[95] In Latino/a/x theology such discernment and witness to justice is experienced in movements of personal and community renewal inspired by the hope of a *mañana* vision—"a radical questioning of the present by the future as envisioned by God."[96] Such discernment is situated in *fronteras*, exile, and diaspora; it moves amid migrations and immigrations; and it points toward further and emerging work. Gilberto Cavazos-González calls the church to move beyond piety and into the embodiment of Christian spiritual life that is justice and liberation:

> If the Spirit of Christ that dwells in each Christian is to sing, whistle, whisper, or moan effectively in the Church and in the world,

---

92. Henderson-Espinoza, "Queer Theory and Latina/o Theologizing," 329.

93. Henderson-Espinoza, "Queer Theory and Latina/o Theologizing," 341. Henderson-Espinoza thanks Carmen Nanko-Fernández for gift of the term "MezQueerTaje" in the winter of 2013 and the invitation to use this play on words in the work on queer *mestizaje*.

94. Henderson-Espinoza, "Queer Theory and Latina/o Theologizing," 343.

95. See García-Johnson, *Mestizo/a Community*, 120–34; Alfaro, *Divino Compañero*, 128–31, 147–48.

96. García-Johnson, *Mestizo/a Community*, 122.

La Justicia

it must be allowed to blow away the chains that keep people poor, bound, blind and imprisoned. Christian spirituality is about traditional piety and devotional practices, but these are worthless if it is not also about justice, peace and liberation. To live our Gospel calling as disciples of Jesus in the world, we need a clearer understanding of Christian spirituality as a liberating spirituality.[97]

La justicia requires a grounding in context and an attentiveness to relationships. It requires an intercultural and interdisciplinary competency that demonstrates awareness of complex, interwoven layers of oppression and injustice in society. It requires time to build trust so that testimonies and counter-testimonies of resistance, survival, and flourishing are heard. Faith in the public square is faith that seeks to find the Spirit of God at work in the world and join in that work. For some, the "public square" of life is the relationship between academics and policymakers.[98] For some it may be the relationship between church and culture. For some it may be working for the common good across distinct communities. Latino/a/x theologians are committed to an integral approach.[99] Whatever the context, whoever the community, the gospel of Jesus Christ calls all toward the justice of God, in the power of the Spirit.

> The Spirit groans, moans, cries and feels the pain together with the victims of exclusion, violence and injustice. In these difficult contexts, it is also the Spirit that empowers people to resist both through large systematic acts of resistance and with small, day-to-day acts of subversion/of nonconformism with the status quo. . . . It is this Spirit who invites us to celebrate life in *convivencia*: the call to *convivencia* is simultaneously a form of protest against social structures that focus on individualism at the expense of community, and an eschatological and prophetic reorientation of the world.[100]

---

97. Cavazos-González, *Beyond Piety*, 2.

98. See, for example, Hinojosa, *Apostles of Change: Latino Radical Politics*, and Hinojosa, Elmore, and Sergio González, *Faith and Power: Latino Religious Politics since 1945*.

99. See Dávila, "Making Spirits Whole," 297–315, and Mata, "And I Saw Googleville Descend from Heaven," 316–30, in Costoya, *Land of Stark Contrasts*. This is also well illustrated in the essays and responses presented in Recinos, *Wading through Many Waters*.

100. Medina, "Theological Musings toward a Latina/o Pneumatology," 183.

Engaging Latino/a/x Theologies

IN CONVERSATION

Daisy Colon

> Ustedes son la luz del mundo. Una ciudad en lo alto de una colina no puede esconderse. Ni se enciende una lámpara para cubrirla con un cajón. Por el contrario, se pone en la repisa para que alumbre a todos los que están en la casa. Hagan brillar su luz delante de todos, para que ellos puedan ver las buenas obras de ustedes y alaben al Padre que está en el cielo.
>
> MATEO 5:14–16

> *I was born in Puerto Rico and raised in the Roman Catholic Church where I participated in different ministries at the beginning of my spiritual life. I graduated from college with a BA in Business Administration and two years of Accounting credits. I worked as an accountant for the government from 1993 to 2001. I have two sons from my first marriage. I moved to Tallahassee, Florida, in 2005 with my children. I worked for the DMV in the State of Florida for four years. In 2009 I reunited with a high-school classmate, and we were married in the Episcopal Church. We moved to Charlotte, NC, in 2012. I found a home parish where I participated in many ministries and graduated from the Education for Ministry program in 2017. During my last year of EFM, I discerned my call to the priesthood. I am now a candidate for Holy Orders completing my MDiv at Virginia Theological Seminary. When people ask how I prefer to be identified, I say I am happy to be called Hispana, Latina, Latinx, or Latine.*

Given my experience, for me, the most important thing in this chapter is that we must learn stories about the experiences of those who come to the United States, their experiences with the immigration system, and their experiences on the *frontera*. So often, those who speak about justice never experience injustice, persecution, or discrimination. When we hear stories of immigration, for example, we watch the stories unfold from afar on the television or in the news. However, as Christians, we are called to come alongside others, and accompany others in their journey. We need to draw closer.

I migrated to the "mainland" United States when my son was diagnosed with autism. I desperately needed education and good services for him that were unavailable in Puerto Rico. I left my career, my family and friends, my culture, and somehow my identity. I was committed to my two small boys who were only four and seven years old. I worked hard, struggling with the language, and learning how to interact with a new culture. There was only a small Hispanic community in Tallahassee and so it was hard to create relationships and to get advice from those who had arrived in the United States before me. After much effort during my first year here to show my intentions behind coming to the United States to white Americans and African Americans, my co-workers and neighbors became more friendly and supportive.

We often make judgements based on our assumptions about others we encounter. However, we must hear the experiences from the other person's perspective. I am learning the importance of listening more deeply. Recently, in my chaplaincy work in the hospital, I met a Hispanic woman. Language is the only thing that we actually have in common because her experience of journeying to the United States was so different to mine. She shared with me her story of coming to the States. She came to find a better place for her children who she left behind in her country until she found a place for them. How difficult it was for her to be separated from her children! Her story is a story of sheer survival.

As Christians, we need to lean into relationships with people who are not like us. We must learn to support others, to lift up their voices and to include them in our community. We need to learn to speak to one another, and we need to learn to speak up on behalf of others. We do not simply follow protocols in the pursuit of justice—we need to invite our hearts and Jesus into this work. We must be committed to being in genuine community with others. As Christians, we need to become more aware and conscious of our own intentions and purpose. The story of the church is incomplete without these people. Our community is incomplete, and our ministry is incomplete without a commitment to inclusion.

In my home church, we have a ministry called *A tu lado*, by your side, that offers support in a spirit of love. It is a ministry that seeks to come alongside others, accompanying people to immigration appointments, providing transportation, and being present. The volunteers in *A tu lado* do not speak Spanish but have compassionate and intentional hearts which moved them to action in their local community with immigrants and their families. I have to say that I would give some other churches a failing grade for their vague attitudes toward the Hispanic population. It is sad to acknowledge that churches who speak about justice in their pulpit do not work for justice in their community.

The Spirit of God calls us to do justice and to tell the truth that testifies to God's love and God's mercy. The love of God is not in a bulletin or on a to-do list. It is a serious matter of our hearts. We realize that we need one another to live in community together. The kingdom of God is all people together, no matter their culture, their race, their language, or any other worldly division. Because for God, all life matters. The importance of the conversation in this chapter about LGBTQI+ issues is also essential. In my experience in the church in Puerto Rico, there is no support for the LGBTQI+ community. But in our families, our congregations, and our communities, there are people with all kinds of stories. We need to learn more, listen more, and, when it is necessary, speak up for greater justice. We must be aware that there is so much pressure and pain for LGBTQI+ communities here in the United States. They may also be here alone if they are people of Latin American heritage. They may be here without language. They may be here without support. Our responsibility is to broaden the message of compassion and care and inclusion. We need to look to the future and awaken our future leaders. We need to draw these young people in and raise them up.

As a candidate for Holy Orders, I want to remain open to the Spirit of God in ministry. Ministry is more than programs. I do not make plans, because when I make plans, God always has other plans for me. I want to learn and to be prepared for any ministry in any community when God calls me. A vision for ministry in the pursuit of justice is more than speaking about it in the pulpit while forgetting to work for it in community. We carry a profound message to love our neighbors as we love ourselves. The way that we treat and love our siblings in Christ grounds us in the love of God and in our love for others through the gospel of Jesus Christ. Our faith community is more complete with the inclusion of Hispanic, Latino, and LGBTQI+ communities. For their stories, their faith, and their voices are a missing part of the kingdom of God here on earth.[101]

FOUNDATIONAL READING

Carroll R., M. Daniel. *The Bible and Borders: Hearing God's Word on Immigration*. Grand Rapids: Brazos, 2020.

101. Translation and interpretation provided by Sharon E. Heaney.

Espín, Orlando. *Grace and Humanness: Theological Reflections Because of Culture.* Maryknoll, NY: Orbis, 2007.
Maldonado Pérez, Zaida, Loida I. Martell-Otero, and Elizabeth Conde-Frazier. "Dancing with the Wild Child: Evangélicas *and the Holy Spirit.*" In *Latina Evangélicas: A Theological Survey from the Margins,* by Loida I. Martell-Otero, Zaida Maldonado Pérez, and Elizabeth Conde-Frazier, 14–32. Eugene, OR: Cascade, 2013.
Medina, Néstor. "Theological Musings toward a Latina/o Pneumatology." In *The Wiley-Blackwell Companion to Latino/a Theology,* edited by Orlando Espín, 174–89. Chichester, UK: Wiley-Blackwell, 2015.
Reyes, Patrick B. *Nobody Cries When We Die: God, Community, and Surviving to Adulthood.* St. Louis: Chalice, 2016.
Rivera-Pagán, Luis. *Essays from the Margins.* Eugene, OR: Cascade, 2014.
Romero, Robert Chao. *Brown Church: Five Centuries of Latino/a Social Justice, Theology, and Identity.* Downers Grove, IL: InterVarsity, 2020.

FURTHER READING

Carmona, Victor. "Theologizing Immigration." In *The Wiley-Blackwell Companion to Latino/a Theology,* edited by Orlando Espín, 365–85. Chichester, UK: Wiley-Blackwell, 2015.
Conde-Frazier, Elizabeth. *Listen to the Children: Conversations with Immigrant Families.* Valley Forge, PA: Judson, 2011.
De La Torre, Miguel A. *Latina/o Social Ethics: Moving beyond Eurocentric Moral Thinking.* Waco, TX: Baylor University Press, 2010.
García-Johnson, Oscar. *Spirit Outside the Gate: Decolonial Pneumatologies of the American Global South.* Downers Grove, IL: InterVarsity, 2019.
Hinojosa, Felipe, Maggie Elmore, and Sergio González, eds. *Faith and Power: Latino Religious Politics since 1945.* New York: New York University Press, 2022.
Nanko-Fernández, Carmen. "Alternately Documented Theologies: Mapping Border, Exile and Diaspora." In *Religion and Politics in America's Borderlands,* edited by Sarah Azaransky, 33–56. Lanham, MD: Lexington, 2013.
Romero, Robert Chao, and Stephen Burris. *Migration, Mission and Ministry: An Introduction.* Skyforest, CA: Urban Loft, 2022.
Salvatierra, Alexia, and Brandon Wrencher. *Buried Seeds: Learning from the Vibrant Resilience of Marginalized Christian Communities.* Grand Rapids: Baker Academic, 2022.
Valentín, Benjamin. *Mapping Public Theology: Beyond Culture, Identity and Difference.* Harrisburg, PA: Trinity, 2002.
Villafañe, Eldin. *The Liberating Spirit: Toward an Hispanic American Pentecostal Social Ethic.* Lanham, MD: University Press of America, 1992.

Conclusion

Colleagues in Conversation

Altagracia Pérez-Bullard

From the beginning, U.S. Latina/o theologians have insisted that their writings are the formal expressions of their communities' struggles for life and the construction of a better world, and against injustice, marginalization, and the assimilatory forces in the dominant Anglo-European culture of the United States.... [T]he existence of U.S. Latina/o theology is one way in which oppressed peoples talk back and break away from the forces that stifle them, which is echoed several times over by the rapid proliferation of people groups reclaiming their right to speak. So U.S. Latina/o theology finds resonances in many places in the world, and its contributions carry implications for many groups and communities attempting to name their identities and describe their faith experiences.[1]

NÉSTOR MEDINA

Sharon and Altagracia became colleagues at Virginia Theological Seminary (VTS) in late summer 2019. Before the COVID pandemic, their offices were next door to one another. Sharon knew she had met a friend when Altagracia asked, with a glint in her eye, "What exactly is an Irish Protestant girl like you doing with Our Lady of Guadalupe on her office wall?" This was just the beginning of cups of

---

1. Medina, *Mestizaje*, 139.

Conclusion

coffee and meaningful conversations. For Altagracia's wicked good humor, generous spirit, and gracious wisdom, Sharon will always be thankful.

Before coming to VTS, Dr. Altagracia Pérez-Bullard served as the canon for congregational vitality in the Episcopal Diocese of New York. Through church leadership development, both lay and clergy, she assisted congregations as they engaged and collaborated with their changing contexts to bring new life to their communities. Altagracia holds a PhD in practical theology from Claremont School of Theology, and MDiv and STM from Union Theological Seminary, New York and a BS in educational psychology from New York University. She has served the church for thirty years as a community leader, youth minister, and priest in the Dioceses of New York, Chicago, and Los Angeles. As the rector of St. Philip's, LA, and Holy Faith, Inglewood, she led multicultural, bilingual congregations engaged in serving and ministering to the wider community. She also served as the dean for Deanery IV, El Centro, and director of the Episcopal Urban Intern Program. Altagracia has brought leadership to the issues of HIV/AIDS, youth violence, worker justice and a living wage, health disparities in communities of color, housing, and community-empowerment. In each of these areas she has sought to build bridges and create alliances between communities across lines of difference, whether they are characterized by race, ethnicity, class, gender, sexuality, or physical and mental abilities. She and her wife Cynthia Bullard-Pérez enjoy the blessings and challenges that are their children Santana, Altagracia Immanuel, Joshua, and Jasmine.

Sharon, I knew how resistant you were about centering your own context in the introduction. But it is lovely to read it, and it makes our conversation together so much more powerful. The reason I think it is essential to share our contexts with one another is because there will always be curiosity about why this Irish woman is interested in Latin American and Latino/a/x theologies. As a Puerto Rican and Dominican Afro-Latina, I see connections between the Irish and the Puerto Rican realities. The island homes. Nations united but divided. Controversy around the relationship with the United States for us, and around the United Kingdom and the Republic of Ireland for you. I have this sense that you, and those from your context, would see echoes in some of our struggles. You would recognize other people shaped by and dealing with colonialism. Of course, it looks different in your context. Colonialism looks different in many of our contexts. But a thread of connectedness exists. What you write in the introduction also shows something that I already know from talking with you and teaching with you. You love and respect this theology. I see what it has meant for you to engage these theologians. That matters. It is not just an intellectual exercise. You were already in conversation with these contexts and these theologians before you decided to pursue theology on these contexts and by these theologians. They have been speaking to your heart. They opened a way for you to see yourself in a bigger context. That is what you want for the people who are reading your book.

Teología en conjunto is collaboration. We interrogate our contexts. We remain connected with our communities. We are committed to the pursuit of justice. And so, our stories matter. As Latino/a/x scholars and practitioners, we are expected to expose ourselves, our culture, and our heritages. There is no hiding. There should be no hiding for you either. I feel my strongest self as a scholar that is in this body when I recognize that the voices saying "you are talking too much about yourself in this space" are, in fact, voices of Western cultural imperialism. We have been educated in that system and we understand that system. Western cultural imperialism is a boy's project of the Enlightenment that created these educational spaces with certain assumptions about objectivity, about knowledge, about intelligence. They wrote us out of it. They wrote women out of it. They wrote people of color out of it. They wrote indigenous people out of it. They wrote Black people out of it. They made us invisible. In Latino/a/x theologies, we talk from a grounded place that understands *mestizaje*, a complex and contested site. When we ground our theological work in our contexts and in our lives, we can be made to feel like we are somehow embarrassing, we are doing something wrong—"cover yourself, you are talking about private things." But this is the very attitude that we want to disrupt. This approach hides how a dominant tradition serves dominant scholars. Such scholars proceed and continue to have a theological conversation in the dominant way. We have seen what this has done. Such disembodied knowledge is destroying the planet. We cannot be a part of that.

You recognize that this space in the United States is fraught with complexity, Sharon. It is not going to be resolved. That you, as a white woman, are living with the complexity, is honest. That is what I am asking of you. Because you are an immigrant from a nation with a colonial history, there are some ways that you see racial things here in the United States that many white people raised in this country do not see. There are deep complexities of race, of class, of access, and of education. If you talk about this complexity and how you recognize that complexity, from your perspective, that is

Conclusion

an interesting nuance to offer. When you open your mouth and you have an accent that does not get the love that the English accent might get, that is nuance. You live it. You have a sharper lens. You are developing a sharper lens. You are learning to notice things. You cannot fix these complexities. When we do not provide a solution, this annoys those in the dominant culture. So to be prepared to hear stories of *la lucha*, and to name the complexities of this struggle, as teachers and as scholars, is a good place to begin together.

You asked me the question, how might those from the dominant culture be changed through this engagement with Latino/a/x theologies? We name our context of work and life together as an Episcopal seminary in Northern Virginia. Our priorities here are learning, teaching, and preparing Christian leaders. Grounded in this setting, there would be two things that I would want to emphasize. First, just because theology is particular does not mean that this theology cannot apply elsewhere. The argument that Latino/a/x theologians make is that this theology will help and strengthen you to work in your own context, wherever that may be. In looking at our particularity, our contexts and reality, the problems we face as Latino/a/x communities, you in turn can learn to deal better with your own context of ministry or with that challenging theological issue. Some questions are the same. Some questions are different. If we are forming Christian leaders, we need to help them listen to the stories of other people in order to make their own thinking and ministry more excellent. I find it frustrating in the academy and in the classroom, that in order to be "inclusive," teachers and writers simply throw in a couple of additional scholars. It is as if those from the dominant culture are using two or three scholars of color, or global thinkers, to "sprinkle on the top" as decoration. What I long for is that those in the dominant culture would want to cook with us. The dish, no doubt, will be different than expected but it will be a better dish. Engagement with scholars and practitioners beyond the dominant culture cannot be an afterthought in our teaching, in our research, or in our ministry.

Second, if you are in the dominant culture, you especially need to recognize that formation in the spiritual life is an ongoing reality. This is an ongoing commitment. This engagement, Sharon, is the practice of our lives as we journey with God and as we journey with one another. This is not a project that you will complete. This is not a problem that you are going to fix. You are not ever going to finish this work. To continue to engage marginalized voices, the misrepresented, and the misunderstood, will take all of us to new places on the journey. We will find new places in our pedagogy, in our theological growth, in our scholarship, and in our practices of ministry. We are responsible for persevering in this engagement. If I am a scholar with a particular focus on Schleiermacher, for example, these conversations can and should influence my scholarship and response to Schleiermacher's work. The compartmentalizing that takes place in theology is difficult for me. Our students often have no idea of scholarship or practice beyond the dominant tradition. I am so grateful that I am part of a wider community of scholars who began a journey together during my own doctoral studies. After many years in ministry, I was reintroduced to a broader theological conversation and education through their work. It is exciting work. It is an exciting journey. It changes us.

You asked me a second question, Sharon, and this is a hard one for me to answer. How might those from the dominant culture be committed to the necessary work of imagining and realizing resistance and justice? Everyone will respond to this in their own way because everybody has different gifts in resistance and justice. "I'm not an activist like you" people will often say to me. But when I am having a conversation with you about your scholarship, your teaching, or your ministry, I am listening for the passion you have, the focus God has given you, the justice you are called to pursue. I am inviting you to share with me how you have centered yourself on whatever God has called you to be about. Then I want to know who you are reading or engaging with from other communities that shares your passion but not your context? I am a United States person. I am completely formed and shaped by this education system. The only way for me to have learned to do what I do is through an education system constructed by the dominant culture. I understand the system. I was taught that scholarship and knowledge require curiosity. Scholarship requires us to interrogate ourselves and interrogate our own work. I do not understand, then, why we are not doing this. Our work is deficient if we do not know the other voices working and writing in this context of the United States. We need to expand more globally too, but at least we need to begin with the diversity of scholarship in the United States. If you care about LGBTQIA+ rights, for example, who are the African American, or Latine scholars and practitioners who are researching and writing about that? Whatever your passion is, it is important to know how others are also dealing with that issue. I do not want to have a conversation with someone in which I am the one expected to introduce them to this breadth. If you care about your area of expertise,

Conclusion

your work is not complete if you are not curious about, and have not interrogated, what others in your field care about. As a Black Latina, I cannot be responsible for your engagement in your field. I am responsible for the intersections in my research and in my field. If theologians can find ancient texts and rare documents, theologians can find Latinx scholars and other thinkers who are writing and making a contribution. How is it possible that teachers and scholars can possess all these tools and capacities, yet in a context as diverse as the United States, they do not listen to any other voices? I am sorry that they do not see it as important work. Because this is justice work. In this country and in this decade, a good scholar, an excellent scholar, cannot simply continue to write white things. I acknowledge their hard work. They have accomplished many things. But they are operating with a deficit. We cannot celebrate scholarship and celebrate practice that is deficit.

If we can learn to be more aware, and more expansive, then our students would also learn this. Of course, in our context we want our students to embrace the Episcopal tradition. I chose the Episcopal Church for the beauty and theology I saw there. However, this tradition can bind our students so that they are terrified of making mistakes. When they read beyond themselves, when they hear marginalized voices, they hear others who as an act of resistance and survival have taken the tradition and made it their own. I think our students need to imagine how to do that. We need to teach them to be curious about the tradition beyond the dominant cultural ways. A canon prescribed by whiteness, middle class-ness, and privilege, in many ways, can provide a contrast that helps define ways to resist the dominant narrative. In the intersections, in the difference, in the contrast, I find the nuance in my own voice. I interpret and do theology *latinamente*. This is a legitimate Christian project. This, to me, is a more authentic voice and expression of how I live with God and how I see God.

I take teaching seriously. It is my central and primary concern in this space. That means my primary role is not to be the guardian of my field and my Episcopal tradition. My students have questions and queries and concerns that they should be encouraged to explore more widely. I need to let them know that others are out there. We might just get right what being a Christian in this time and place means if we were concerned with engaging the other. Engaging the issues imaginatively, in light of our intersection with the thinking of others, might help us get it right. We would be stronger ministers. Our preaching, our teaching, and our evangelism would be informed by a living church around us. I often ask, do we want to be a museum full of artefacts, knowing what, and when, and where? Or do we want to be a living church? A living church teaches us to engage contexts, encounter cultures, and be ministers in our world today. We need to be reminded that students can be changed, teachers can be changed, and the church can be changed by the power of the Spirit of God at work in our conversations and with the witness to one another.

As our students go out into the world, they need to know that their *lo cotidiano* is a valuable source for theology. They need to know that the particularity of their story, their everyday lives, their community's context, and reality are valuable sources for theological reflection. There are many margins in our church where they will serve. The dominance of white, suburban, middle-class values in our church means there are a lot of people who feel marginalized. I want our students to leave seminary equipped, feeling like they have the competency and strength they need to serve in these times. They will serve in communities that have a right to delve into their heritage, to look at their histories, and to see where God has been at work. Then these communities of faith can share with the wider community what it honestly means to cross *fronteras* of every kind, to pursue justice, and to seek the places where the Spirit of God is at work in the world. Engaging across difference changes us. Engaging with broader theology makes us stronger. It prepares us. It empowers us. Sharon, engaging Latino/a/x theologies is not a side conversation. This journey, this walking together in faith, this *is* the conversation. This is collegiality, this is our witness to the gospel.

FOUNDATIONAL READING

Conde-Frazier, E. *Atando Cabos: Latinx Contributions to Theological Education*. Grand Rapids: Eerdmans, 2021.

Dace, Karen L., ed. *Unlikely Allies in the Academy: Women of Color and White Women in Conversation*. London: Routledge, 2012.

Fernandez, Eleazar S., ed. *Teaching for a Culturally Diverse and Racially Just World*. Eugene, OR: Cascade, 2014.

Kwok, Pui-Lan, Cecelia González-Andrieu, and Dwight N. Hopkins, eds. *Teaching Global Theologies: Power and Praxis*. Waco, TX: Baylor University Press, 2015.

Pérez-Bullard, Altagracia. "In Times Like These: Comfort and Courage for Change." In *Fearful Times: Living Faith*, edited by Robert Boak Slocum and Martyn Percy, 73–80. Eugene, OR: Wipf and Stock, 2021.

———. "Liderazgo en Conjunto: A Leadership Development Model for the Twenty-First Century." *Anglican Theological Review* 101.4 (2019) 625–50.

CONCLUSION

Peters, Rebecca Todd, and Grace Y. Kao, eds. "Feminist Theology as Conversation and Invitation." Introduction to *Encountering the Sacred: Feminist Reflections on Women's Lives*, edited by Rebecca Todd Peters and Grace Y. Kao, 1–16. London: T. & T. Clark, 2019.

FURTHER READING

Pérez-Bullard, Altagracia. "Aspiring to Un Liderazgo en Conjunto: Leadership Development for Latine Congregations." In *The Wiley-Blackwell Companion to Latinoax Theology*, edited by Orlando Espín. 2nd ed. Chichester, UK: Wiley-Blackwell, forthcoming.
———. "Latina/o Practical Theology: Reflections on Faith Based Organizing as a Religious Practice." In *The Wiley-Blackwell Companion to Latino/a Theology*, edited by Orlando O. Espín, 439–52. Chichester, UK: Wiley-Blackwell, 2015.
———. "Living into Multicultural Inclusive Ministry." *Anglican Theological Review* 93.4 (2011) 659–67.
———. "Pastoral Care in Contexts of Pandemic: The Ongoing Reality of HIV/AIDS." In *Injustice and the Care of Souls!*, edited by Sheryl A. Kujawa-Holbrook and Karen B. Montagno. 2nd ed. Minneapolis: Fortress, forthcoming.
———. "Pastoral Care with Persons Living with HIV/AIDS." In *Injustice and the Care of the Souls: Taking Oppression Seriously in Pastoral Care*, edited by Sheryl Kujawa-Holbrook and Karen Montagno, 119–210. Minneapolis: Fortress, 2009.
Roland Guzmán, Carla E. *Unmasking Latinx Ministry for Episcopalians: An Anglican Approach*. New York: Church Publishing, 2020.

Bibliography

Abalos, D. *Latinos in the United States: The Sacred and the Political.* Notre Dame, IN: University of Notre Dame Press, 1986.
Adams, M. Minerva Carcaño, Gerald Kikanas, et al. *Bishops on the Border: Pastoral Responses to Immigration.* New York: Moorehouse, 2013.
Agosto, Efraín. "Revelation." In *The Wiley-Blackwell Companion to Latino/a Theology*, edited by Orlando Espín, 91–110. Chichester, UK: Wiley-Blackwell, 2015.
———. "Sola Scriptura and Latino/a Protestant Hermeneutics." In *Building Bridges, Doing Justice: Constructing a Latino/a Ecumenical Theology*, edited by Orlando Espín, 69–90. Maryknoll, NY: Orbis, 2009.
Agosto, Efraín, and Jacqueline M. Hidalgo. *Latinxs, the Bible and Migration.* New York: Palgrave Macmillan, 2020.
Alcántara, Jared. E. *Crossover Preaching: Intercultural-Improvisational Homiletics in Conversation with Gardner C. Taylor.* Downers Grove, IL: IVP Academic, 2015.
———. "'I Can't Breathe': The Adverse Impact of Racialization on Seminarians of Color and Its Import for the Homiletics Classroom." *Journal of Evangelical Homiletics Society* 20.2 (2020) 30–65.
———. "Pedagogy That Purifies the Air: Recognizing and Reducing 'Stereotype Threat' in the Preaching Classroom." *Homiletic* 46.2 (2021) 20–30.
———. *The Practices of Christian Preaching: Essentials for Effective Proclamation.* Grand Rapids: Baker Academic, 2019.
———. "Sermons with 'Local Soil': Cultivating Contextually Responsive Preachers." *Trinity Journal* 41.2 (2020) 185–98.
Alcoff, Linda Martín. *Visible Identities: Race, Gender and the Self.* Oxford: Oxford University Press, 2006.
Alfaro, Sammy. *Divino Compañero: Toward a Hispanic Pentecostal Christology.* Eugene, OR: Pickwick, 2010.
———. "Reading and Hearing Scripture in the Latina/o Pentecostal Community." In *Latino/a Theology and the Bible: Ethnic-Racial Reflections on Interpretation*, edited by Francisco Lozada and Fernando Segovia, 34–38. Lanham, MD: Lexington, 2021.
Althaus-Reid, Marcella. *Controversies in Feminist Theology.* London: SCM, 2007.
———. *From Feminist Theology to Indecent Theology.* London: SCM, 2004.
———. *Indecent Theology: Theological Perversions in Sex, Gender and Politics.* London: Routledge, 2000.
———. *Liberation Theology and Sexuality.* Aldershot, UK: Ashgate, 2006.
———. *Trans/formations.* London: SCM, 2009.

Bibliography

Alvarez, Carmelo. "Hispanic Pentecostals in the United States." In *Pentecostal Power: Expressions, Impact and Faith of Latin American Pentecostalism*, edited by Calvin L. Smith, 63–84. Leiden: Brill, 2011.

Alvarez, Emilio. *Pentecostal Orthodoxy: Toward an Ecumenism of the Spirit*. Downers Grove, IL: IVP Academic, 2022.

Anzaldúa, Gloria. *Borderlands/La Frontera: The New Mestiza*. 25th anniversary ed. San Francisco: Aunt Lute, 2012.

———. *Light in the Dark/Luz en lo oscuro: Rewriting Identity, Spirituality, Reality*. Durham, NC: Duke University Press, 2015.

Aponte, Edwin David. *¡Santo! Varieties of Latino/a Spirituality*. Maryknoll, NY: Orbis, 2012.

Aponte, Edwin David, and Miguel A. De La Torre. *Introducing Latinx Theologies*. Maryknoll, NY: Orbis, 2020.

———. *Introducing Latino/a Theologies*. Maryknoll, NY: Orbis, 2001.

———, eds. *Handbook of Latina/o Theologies*. St. Louis: Chalice, 2006.

Aquino, Jorge A. "*Mestizaje*: The Latina/o Religious Imaginary in the North American Racial Crucible." In *The Wiley-Blackwell Companion to Latino/a Theology*, edited by Orlando Espín, 283–312. Chichester, UK: Wiley-Blackwell, 2015.

Aquino, María Pilar. "Latina Feminist Theology: Central Features." In *A Reader in Latina Feminist Theology: Religion and Justice*, edited by María Pilar Aquino, Daisy L. Machado and Jeanette Rodríguez, 133–60. Austin: University of Texas, 2002.

———. *Love That Produces Hope: The Thought of Ignacio Ellacuría*. Collegeville, MN: Liturgical, 2006.

———. *Nuestro Clamo por la Vida: Teología latinoamericana desde la perspectiva de la mujer*. San José: Editorial DEI, 1992.

———. *Our Cry for Life: Feminist Theology from Latin America*. Maryknoll, NY: Orbis, 1993.

———. "Theology and Identity in the Context of Globalization." In *The Oxford Handbook of Feminist Theology*, edited by Mary McClintock Fulkerson and Sheila Briggs, 418–40. Oxford: Oxford University Press, 2012.

Aquino, María Pilar, D. Machado, and J. Rodríguez, eds. *A Reader in Latina Feminist Theology: Religion and Justice*. Austin: University of Texas, 2002.

Aquino, María Pilar, and Elisabeth Schüssler Fiorenza, eds. *In the Power of Wisdom*. Concilium (Glen Rock, NJ). London: SCM, 2000.

Aquino, María Pilar, and Maria José Rosado-Nunes, eds. *Feminist Intercultural Theology: Latina Explorations for a Just World*. Maryknoll, NY: Orbis, 2007.

Armas, Kat. *Abuelita Faith: What Women on the Margins Teach Us about Wisdom, Persistence and Strength*. Grand Rapids: Brazos, 2021.

Arreola, D., ed. *Hispanic Spaces, Latino Places: Community and Cultural Diversity in Contemporary America*. Austin: University of Texas, 2004.

Avalos, Hector. *This Abled Body: Rethinking Disabilities in Biblical Studies*. Semeia Studies 55. Leiden: Brill, 2007.

———. *The Bad Jesus: The Ethics of New Testament Ethics*. Sheffield, UK: Sheffield Phoenix, 2015.

———, ed. *Introduction to the U.S. Latina and Latino Religious Experience*. Boston: Brill, 2004.

———. *Slavery, Abolitionism, and the Ethics of Biblical Scholarship*. Sheffield, UK: Sheffield Phoenix, 2011.

Bibliography

———. *Strangers in Our Own Land: Religion in Contemporary U.S. Latina/o Literature*. Nashville: Abingdon, 2005.
Azcuy, Virginia. *La teología Argentina del pueblo / Lucio Gera*. Edición Virginia Azcuy. Santiago: Universidad Alberto Hurtado, 2015.
Azcuy, Virginia R., Nancy E. Bedford, and Mercedes L. García B. *Teología feminista a tres voces*. Santiago de Chile: Ediciones Universidad Alberto Hurtado, 2016.
Badillo, David A. *Latinos and the New Immigrant Church*. Baltimore: Johns Hopkins University Press, 2006.
Baer, James A. *A Social History of Cuba's Protestants*. Lanham, MD: Lexington, 2019.
Bailey, Randall C., Tat-Siong Benny Liew, and Fernando F. Segovia, eds. *They Were All Together in One Place? Toward Minority Biblical Criticism*. Leiden: Brill, 2009.
Bañuelas, Arturo J., ed. *Mestizo Christianity: Theology from the Latino Perspective*. 1995. Reprint, Eugene, OR: Wipf and Stock, 2004.
Barba, Loida. "Latina/o Pentecostalisms." In *The Oxford Handbook of Latinx Christianities in the United States*, edited by Kristy Nabhan-Warren, 130–50. Oxford: Oxford University Press, 2022.
Barber, Marian Jean. "How the Irish, Germans and Czechs became Anglo: Race and Identity in the Texas-Mexico Borderlands." PhD thesis, University of Texas at Austin, 2010.
Barreto, Raimundo, and Roberto Sirvent, eds. *Decolonial Christianities: Latinx and Latin American Perspectives*. New York: Palgrave Macmillan, 2020.
Barton, Paul, and David Maldonado, eds. *Hispanic Christianity within Mainline Protestant Traditions: A Bibliography*. Decatur, GA: Asociación para la Educación Teológica, 1998.
Bebbington, David W., ed., *The Gospel in Latin America: Historical Studies in Evangelicalism and the Global South*. Waco, TX: Baylor University Press, 2022.
Bedford, Nancy Elizabeth. *Galatians*. Louisville: Westminster John Knox, 2016.
———. "Making Spaces: Latin American and Latina Feminist Theologies on the Cusp of Interculturality." In *Feminist Intercultural Theology: Latina Explorations for a Just World*, edited by María Pilar Aquino and Maria José Rosado-Nunes, 49–69. Maryknoll, NY: Orbis, 2007.
———. *La porfía de la resurrección: ensayos desde el feminismo teológico latinoamericano*. Buenos Aires: Ediciones Kairós, 2008.
———. *Sigamos a Jesús en su reino de vida: Cuaderno de Participación de CLADE V*. Buenos Aires: Ediciones Kairós, 2011.
———. *Who Was Jesus and What Does It Mean to Follow Him?* Harrisonburg, VA: Herald, 2021.
Benavides, Luis. "The Spirit." In *Handbook to Latina/o Theologies*, edited by Edwin David Aponte and Miguel De La Torre, 25–32. St. Louis: Chalice, 2006.
Boff, Leonardo, et al.; entrevistas Elsa Tamez. *Teologos de la liberación hablan sobre la mujer*. San José: Editorial DEI, 1986.
Boff, Leonardo et al.; interviews Elsa Tamez. *Against Machismo: Theologians of Liberation Talk about the Struggle of Women*. Oak Park: Meyer-Stone, 1987.
Bordas, Juana. *The Power of Latino Leadership*. Oakland, CA: Berrett-Koehler, 2013.
———. *Salsa, Soul and Spirit: Leadership for a Multicultural Age*. 2nd ed. Oakland, CA: Berrett-Koehler, 2012.
Bousier, Helen. *An Interfaith Response to US Immigration Policies: The Ethics of Hospitality*. Lanham, MD: Lexington, 2019.

Bibliography

Brazal, A., and M. T. Dávila, eds. *Living with(out) Borders: Catholic Theological Ethics on the Migration of Peoples*. Maryknoll, NY: Orbis, 2016.

Breen, Louise A., ed. *Converging Worlds: Communities and Cultures in Colonial America. A Sourcebook*. London: Routledge, 2012.

Brimelow, Peter. *Alien Nation: Common Sense about America's Immigrant Disaster*. New York: Harper Perennial, 1996.

Bryant, S., R. O'Toole, and B. Vinson, eds. *Africans to Spanish America: Expanding the Diaspora*. Urbana: University of Illinois, 2014.

Campese, Gioacchino, and Pietro Ciallella, eds. *Migration, Religious Experience and Globalization*. New York: Center for Migration Studies, 2003.

Candelaria, Michael. *The Latino Christ in Art, Literature, and Liberation Theology*. Albuquerque: University of New Mexico Press, 2018.

———. *Popular Religion and Liberation: The Dilemma of Liberation*. Albany: State University of New York Press, 1990.

Carmona, Victor. "Theologizing Immigration." In *The Wiley-Blackwell Companion to Latino/a Theology*, edited by Orlando Espín, 365–85. Chichester, UK: Wiley-Blackwell, 2015.

Carroll R., Daniel M. *The Bible and Borders: Hearing God's Word on Immigration*. Grand Rapids: Brazos, 2020.

———. *The Book of Amos*. Grand Rapids: Eerdmans, 2020.

———. *Christians at the Border: Immigration, the Church and the Bible*. 2nd ed. Grand Rapids: Brazos, 2013.

———. "The Image and Mission of God: Genesis as a Lens for a Biblical Discussion of Migration." In *Global Migration and Christian Faith: Implications for Identity and Mission*, edited by M. Daniel Carroll R. and Vincent E. Bacote, 37–52. Eugene, OR: Wipf & Stock, 2021.

———. "Reading the Bible through Other Lenses: New Vistas from a Hispanic Diaspora Perspective." In *Global Voices: Reading the Bible in the Majority World*, edited by Craig Keener and M. Daniel Carroll R., 5–26. Peabody, MA: Hendrickson, 2013.

Carroll R., Daniel M., and Vincent E. Bacote, eds. *Global Migration and Christian Faith: Implications for Identity and Mission*. Eugene, OR: Cascade, 2021.

Casimir, Jean. *The Haitians: A Decolonial History*. Chapel Hill: University of North Carolina Press, 2020.

Castelo, Daniel. "Latinx Perspectives." In *T. & T. Clark Handbook of Pneumatology*, edited by Daniel Castelo and Kenneth Loyer, 319–26. London: T. & T. Clark, 2020.

Castillo, Ana, ed. *Goddess of the Americas—La diosa de las Américas: Writings on the Virgin of Guadalupe*. New York: Riverhead, 1997.

Chasteen, John Charles. *Born in Blood and Fire: A Concise History of Latin America*. 2nd ed. New York: Norton, 2006.

Chavez, Patricia Cuyatti. *Hanging On and Rising Up: Renewing, Re-envisioning, and Rebuilding the Cross from the "Marginalized."* Eugene, OR: Pickwick, 2019.

Chavez, Leo. *The Latino Threat Narrative: Constructing Immigrants, Citizen and the Nation*. Stanford, CA: Stanford University Press, 2008.

Cleary, Edward L. *The Rise of Charismatic Catholicism in Latin America*. Gainsville: University Press of Florida, 2011.

Conde-Frazier, Elizabeth. *Atando Cabos: Latinx Contributions to Theological Education*. Grand Rapids: Eerdmans, 2021.

Bibliography

———. *Hispanic Bible Institutes: A Community of Theological Construction.* Scranton, PA: University of Scranton Press, 2004.

———. "Latina Women and Immigration." *Journal of Latin American Theology* 3.2 (2008) 54–75.

———. *Listen to the Children/Escuchemos a los niños: Conversations with Immigrant Families.* Valley Forge, PA: Judson, 2011.

———. "Participatory Active Research." In *The Wiley-Blackwell Companion to Practical Theology*, edited by Bonnie Miller-McLemore, 234–44. Malden, MA: Wiley-Blackwell, 2012.

Conde-Frazier, Elizabeth, S. Steve Kang, and Gary A. Parrett. *A Many Colored Kingdom: Multicultural Dynamics for Spiritual Formation.* Grand Rapids: Baker Academic, 2004.

Costas, Orlando. *Christ outside the Gate: Mission beyond Christendom.* Maryknoll, NY: Orbis, 1982.

———. *The Church and Its Mission: A Shattering Critique from the Third World.* Wheaton, IL: Tyndale, 1974.

———. *The Integrity of Mission: The Inner Life and Outreach of the Church.* San Francisco: Harper & Row, 1979.

———. *Liberating News: A Theology of Contextual Evangelization.* Grand Rapids: Eerdmans, 1989.

Countryman, Edward. *Enjoy the Same Liberty: Black Americans and the Revolutionary Era.* Lanham, MD: Rowman & Littlefield, 2012.

Crespo, Orlando. *Being Latino in Christ: Finding Wholeness in Your Ethnic Identity.* Downers Grove, IL: InterVarsity, 2003.

Crozier, Karen, and Elizabeth Conde-Frazier. "A Narrative of Children's Spirituality: African American and Latino Theological Perspectives." In *Children's Spirituality: Christian Perspectives, Research and Applications*, edited by Kevin E. Lawson and Scottie May, 286–312. 2nd ed. Eugene, OR: Cascade, 2019.

Cruz, Joel Morales. *The Histories of the Latin American Church: A Brief Introduction.* Minneapolis: Fortress, 2014.

———. *The Histories of the Latin American Church: A Handbook.* Minneapolis: Fortress, 2014.

Cruz, Gemma Tulud. *Christianity across Borders.* Abingdon, UK: Routledge, 2021.

Cruz, Samuel. "A Rereading of Latino(a) Pentecostalism." In *New Horizons in Hispanic/Latino(a) Theology*, edited by Benjamín Valentín, 201–16. Cleveland, OH: Pilgrim, 2003.

Cuéllar, Gregory L. *Resacralizing the Other at the US-Mexico Border: A Borderland Hermeneutic.* London: Routledge, 2020.

Cuyatti Chávez, P. *Hanging On and Rising Up: Renewing, Re-envisioning, and Rebuilding the Cross from the "Marginalized."* Eugene, OR: Pickwick, 2019.

Dace, Karen L. *Unlikely Allies in the Academy: Women of Color and White Women in Conversation.* London: Routledge, 2012.

Dahm, Charles. *Parish Ministry in a Hispanic Community.* New York: Paulist, 2004.

Dávila, María Teresa. "Making Spirits Whole: Homeless Ministries as a Tool for Integral Development." In *Land of Stark Contrasts: Faith-Based Responses to Homelessness in the United States*, edited by Manuel Mejido Costoya, 297–315. New York: Fordham, 2021.

———. "A 'Preferential Option': A Challenge to Faith in a Culture of Privilege." In *The Word Became Culture*, edited by Miguel H. Díaz, 49–70. Maryknoll, NY: Orbis, 2020.

———. "Who Is Still Missing? Economic Justice and Immigrant Justice." In *The Almighty and the Dollar: Reflections on Economic Justice for All*, edited by Mark J. Allman, 214–27. Winona, MN: Anselm, 2012.

Davis, Graham. *Land! Irish pioneers in Mexican and Revolutionary Texas*. College Station: Texas A&M University Press, 2002.

De Anda, Neomi. "Images of God, Imago Dei, and God's Relationship with Humanity through the Image of Mary's Breast Milk: A Focus upon Sor María Anna Agueda de San Ignacio (1695–1756)." PhD diss., Loyola University Chicago, 2011.

———. "Jesus the Christ." In *The Wiley-Blackwell Companion to Latino/a Theology*, edited by Orlando Espín, 155–72. Chichester, UK: Wiley-Blackwell, 2015.

———. "Latina Feminist and *Mujerista* Theologies as Political Theologies?" In *T. & T. Clark Handbook of Political Theology*, edited by Rubén Rosario Rodríguez, 271–84. London: T. & T. Clark, 2020.

De Anda, Neomi, and Néstor Medina. "*Convivencias*: What Have We Learned? Toward a Latino/a Ecumenical Theology." In *Building Bridges, Doing Justice*, edited by Orlando Espín, 185–96. Maryknoll, NY: Orbis, 2009.

Deck, Allan Figueroa, ed. *Frontiers of Hispanic Theology in the United States*. Maryknoll, NY: Orbis, 1992.

Deck, Allan, Yolanda Tarango, and Timothy Matovina, eds. *Perspectivas: Hispanic Ministry*. Kansas City: Sheed & Ward, 1995.

De Genova, N., ed. *Racial Transformations: Latinos and Asians Remaking the United States*. Durham, NC: Duke University Press, 2006.

De La Torre, Miguel A. *Burying White Privilege*. Grand Rapids: Eerdmans, 2019.

———. *The Colonial Compromise: The Threat of the Gospel to the Indigenous Worldview*. Lanham, MD: Lexington, 2021.

———. *Decolonizing Christianity*. Grand Rapids: Eerdmans, 2021.

———. *Embracing Hopelessness*. Minneapolis: Fortress, 2017.

———. *Faith and Reckoning after Trump*. Maryknoll, NY: Orbis, 2021.

———, ed. *Handbook of U.S. Theologies of Liberation*. St. Louis: Chalice, 2004.

———. *Latina/o Social Ethics: Moving beyond Eurocentric Moral Thinking*. Waco, TX: Baylor University Press, 2010.

———. *Liberating Sexuality: Justice between the Sheets*. St. Louis: Chalice, 2016.

———. *Out of the Shadows into the Light: Christianity and Homosexuality*. St. Louis: Chalice, 2009.

———. *The Politics of Jesús: A Hispanic Political Theology*. Lanham, MD: Rowman and Littlefield, 2015.

———. *Reading the Bible from the Margins*. Maryknoll, NY: Orbis, 2002.

———. *Trails of Hope and Terror: Testimonies on Immigration*. Maryknoll, NY: Orbis, 2009.

———. *The U.S. Immigration Crisis: Toward an Ethic of Place*. Eugene, OR: Cascade, 2016.

De La Torre, Miguel, and Gastón Espinosa, eds. *Rethinking Latino(a) Religion and Identity*. Cleveland, OH: Pilgrim, 2006.

De La Torre, Miguel, and Mitri Raheb, eds. *Resisting Occupation: A Global Struggle for Liberation*. Lanham, MD: Lexington, 2021.

Delgadillo, Theresa. *Spiritual Mestizaje: Religion, Gender, Race and Nation in Chicana Narrative*. Durham, NC: Duke University Press, 2011.

Bibliography

Delgado, Teresa. *Augustine and Social Justice*. Lanham, MD: Lexington, 2015.

———. *A Puerto Rican Decolonial Theology: Prophesy Freedom*. New York: Palgrave Macmillan, 2017.

Díaz, Miguel H. "The Life-Giving Reality of God from Black, Latin American and US Hispanic Theological Perspectives." In *The Cambridge Companion to the Trinity*, edited by Peter Phan, 259–73. Cambridge: Cambridge University Press, 2011.

———, ed. *The Word Became Culture*. Maryknoll, NY: Orbis, 2020.

DiPietro, Pedro J., Jennifer McWeeny, and Shireen Roshanravan, eds. *Speaking Face to Face: The Visionary Philosophy of María Lugones*. Albany: State University of New York Press, 2019.

Dunbar-Ortiz, Roxanne, and Dina Gilio-Whitaker, *"All the Real Indians Died Off": And 20 Other Myths about Native Americans*. Boston: Beacon, 2016.

Elizondo, Virgilio. "Elements for a Mexican American *Mestizo* Christology." In *Jesus in the Hispanic Community: Images of Christ from Theology to Popular Religion*, edited by Harold J. Recinos and Hugo Magallanes, 3–15. Louisville: WJK, 2009.

———. *The Future Is Mestizo: Life Where Cultures Meet*. Oak Park, IL: Meyer-Stone, 1988.

———. *Galilean Journey: The Mexican-American Promise*. Maryknoll, NY: Orbis, 1983.

———. *A God of Incredible Surprises: Jesus of Galilee*. Lanham, MD: Rowan and Littlefield, 2003.

———. *Spiritual Writings*. Maryknoll, NY: Orbis, 2010.

———. *The Way of the Cross: The Passion of Christ in the Americas*. Lanham, MD: Rowman and Littlefield, 2002.

Elizondo, Virgilio, Gastón Espinoza, and Jesse Miranda. *Latino Religions and Civic Activism in the United States*. Oxford: Oxford University Press, 2005.

Elizondo, Virgilio, and Timothy Matovina. *Mestizo Worship: A Pastoral Approach to Liturgical Ministry*. Collegeville, MN: Liturgical, 1998.

Empereur, J., and Eduardo Fernandez. *La Vida Sacra: Contemporary Hispanic Sacramental Theology*. Lanham, MD: Rowman and Littlefield, 2006.

Espín, Orlando, ed. *Building Bridges, Doing Justice: Constructing a Latino/a Ecumenical Theology*. Maryknoll, NY: Orbis, 2009.

———. *Grace and Humanness: Theological Reflections because of Culture*. Maryknoll, NY: Orbis, 2007.

———. *Idol and Grace: On Traditioning and Subversive Hope*. Maryknoll, NY: Orbis, 2014.

———. "Immigration and Some of Its Implications for Christian Identity and Doctrine." In *Religion and Politics in America's Borderlands*, edited by Sarah Azaransky, 19–32. Lanham, MD: Lexington, 2013.

———. "Tradition and Popular Religion." In *Mestizo Christianity: Theology from the Latino Perspective*, edited by Arturo J. Bañuelas, 148–74. Maryknoll, NY: Orbis, 1995.

———, ed. *The Wiley-Blackwell Companion to Latinoax Theology*. 2nd ed. Chichester, UK: Wiley-Blackwell, forthcoming.

———, ed. *The Wiley-Blackwell Companion to Latino/a Theology*. Chichester, UK: Wiley-Blackwell, 2015.

Espín, Orlando O., and Gary Macy, eds. *Futuring Our Past: Explorations in the Theology of Tradition*. Maryknoll, NY: Orbis, 2006.

Espín, Orlando O., and Miguel H. Díaz, eds. *From the Heart of Our People: Latino/a Explorations in Catholic Systematic Theology*. Maryknoll, NY: Orbis, 1999.

Bibliography

Espinosa, Gastón. *Latino Pentecostals in America: Faith and Politics in Action.* Oxford: Oxford University Press, 2016.

Espinosa-Miñoso, Yuderkys, María Lugones, and Nelson Maldonado-Torres, eds. *Decolonial Feminism in Abya Yala: Caribbean, Meso, and South American Contributions and Challenges.* Lanham, MD: Rowman & Littlefield, 2021.

Fanning, Tim. *Paisanos: The Forgotten Irish Who Changed the Face of Latin America.* Dublin: Gill, 2017.

Fernández, Eduardo C. *La Cosecha: Harvesting Contemporary United States Hispanic Theology, 1972–1998.* Collegeville, MN: Liturgical, 2000.

Fernandez, Eleazar, ed. *Teaching for a Culturally Diverse and Racially Just World.* Eugene, OR: Cascade, 2014.

Fernandez, Eleazar S., and Fernando F. Segovia. *A Dream Unfinished: Theological Reflections on America from the Margins.* Maryknoll, NY: Orbis, 2001.

Floyd-Thomas, Stacey M., and Anthony B. Pinn, eds. *Liberation Theologies in the United States: An Introduction.* New York: New York University Press, 2010.

Fountain-Stokes, Lawrence La. "De sexilio(s) y diáspora(s) homosexual(es) latina(s): cultura puertorriqueña y lo nuyorican queer." *Debate Feminista* 29 (April 2004) 138–57.

Francis, J. Michael, and Kathleen M. Kole. *Murder and Martyrdom in Spanish Florida: Don Juan and the Guale Uprising of 1597.* New York: Anthropological Papers of the American Museum of Natural History, 2011.

García, Lorena. "Now Why Do You Want to Know about That? Heteronormativity, Sexism, and Racism in the Sexual (Mis)education of Latina Youth." *Gender and Society* 23.4 (2009) 520–41.

García, Sixto J. "The Latino/a Theology of God as the Future of Theodicy." In *The Wiley-Blackwell Companion to Latino/a Theology*, edited by Orlando Espín, 129–54. Chichester, UK: Wiley-Blackwell, 2015.

García-Johnson, Oscar. "In Search of Indigenous Pneumatologies in the Americas." In *The Spirit Over the Earth: Pneumatologies in the Majority World*, edited by Gene Green, Stephen Pardue and K. K. Yeo, 142–64. Grand Rapids: Eerdmans, 2016.

———. *Introducción a la teología del nuevo mundo: el quehacer teológico en siglo XXI.* Barcelona: Editorial CLIE, 2022.

———. *Mestizo/a Community of the Spirit: A Postmodern Latino/a Ecclesiology.* Eugene, OR: Pickwick, 2009.

———. "The Politics of the *Espiritu*: Ethic as Recognition-Assemblage-Decolonial Healing." In *T. & T. Clark Handbook of Political Theology*, edited by Rubén Rosario Rodríguez, 355–72. London: T. & T. Clark, 2020.

———. "The Spirit in the Colonial Difference." In *T. & T. Clark Handbook of Pneumatology*, edited by Daniel Castelo and Kenneth Loyer, 301–10. London: T. & T. Clark, 2020.

———. *Spirit Outside the Gate: Decolonial Pneumatologies of the American Global South.* Chicago: IVP Academic, 2019.

García-Johnson, Oscar, and Milton Acosta, eds. *Conversaciones Teológicas Del Sur Global Americano: Violencia, Desplazamiento y Fe.* Eugene, OR: Puertas Abiertas, 2016.

García-Rivera, Alejandro. *The Community of the Beautiful: A Theological Aesthetics.* Collegeville, MN: Liturgical, 1999.

———. *The Garden of God: A Theological Cosmology.* Minneapolis: Fortress, 2009.

———. *A Wounded Innocence: Sketches for a Theology of Art.* Collegeville, MN: Liturgical, 2003.

Bibliography

García-Rivera, Alejandro, and Thomas Scirghi. *Living Beauty: The Art of Liturgy.* Lanham, MD: Rowman and Littlefield, 2008.

García-Treto, Francisco. *Job, Proverbios, Eclesiastés y Cantar de los Cantares.* Minneapolis: Augsburg Fortress, 2010.

———. *Salmos.* Minneapolis: Augsburg Fortress, 2008.

Garrard, Virginia, and Justin M. Dorran. "Pentecostalism and Neo-Pentecostalism in Latin America: Two Case Studies." In *The Oxford Handbook of Latin American Christianity,* edited by David Thomas Orique, Susan Fitzpatrick-Behrens and Virginia Garrard, 291–308. Oxford: Oxford University Press, 2020.

Gates, Henry Louis. *Life upon These Shores: Looking at African American History, 1513-2008.* New York: Knopf, 2011.

Gebara, Ivone. *Longing for Running Water: Ecofeminism and Liberation.* Minneapolis: Fortress, 1999.

———. *Out of the Depths: Women's Experience of Evil and Salvation.* Minneapolis: Fortress, 2002.

Goizueta, Roberto. *Caminemos Con Jesús: Toward a Hispanic/Latino Theology of Accompaniment.* Maryknoll, NY: Orbis, 1995.

———. "Christ of the Borderlands: Faith and Idolatry in an Age of Globalization." In *Religion, Economics, and Culture in Conflict and Conversation,* edited by Laura Cassidy and Maureen O'Connell, 177–95. Maryknoll, NY: Orbis, 2011.

———. *Christ Our Companion: Toward a Theological Aesthetics of Liberation.* Maryknoll, NY: Orbis, 2009.

———. "The Church: A Latino Catholic Perspective." In *In Our Own Voices: Latino/a Renditions of Theology,* edited by Benjamín Valentín, 133–52. Maryknoll, NY: Orbis, 2010.

———. "*Corpus Verum*: Toward a Borderland Ecclesiology." In *Building Bridges, Doing Justice,* edited by Orlando Espín, 143–66. Maryknoll, NY: Orbis, 2009.

———. "Resisting the Frontier, Meeting at the Border." In *Resist! Christian Dissent for the 21st Century,* edited by Michael G. Long, 98–117. Maryknoll, NY: Orbis, 2008.

———. "The Significance of U.S. Hispanic Experience for Theological Method." In *Mestizo Christianity: Theology from the Latino Perspective,* edited by Arturo J. Bañuelas, 83–103. Maryknoll, NY: Orbis, 1995.

———, ed. *We Are a People! Initiatives in Hispanic-American Theology.* Minneapolis: Fortress, 1992.

Gómez-Ruíz. Raúl. *Mozarabs, Hispanics, and the Cross.* Maryknoll, NY: Orbis, 2007.

Gonzalez, Juan. *Harvest of Empire: A History of Latinos in America.* Rev. ed. New York: Penguin, 2011.

González, Justo L. *¡Alabadle! Hispanic Christian Worship.* Nashville: Abingdon, 1996.

———. *The Changing Shape of Church History.* St. Louis: Chalice, 2002.

———. *Knowing Our Faith: A Guide for Believers, Seekers and Christian Communities.* Grand Rapids: Eerdmans, 2019.

———. "A Latino Perspective." In *Methods for Luke,* edited by Joel Green, 113–43. Cambridge: Cambridge University Press, 2010.

———. *Mañana: Christian Theology from a Hispanic Perspective.* Nashville: Abingdon, 1990.

———. *The Mestizo Augustine: A Theologian between Two Cultures.* Downers Grove, IL: IVP Academic, 2016.

Bibliography

———. *Out of Every Tribe and Nation: Christian Theology at the Ethnic Round Table*. Nashville: Abingdon, 1992.
———. *Santa Biblia: The Bible through Hispanic Eyes*. Nashville: Abingdon, 1996.
———. *The Story Luke tells: Luke's Unique Witness to the Gospel*. Grand Rapids: Eerdmans, 2015.
———. *Teach Us to Pray: The Lord's Prayer in the Early Church and Today*. Grand Rapids: Eerdmans, 2020.
———. *Teología liberadora: enfoque desde la opresión en una tierra*. Buenos Aires: Kairos, 2014.
González, Justo L., and V. Elizondo. *Who Is My Neighbor? Christian Faith and Social Action*. Nashville: Abingdon, 2006.
González, Justo L., and Catherine González. *The Liberating Pulpit*. Nashville: Abingdon, 1994.
———. *Liberation Preaching: The Pulpit and the Oppressed*. Nashville: Abingdon, 1980.
González, Justo L., and Odina E. González. *Christianity in Latin America: A History*. Cambridge: Cambridge University Press, 2008.
———. *Nuestra Fe: A Latin American Church History Sourcebook*. Nashville: Abingdon, 2014.
González, Justo L., and Pablo A. Jiménez. *Púlpito: An Introduction to Hispanic Preaching*. Nashville: Abingdon, 2005.
González, Karen. *Beyond Welcome: Centering Immigrants in Our Christian Response to Immigration*. Grand Rapids: Brazos, 2022.
———. *The God Who Sees: Immigrants, the Bible and the Journey to Belong*. Huntington, TX: Herald, 2019.
Gonzalez, Michelle A. *Afro-Cuban Theology: Religion, Race, Culture and Identity*. Gainesville: University Press of Florida, 2006.
———. *Created in God's Image: An Introduction to Feminist Theological Anthropology*. Maryknoll, NY: Orbis, 2007.
———. *A Critical Introduction to Religion in the Americas: Bridging the Liberation Theology and Religious Studies Divide*. New York: New York University Press, 2014.
———. *Embracing Latina Spirituality: A Woman's Perspective*. Cincinnati: St. Anthony Messenger, 2009.
———. "Jesus." In *Handbook of Latina/o Theologies*, edited by Edwin David Aponte and Miguel A. De La Torre, 17–24. St. Louis: Chalice, 2006.
———. *Shopping*. Minneapolis: Fortress, 2010.
———. *Sor Juana: Beauty and Justice in the Americas*. Maryknoll, NY: Orbis, 2003.
———. "Who We Are: A Latino/a Constructive Anthropology." In *In Our Own Voices: Latino/a Renditions of Theology*, edited by Benjamín Valentín, 64–84. Maryknoll, NY: Orbis, 2010.
Gonzalez, Michelle A., and Ennis B. Edmonds. *Caribbean Religious History: An Introduction*. New York: New York University Press, 2010.
González-Justiniano, Yara. *Centering Hope as a Sustainable Decolonial Practice: Esperanza en Práctica*. Lanham, MD: Lexington, 2022.
———. "Practices of Hope: The Public Presence of the Church in Puerto Rico." PhD thesis, Boston University, 2019.
Gracia, Jorge, and Pablo de Greif, eds. *Hispanics/Latinos in the United States: Ethnicity, Race and Rights*. London: Routledge, 2000.

Bibliography

Griffin, Mark, and Theron Walker. *Living on the Borders: What the Church Can Learn from Ethnic Immigrant Cultures.* Grand Rapids: Brazos, 2004.

Groody, Daniel. *Border of Death, Valley of Life: An Immigrant Journey of Heart and Spirit.* Lanham, MD: Rowan and Littlefield, 2002.

Guasco, Michael. *Slaves and Englishmen: Human Bondage in the Early Modern Atlantic World.* Philadelphia: University of Pennsylvania Press, 2014.

Gutiérrez, Gustavo. *A Theology of Liberation.* 15th anniversary ed. Maryknoll, NY: Orbis, 1988.

Gutiérrez, Verónica A. "Indigenous Christianities: Ritual, Resilience, and Resistance among the Nahuas in Sixteenth-Century Mexico." In *Decolonial Christianities: Latinx and Latin American Perspectives*, edited by Raimundo Barreto and Roberto Sirvent, 107–27. New York: Palgrave Macmillan, 2019.

Harris, Max. *Carnival and Other Christian Festivals: Folk Theology and Folk Performance.* Austin: University of Texas Press, 2003.

Haynes, Sam W., and Cary D. Wintz, eds. *Major Problems in Texas History: Documents and Essays.* 2nd ed. Boston: Cengage Learning, 2017.

Heaney, Sharon E. *Contextual Theology for Latin America: Liberation Themes in Evangelical Perspective.* Eugene, OR: Wipf and Stock, 2008.

Henderson-Espinoza, R. *Activist Theology.* Minneapolis: Fortress, 2019.

———. *Body Becoming: A Path to Our Liberation.* Minneapolis: Broadleaf, 2022.

———. "Queer Theory and Latina/o Theologizing." In *The Wiley-Blackwell Companion to Latino/a Theology*, edited by Orlando Espín, 329–46. Chichester, UK: Wiley-Blackwell, 2015.

Heywood, Linda, and John Thornton. *Central Africans, Atlantic Creoles, and the Foundations of the Americas, 1585–1660.* Cambridge: Cambridge University Press, 2007.

Hidalgo, Jacqueline M. *Latina/o/x Studies and Biblical Studies.* Leiden: Brill, 2020.

Hill, Graham J., ed. *Relentless Love: Living Out Integral Mission to Combat Poverty, Injustice and Conflict.* London: Langham Global Library, 2020.

Hinojosa, Felipe. *Apostles of Change: Latino Radical Politics, Church Occupations and the Fight to Save the Barrio.* Austin: University of Texas Press, 2021.

———. *Latino Mennonites: Civil Rights, Faith and Evangelical Culture.* Baltimore: Johns Hopkins University Press, 2014.

Hinojosa, Felipe, Maggie Elmore, and Sergio M. González. *Faith and Power: Latino Religious Politics since 1945.* New York: New York University Press, 2022.

Hoxie, Frederick E., ed. *The Oxford Handbook of American Indian History.* New York: Oxford University Press, 2016.

Hughes, Jennifer Scheper. "Mapping the Autochthonous Indigenous Church: Toward a Decolonial History of Christianity in las Américas." In *Decolonial Christianities: Latinx and Latin American Perspectives*, edited by Raimundo Barreto and Roberto Sirvent, 91–105. New York: Palgrave Macmillan, 2019.

Huntington, Samuel. *Who Are We? The Challenges to America's National Identity.* New York: Simon and Schuster, 2004.

Igartua, José E. *Communities of the Soul: A Short History of Religion in Puerto Rico.* Montreal: McGill-Queen's University Press, 2021.

Ignatiev, Noel. *How the Irish Became White.* Abingdon, UK: Routledge, 1995.

Imperatori-Lee, Natalia. *Cuéntame: Narrative in the Ecclesial Present.* Maryknoll, NY: Orbis, 2018.

Bibliography

Isasi-Díaz, Ada María. "By the Rivers of Babylon: Exile as a Way of Life." In *Reading from this Place*, edited by Fernando Segovia and Mary Ann Tolbert, 149–64. Minneapolis: Fortress, 1995.

———. "Christ in *Mujerista* Theology." In *Thinking of Christ: Proclamation, Explanation, Meaning*, edited by Tatha Wiley, 157–76. New York: Continuum, 2003.

———. *La Lucha Continues: Mujerista Theology*. Maryknoll, NY: Orbis, 2004.

———. *En la Lucha: Elaborating a Mujerista Theology*. Minneapolis: Fortress, 1993.

———. *Mujerista Theology: A Theology for the Twenty-First Century*. Maryknoll, NY: Orbis, 1996.

Isasi-Díaz, Ada María, Timothy Matovina, and Nina Torres-Vidal. *Camino a Emaús: Compartiendo el Ministerio de Jesús*. Minneapolis: Fortress, 2002.

Isasi-Díaz, Ada María, and E. Mendieta, eds. *Decolonizing Epistemologies: Latina/o Theology and Philosophy*. New York: Fordham University Press, 2012.

Isasi-Díaz, Ada María, and Fernando Segovia, eds. *Hispanic/Latino Theology: Challenge and Promise*. Minneapolis: Fortress, 1996.

Isasi-Díaz, Ada María, and Yolanda Tarango. *Hispanic Women Prophetic Voice in the Church: Toward a Hispanic Women's Liberation Theology*. San Francisco: Harper & Row, 1988.

Jeyaraj, Daniel, Robert W. Pazmiño, and Rodney L. Petersen. *Antioch Agenda. Essays on the Restorative Church in Honor of Orlando E. Costas*. New Dehli: Indian Society for the Promotion of Christian Knowledge for Andover Newton Theological School and the Boston Theological Institute, 2007.

Jiménez, F., and G. Keller. *Hispanics in the United States: An Anthology of Creative Literature*. Vol. 1. Ypsilanti: Bilingual Preview, 1982.

———. *Hispanics in the United States: An Anthology of Creative Literature*. Vol. 2. Ypsilanti: Bilingual Preview, 1982.

Johnson, Elizabeth A., ed. *The Strength of Her Witness: Jesus Christ in the Global Voices of Women*. Maryknoll, NY: Orbis, 2016.

Keener, Craig, and M. Daniel Carroll R., eds. *Global Voices: Reading the Bible in the Majority World*. Peabody, MA: Hendrickson, 2013.

Kendi, Ibram X., and Keisha N. Blain, eds. *Four Hundred Souls: A Community History of African America, 1619–2019*. New York: One World, 2021.

Kidd, Thomas A. *American Colonial History: Clashing Cultures and Faiths*. New Haven, CT: Yale University Press, 2016.

Kirby, Peadar. *Ireland and Latin America, Links and Lessons*. Dublin: Gill and Macmillan, 1993.

———. "Latin America: The Region That Ireland Forgot" *History Ireland* 16.4, Ireland and Latin America (2008) 10–11. https://www.jstor.org/stable/27725822.

Kwok, Pui-lan, ed. *Hope Abundant: Third World and Indigenous Women's Theology*. Maryknoll, NY: Orbis, 2010.

———, ed. *Women and Christianity*. London: Routledge, 2010.

Kwok, Pui-lan, Cecilia González-Andrieu, Dwight N. Hopkins, eds. *Teaching Global Theologies: Power and Praxis*. Waco, TX: Baylor University Press, 2015.

Lazo, Rodrigo, and Jesse Alemán, eds. *The Latino Nineteenth Century*. New York: New York University Press, 2016.

Lee, Erika. *The Making of Asian America: A History*. New York: Simon & Schuster, 2015.

Bibliography

León, Luis. "Latino Men, Machismo, and Christianity." In *The Oxford Handbook of Latinx Christianities in the United States*, edited by Kristy Nabhan-Warren, 279–95. Oxford: Oxford University Press, 2022.

Liew, Tat-siong Benny, and Fernando Segovia, eds. *Reading Biblical Texts Together: Pursuing Minoritized Biblical Criticism*. Atlanta: SBL, 2022.

Lin, Tony Tian-Ren. *Prosperity Gospel Latinos and Their American Dream*. Chapel Hill: University of North Carolina Press, 2020.

Lozada, Francisco. *John: An Introduction and Study Guide—History, Community and Ideology*. London: T. & T. Clark, 2018.

———. "Teaching the New Testament: Toward an Expanded Contextual Approach." In *Soundings in Cultural Criticism: Perspectives and Methods in Culture, Power and Identity in the New Testament*, edited by Francisco Lozada and Greg Carey, 151–64. Minneapolis: Fortress, 2013.

———. *Toward a Latino/a Biblical Interpretation*. Atlanta: SBL, 2017.

Lozada, Francisco, and Greg Carey. *Soundings in Cultural Criticism: Perspectives and Methods in Culture, Power and Identity in the New Testament*. Minneapolis: Fortress, 2013.

Lozada, Francisco, and Fernando F. Segovia, eds. *Latino/a Theology and the Bible: Ethnic-Racial Reflections on Interpretation*. Lanham, MD: Lexington, 2021.

———, eds. *Latino/a Biblical Hermeneutics: Problematics, Objectives, Strategies*. Atlanta: SBL, 2014.

Lozano, Nora O. "Is It Truly a 'Good' Book? The Bible, Empowerment and Liberation." In *Latino/a Theology and the Bible: Ethnic-Racial Reflections on Interpretation*, edited by Francisco Lozada and Fernando Segovia, 89–102. Lanham, MD: Lexington, 2021.

Lozano, Rosina. *An American Language: The History of Spanish in the United States*. Oakland: University of California Press, 2018.

Lugones, María. *Pilgrimages/Peregrinajes: Theorizing Coalition against Multiple Oppressions*. Lanham, MD: Rowman & Littlefield, 2003.

Luiz Carlos, Susin, and María Pilar Aquino, eds. *Reconciliation in a World of Conflicts*. London: SCM, 2003.

Lynch, John. *New Worlds: A Religious History of Latin America*. New Haven, CT: Yale University Press, 2012.

Machado, Daisy. "History and Latino/a Identity: Mapping a Past That Leads to Our Future." In *The Wiley-Blackwell Companion to Latino/a Theology*, edited by Orlando Espín, 35–52. Chichester, UK: Wiley-Blackwell, 2015.

———. *Of Borders and Margins: Hispanic Disciples in Texas, 1888–1945*. Oxford: Oxford University Press, 2003.

———. "The Unnamed Woman: Justice, Feminists and the Undocumented Woman." In *A Reader in Latina Feminist Theology: Religion and Justice*, edited by María Pilar Aquino, Daisy Machado and Jeanette Rodríguez, 161–76. Austin: University of Texas Press, 2002.

Madrazo, Tito. "Preaching and the Wounds of Migration." *Liturgy* 36.2 (2021) 45–50.

———. *Predicadores: Hispanic Preaching and Immigrant Identity*. Waco, TX: Baylor University Press, 2021.

Madrazo, Tito, and Alma Tinoco Ruiz. "Preaching from Sanctuary." In *Preaching the Fear of God in a Fear-Filled World: Proceedings from the 13th Conference of Societas Homiletica, Durham 2018*, edited by Dawn Ottoni-Wilhelm, 119–33. Zurich: LIT Verlag, 2020.

Bibliography

Madsen, Deborah Lea. "The West and Manifest Destiny." In *A Concise Companion to American Studies*, edited by John Carlos Rowe, 369–88. Oxford: Wiley-Blackwell, 2010.

Maldonado, David. *Crossing Guadalupe Street: Growing up Hispanic and Protestant*. Albuquerque: University of New Mexico Press, 2001.

———. *Protestantes/Protestants: Hispanic Christianity within Mainline Traditions*. Nashville: Abingdon, 1999.

Maldonado, David, and Paul Barton. *Hispanic Christianity within Mainline Protestant Traditions: A Bibliography*. Decatur, GA: AETH, 1998.

Mamdani, Mahmood. *Neither Settler nor Native: The Making and Unmaking of Permanent Minorities*. Cambridge, MA: Belknap, 2020.

Marrow, H. B. "In Ireland 'Latin Americans Are Kind of Cool': Evaluating a National Context of Reception with a Transnational Lens. Ethnicities." *Sage Journals* 13.5 (2013) 645–66. https://doi.org/10.1177/1468796812463188.

Marshall, Oliver. *English, Irish and Irish-American Pioneer Settlers in Nineteenth-Century Brazil*. Oxford: University of Oxford, 2005.

Martell, Loida. "Reading against the Grain: Scripture and Constructive Evangélica Theology." In *Latino/a Theology and the Bible: Ethnic-Racial Reflections on Interpretation*, edited by Francisco Lozada Jr. and Fernando F. Segovia, 103–26. Lanham, MD: Lexington/Fortress Academic, 2021.

Martell-Otero, Loida. "*Encuentro con el Jesús Sato*: An *Evangélica Soter*-ology." In *Jesus in the Hispanic Community: Images of Christ from Theology to Popular Religion*, edited by Harold J. Recinos and Hugo Magallanes, 74–91. Louisville: WJK, 2009.

———. "From Foreign Bodies in Teacher Space to Embodied Spirit in *Personas Educadas*: or, How to Prevent 'Tourists of Diversity' in Education." In *Teaching for a Culturally Diverse and Racially Just World*, edited by Eleazar S. Fernandez, 52–68. Eugene, OR: Cascade, 2014.

———. "From *Satas* to *Santas*—*Sobrajas* No More: Salvation in the Spaces of the Everyday." In *The Strength of Her Witness: Jesus Christ in the Global Voices of Women*, edited by Elizabeth Johnson, 232–42. Maryknoll, NY: Orbis, 2016.

———. "*Hablando Se Entiende la Gente*: Tower of Babble or Gift of Tongues." In *Teaching Global Theologies: Power and Praxis*, edited by Kwok Pui Lan, Cecelia González-Andrieu and Dwight Hopkins, 143–62. Waco, TX: Baylor University Press, 2015.

Martell-Otero, Loida, Zaida Maldonado Pérez, and Elizabeth Conde-Frazier. *Latina Evangélicas: A Theological Survey from the Margins*. Eugene, OR: Cascade, 2013.

Martínez, Juan Francisco. *Los Protestantes: An Introduction to Latino Protestantism in the United States*. Santa Barbara, CA: Praeger, 2011.

———. *Walk with the People: Latino Ministry in the United States*. Eugene, OR: Wipf and Stock, 2016.

Mata, Roberto. "And I Saw Googleville Descend from Heaven: Reading the New Jerusalem in Gentrified Latinx Communities of Silicon Valley." In *Land of Stark Contrasts: Faith-Based Responses to Homelessness in the United* States, edited by Manuel Mejido Costoya, 316–30. New York: Fordham, 2021.

Matovina, T. *Beyond Borders: Writings of Virgilio Elizondo and Friends*. Maryknoll, NY: Orbis, 2000.

———. *Latino Catholicism: Transformation in America's Largest Church*. Princeton: Princeton University Press, 2012.

BIBLIOGRAPHY

———. *Theologies of Guadalupe: From the Era of Conquest to Pope Francis*. New York: Oxford University Press, 2019.
Matovina, Timothy, and Hosffman Ospino. *Reflexiones: Hispanic Ministry*. New York: Paulist, 2021.
Matsuoka, Fumitaka. *Out of Silence: Emerging Themes in Asian American Churches*. Cleveland, OH: United Church, 1995.
Matsuoka, Fumitaka, and Eleazar S. Fernandez, eds. *Realizing the America of our Hearts: Theological Voices of Asian Americans*. St. Louis: Chalice, 2003.
Maynard-Reid, Pedrito U. *Diverse Worship: African American, Caribbean and Hispanic Perspectives*. Downers Grove, IL: InterVarsity, 2000.
McDevitt, Patrick "Ireland, Latin America, and an Atlantic Liberation Theology." In *The Atlantic Global History 1500–2000*, edited by Jorge Cañizares-Esguerra and Erik R. Seeman, 248–61. London: Routledge, 2017.
McKnight, Kathryn Joy, and Leo J. Garofalo, eds. *Afro-Latino Voices: Narratives from the Early Modern Ibero-Atlantic World, 1550–1812*. Indianapolis: Hackett, 2009.
Medina, Lara. "*Nepantla* Spirituality: Negotiating Multiple Religious Identities among U.S. Latinas." In *Rethinking Latino(a) Religion and Identity*, edited by Miguel De La Torre and Gastón Espinosa, 249–66. Cleveland, OH: Pilgrim, 2006.
Medina, Lara, and Martha R Gonzales. *Voices from the Ancestors: Xicanx and Latinx Spiritual Expressions and Healing Practices*. Tucson: University of Arizona Press, 2019.
Medina, Néstor. *Christianity, Empire and the Spirit: (Re)Configuring Faith and the Cultural*. Leiden: Brill, 2018.
———. "(De)Ciphering *Mestizaje*: Encrypting Lived Faith." In *The Word Became Culture*, edited by Miguel H. Díaz, 71–92. Maryknoll, NY: Orbis, 2020.
———. "Ethics, Theology and Mestizaje." In *The Oxford Handbook of Latinx Christianities in the United States*, edited by Kristy Nabhan-Warren, 207–24. Oxford: Oxford University Press, 2022.
———. "Latin America." In *The Oxford Handbook of Ecumenical Studies*, edited by Geoffrey Wainwright and Paul McPartlan, 527–35. Oxford: Oxford University Press, 2021.
———. *Mestizaje: (Re)Mapping Race, Culture and Faith in Latina/o Catholicism*. Maryknoll, NY: Orbis, 2009.
———. "Theological Musings toward a Latina/o Pneumatology." In *The Wiley-Blackwell Companion to Latino/a Theology*, edited by Orlando Espín, 173–89. Chichester, UK: Wiley-Blackwell, 2015.
Medina, Néstor, and Sammy Alfaro, eds. *Pentecostals and Charismatics in Latin America and Latino Communities*. New York: Palgrave Macmillan, 2015.
Medina, Néstor, and Jeff Nowers, eds. *Theology and the Crisis of Engagement: Essays on the Relationship of Theology and the Social Sciences in Honor of Lee Cormie*. Eugene, OR: Pickwick, 2013.
Medrano, Ethelia Ruiz, and Susan Kellogg, eds. *Negotiation within Domination: New Spain's Indian Pueblos Confront the Spanish State*. Boulder: University of Colorado Press, 2010.
Miller, Donald E., and Tetsauno Yamamori. *Global Pentecostalism: The New Face of Christian Social Engagement*. Berkeley: University of California Press, 2007.
Mize, Ronald. *Latina/o Studies*. Cambridge: Polity, 2019.

Bibliography

Morales, Harold. *Latino and Muslim in America: Race, Religion and the Making of New Minority*. Oxford: Oxford University Press, 2018.

Morello, Gustavo. *Lived Religion in Latin America: An Enchanted Modernity*. Oxford: Oxford University Press, 2021.

Moraga, Cherríe, and Gloria Anzaldúa. *This Bridge Called My Back: Writings by Radical Women of Color*. 4th ed. Albany: State University of New York Press, 2015.

Moros, Matilde. "Theologizing Social and Economic Justice." In *The Wiley-Blackwell Companion to Latino/a Theology*, edited by Orlando Espín, 313–27. Chichester, UK: Wiley-Blackwell, 2015.

Mulder, Mark T., Aida I. Ramos, and Gerardo Martí. *Latino Protestants in America: Growing and Diverse*. Lanham, MD: Rowman and Littlefield, 2017.

Murray, Edmundo. *Devenir irlandés. Narrativas intimas de la emigración irlandesa a la Argentina (1844–1912)*. Buenos Aires: Editorial Universitaria Buenos Aires, 2000. Available in English as *Becoming Irlandés: Private Narratives of the Irish Emigration to Argentina, 1844–1912*. Buenos Aires: Editorial Universitaria Buenos Aires, 2005.

———. "Ireland and Latin America." *Society for Irish Latin American Studies*, 2005. http://www.irlandeses.org/murrayintro.htm.

———. "The Irish in Latin America and Iberia: An Annotated Bibliography." https://hcommons.org/deposits/item/hc:30333.

———. "Secret Diasporas: The Irish in Latin America and the Caribbean." *History Ireland* 4 (Jul/Aug 2008). https://www.historyireland.com/secret-diasporas-the-irish-in-latin-america-and-the-caribbean.

Nabhan-Warren, Kristy. *Américan Woman: The Virgin of Guadalupe, Latinas and Accompaniment*. Los Angeles: Loyola Marymount University Press, 2018.

———. *Meatpacking America: How Migration, Work and the Faith Unite and Divide in the Heartland*. Chapel Hill: University of North Carolina Press, 2018.

———, ed. *The Oxford Handbook of Latinx Christianities in the United States*. New York: Oxford University Press, 2022.

Nanko-Fernández, Carmen. "Alternately Documented Theologies: Mapping Border, Exile and Diaspora." In *Religion and Politics in America's Borderlands*, edited by Sarah Azaransky, 33–56. Lanham, MD: Lexington, 2013.

———. *Campus Ministry: Identity, Mission and Praxis*. Washington, DC: National Catholic Educational Association, 1997.

———. "Lo Cotidiano as Locus Theologicus." In *The Wiley-Blackwell Companion to Latino/a Theology*, edited by Orlando Espín, 15–33. Chichester, UK: Wiley-Blackwell, 2015.

———. "From *Pájaro* to Paraclete: Retrieving the Spirit of God in the Company of Mary." In *Building Bridges, Doing Justice*, edited by Orlando Espín, 13–28. Maryknoll, NY: Orbis, 2009.

———. "Playing en los Márgenes. Lo Popular as *Locus Theologicus*." In *The Word Became Culture*, edited by Miguel H. Díaz, 93–114. Maryknoll, NY: Orbis, 2020.

———. *Theologizing en Espanglish*. Maryknoll, NY: Orbis, 2010.

Nobasco, Vianny Jasmin. "Doing Latinidad While Black: Afro-Latino Identity and Belonging." PhD thesis, University of Arkansas, 2020.

Oliver, Juan. *A House of Meanings: Christian Worship in Plain Language*. New York: Church Publishing, 2020.

———. *Ripe Fields: The Promise and Challenge of Latino Ministry*. New York: Church Publishing, 2009.

Bibliography

Ortega, Ofelia. *Cuban Feminist Theology: Visions and Praxis.* Lanham, MD: Lexington, 2022.
Ortiz, Manuel. *The Hispanic Challenge: Opportunities Confronting the Church.* Downers Grove, IL: InterVarsity, 1993.
Ortiz, Paul. *An African American and Latinx History of the United States.* Boston: Beacon, 2018.
Padilla, Alvin, Roberto Goizueta, and Eldin Villafañe. *Hispanic Christian Thought at the Dawn of the 21st Century: Apuntes in Honor of Justo L. González.* Nashville: Abingdon, 2005.
Padilla, Elaine. *Theology of Migration in Abrahamic Religions.* New York: Springer, 2014.
Padilla, Elaine, and Peter C. Phan, eds. *Contemporary Issues of Migration and Theology.* New York: Palgrave Macmillan, 2013.
Panich, Lee M., and Tsim D. Schneider, eds. *Indigenous Landscapes and Spanish Missions: New Perspectives from Archaeology and Ethnohistory.* Tucson: University of Arizona Press, 2014.
Pazmiño, R. *Latin American Journey: Insights for Christian Education in North America.* Cleveland, OH: United Church, 1994.
Pedraja Luis. *Jesus Is My Uncle: Christology from a Hispanic Perspective.* Nashville: Abingdon, 1999.
———. *Teología: An Introduction to Hispanic Theology.* Nashville: Abingdon, 2003.
Perea, Stan, ed. *A Legacy of Fifty Years: The Life and Work of Justo González.* Nashville: Abingdon, 2013.
Peres, Tanya M., and Rochelle A. Marrinan. *Unearthing the Missions of Spanish Florida.* Gainesville: University Press of Florida, 2021.
Pérez, Altagracia. "Latina/o Practical Theology: Reflections on Faith Based Organizing as a Religious Practice." In *The Wiley-Blackwell Companion to Latino/a Theology*, edited by Orlando O. Espín, 439–52. Chichester, UK: Wiley-Blackwell, 2015.
———. "Pastoral Care with Persons Living with HIV/AIDS." In *Injustice and the Care of the Souls: Taking Oppression Seriously in Pastoral Care*, edited by Sheryl Kujawa-Holbrook and Karen Montagno, 119–210. Minneapolis: Fortress, 2009.
Pérez, Arturo, Consuelo Coyarrubias, and Edward Foley, eds. *Así Es: Stories of Hispanic Spirituality.* Collegeville, MN: Liturgical, 1994.
Perez, Elizabeth. *Religion in the Kitchen: Cooking, Talking and the Making of Black Atlantic Traditions.* New York: New York University Press, 2016.
Pérez-Bullard, Altagracia. "Aspiring to Un Liderazgo en Conjunto: Leadership Development for Latine Congregations." In *The Wiley-Blackwell Companion to Latinoax Theology*, edited by Orlando Espín. 2nd ed. Chichester, UK: Wiley-Blackwell, forthcoming.
———. "In Times Like These: Comfort and Courage for Change." In *Fearful Times; Living Faith*, edited by Robert Boak Slocum and Martyn Percy, 73–80. Eugene, OR: Wipf and Stock, 2021.
———. "Liderazgo en Conjunto: A Leadership Development Model for the Twenty-First Century." *Anglican Theological Review* 101.4 (2019) 625–50.
———. "Living into Multicultural Inclusive Ministry." *Anglican Theological Review* 93.4, 659–67.
Peters, Rebecca Todd, and Grace Y. Kao, eds. *Encountering the Sacred: Feminist Reflections on Women's Lives.* London: T. & T. Clark, 2019.

Bibliography

———. "Feminist Theology as Conversation and Invitation." Introduction to *Encountering the Sacred: Feminist Reflections on Women's Lives*, edited by Rebecca Todd Peters and Grace Y. Kao, 1–16. London: T. & T. Clark, 2019.

Pineda-Madrid, Nancy. "Feminist Theory and Latina Feminist/Mujerista Theologizing." In *The Wiley-Blackwell Companion to Latino/a Theology*, edited by Orlando Espín, 347–64. Chichester, UK: Wiley-Blackwell, 2015.

———. Foreword to *Fragile Resurrection: Practicing Hope after Domestic Violence*, edited by Ashley Theuring, ix–xii. Eugene, OR: Cascade, 2021.

———. *Suffering and Salvation in Ciudad Juárez*. Minneapolis: Fortress, 2011.

Pinn, A., and B. Valentín, eds. *Creating Ourselves: African Americans and Hispanic Americans on Popular Culture and Religious Expression*. Durham, NC: Duke University Press, 2009.

———, eds. *The Ties That Bind: African American and Hispanic American/Latino/a Theologies in Dialogue*. New York: Continuum, 2001.

Pitts, Andrea. "Latina/x Feminist Philosophy." In *The Oxford Handbook of Feminist Philosophy*, edited by Kim Q. Hall and Ásta, 120–35. Oxford: Oxford University Press, 2021.

———. *Nos/Otras: Gloria Anzaldúa, Multiplicitous Agency and Resistance*. Albany: State University of New York Press, 2021.

Pitts, Andrea, Mariana Ortega, and José M. Medina, eds. *Theories of the Flesh: Latinx and Latin American Feminisms, Transformation and Resistance*. Oxford: Oxford University Press, 2020.

Ramirez, Daniel. *Migrating Faith: Pentecostalism in the United States and Mexico, 1906–1966*. Chapel Hill: University of North Carolina Press, 2015.

Ramos, Aida, Gerardo Martí, and Mark Mulder. "Latino/a Protestantisms: Historical and Sociological Overviews." In *The Oxford Handbook of Latinx Christianities in the United States*, edited by Kristy Nabhan-Warren, 109–29. Oxford: Oxford University Press, 2022.

Recinos, Harold J. *Good News from the Barrio: Prophetic Witness for the Church*. Louisville: Westminster John Knox, 2006.

———, ed. *Wading through Many Voices: Toward a Theology of Public Conversation*. Lanham, MD: Rowman & Littlefield, 2011.

Recinos, Harold J., and Hugo Magallanes, eds. *Jesus in the Hispanic Community: Images of Christ from Theology to Popular Religion*. Louisville: Westminster John Knox, 2009.

Reid, B. *Taking Up the Cross: New Testament Interpretations through Latina and Feminist Eyes*. Minneapolis: Fortress, 2007.

Reinhard, Wolfgang. *Empires and Encounters: 1350–1750*. Cambridge, MA: Bleknap, 2015.

Ress, Mary Judith. *Ecofeminism in Latin America*. Maryknoll, NY: Orbis, 2006.

Restall, Matthew, and Amara Solari. *The Maya Apocalypse and Its Western Roots*. Lanham, MD: Rowman & Littlefield, 2022.

Reyes, Patrick. *Nobody Cries When We Die: God, Community and Surviving to Adulthood*. St. Louis: Chalice, 2016.

Rivera, Luis N. *A Violent Evangelism: The Political and Religious Conquest of the Americas*. Louisville: Westminster John Knox, 1992.

Rivera-Pagán, Luis. *Essays from the Margins*. Eugene, OR: Cascade, 2014.

———. "A New Pentecost: Conversion in the Caribbean." In *The Oxford Handbook of Latin American Christianity*, edited by David Thomas Orique, Susan Fitzpatrick-Behrens, and Virginia Garrard, 329–46. Oxford: Oxford University Press, 2020.

Bibliography

———. "The Political Praxis of Bartolomé de Las Casas." In *The T. & T. Clark Handbook of Political Theology*, edited by Rubén Rosario Rodríguez, 131–45. London: T. & T. Clark, 2020.

Rivera Rivera, Mayra. *Poetics of the Flesh*. Durham, NC: Duke University Press, 2015.

———. "Thinking Bodies: The Spirit of a Latina Incarnational Imagination." In *Decolonizing Epistemologies: Latina/o Theology and Philosophy*, edited by Ada María Isasi-Díaz and Eduardo Mendieta, 207–25. New York: Fordham, 2012.

———. *Touch of Transcendence: A Postcolonial Theology of God*. Louisville: Westminster John Knox, 2007.

Robeck, John Mark. *Toward a Pentecostal Theology of Praxis: A Case Study*. Lanham, MD: Lexington, 2021.

Rodríguez, Daniel. *A Future for the Latino Church: Models for Multilingual, Multigenerational Hispanic Congregations*. Downers Grove, IL: InterVarsity, 2011.

Rodríguez, Havidan, Rogelio Saenz, and Cecilia Menivar, eds. *Latinos/as/xs in the United States: Changing the Face of America*. New York: Springer, 2008.

Rodríguez, Jeanette. *Our Lady of Guadalupe: Faith and Empowerment among Mexican-American Women*. Austin: University of Texas Press, 1994.

———. *Stories We Live/Cuentos que Vivimos: Hispanic Women's Spirituality*. New York: Paulist, 1996.

Rodríguez, Jeanette, and Ted Fortier. *Cultural Memory: Resistance, Faith and Identity*. Austin: University of Texas, 2007.

Rodríguez, José David, and Loida I. Martell-Otero, eds. *Teología en Conjunto: A Collaborative Hispanic Protestant Theology*. Louisville: Westminster John Knox, 1997.

Rodríguez, Rubén Rosario. *Christian Martyrdom and Political Violence: A Comparative Theology with Judaism and Islam*. New York: Cambridge University Press, 2017.

———. "Liberation Hermeneutics in Jewish, Christian and Muslim Exegesis: A Latino/a Perspective." In *Latino/a Theology and the Bible: Ethnic-Racial Reflections on Interpretation*, edited by Francisco Lozada and Fernando Segovia, 169–88. Lanham, MD: Lexington, 2021.

———. *Racism and God-Talk: A Latino/a Perspective*. New York: New York University Press, 2008.

———, ed. *The T. & T. Clark Handbook of Political Theology*. London: T. & T. Clark, 2020.

Roediger, David R. *Working Toward Whiteness: How America's Immigrants Became White; The Strange Journey from Ellis Island to the Suburbs*. New York: Basic, 2005.

Roland Guzmán, Carla E. *Unmasking Latinx Ministry for Episcopalians: An Anglican Approach*. New York: Church Publishing, 2020.

Romero, C. Gilbert. *Hispanic Devotional Piety: Tracing the Biblical Roots*. Maryknoll, NY: Orbis, 1991.

Romero, Robert Chao. *Brown Church: Five Centuries of Latina/o Social Justice, Theology and Identity*. Downers Grove, IL: InterVarsity, 2020.

Romero, Robert Chao, and Stephen Burris, eds. *Migration, Mission and Ministry: An Introduction*. Skyforest, CA: Urban Loft, 2022.

Roorda, Eric P., Lauren Derby, and Raymundo González, eds. *The Dominican Republic Reader: History, Culture, Politics*. Durham, NC: Duke University Press, 2014.

Roper, G., and J. R. Middleton. *A Kairos Moment for Caribbean Theology: Ecumenical Voices in Dialogue*. Eugene, OR: Pickwick, 2013.

Ross, Kenneth, Ana María Bidegain, and Todd M Johnson, eds. *Christianity in Latin America and the Caribbean*. Edinburgh: Edinburgh University Press, 2022.

Bibliography

Ruiz, Jean-Pierre. "Beyond Borders and Boundaries: Rethinking Eisegesis and Rereading Ruth 1:16–17." In *The Word Became Culture*, edited by Miguel H. Díaz, 25–48. Maryknoll, NY: Orbis, 2020.

———. "The Bible and Latino/a Theology." In *The Wiley-Blackwell Companion to Latino/a Theology*, edited by Orlando Espín, 111–28. Chichester, UK: Wiley-Blackwell, 2015.

———. *Reading from the Edges: The Bible and People on the Move*. Maryknoll, NY: Orbis, 2011.

———. *Revelation in the Vernacular*. Maryknoll, NY: Orbis, 2021.

Salvatierra, Alexia, and Brandon Wrencher. *Buried Seeds: Learning from the Vibrant Resilience of Marginalized Christian Communities*. Grand Rapids: Baker Academics, 2022.

Sánchez, David A. "The Apocalyptic Legacy of Early Christianity." In *Fortress Commentary on the Bible: The New Testament*, edited by Margaret Aymer, Cynthia Briggs Kittredge, and David A. Sánchez, 63–82. Minneapolis: Fortress, 2014.

———. *From Patmos to the Barrio: Subverting Imperial Myths*. Minneapolis: Fortress, 2008.

———. "Interpretive World Making: Formulating a Space for a Critical Latino/a Cultural and Biblical Discourse." In *Latino/a Hermeneutics: Problematics, Objectives, Strategies*, edited by Francisco Lozada and Fernando F. Segovia, 246–62. Atlanta: SBL, 2014.

———. "'It Is No Longer Because of Your Words . . .': Interrogating John 4 through the Lens of *Malinchismo* and the Vanquished Woman Motif." In *Reading Biblical Texts Together: Pursuing Minoritized Biblical Criticism*, edited by Tat-siong Benny Liew and Fernando Segovia, 309–22. Atlanta: SBL, 2022.

———. "Troubled Northern Ireland: Talking Walls, Open Wounds." *Political Theology*, March 4, 2019. https://politicaltheology.com/troubled-northern-ireland-talking-walls-open-wounds.

Sánchez-Walsh, Arlene M. *Latino Pentecostal Identity: Evangelical Faith, Self and Society*. New York: Columbia University Press, 2003.

———. *Pentecostals in America*. New York: Columbia University Press, 2018.

Sandoval, Moises. *On the Move: A History of the Hispanic Church in the United States*. Maryknoll, NY: Orbis, 2006.

Scharrón-del Río, María R., and Alan A. Aja. "*Latinx*: Inclusive Language as Liberative Praxis." *Journal of Latinx Psychology* 8.1 (2020) 7–20.

Schnieder, Nicolas Iglesias. "Pentecostals/Charismatics." In *Christianity in Latin America and the Caribbean*, edited by Kenneth Ross, Ana María Bidegain and Todd Johnson, 322–36. Edinburgh: Edinburgh University Press, 2022.

Schroeder, Joy A., and Marion Ann Taylor. *Voices Long Silenced: Women Biblical Interpreters through the Centuries*. Louisville: Westminster John Knox, 2022.

Schultze, George E. *Strangers in a Foreign Land: The Organizing of Catholic Latinos in the United States*. Lanham, MD: Lexington, 2007.

Segovia, Fernando F. *Decolonizing Biblical Studies: A View from the Margins*. Maryknoll, NY: Orbis, 2000.

———. *Interpreting beyond Borders*. Sheffield, UK: Sheffield Academic, 2000.

———. *Postcolonial Biblical Criticism: Interdisciplinary Intersections*. London: T. & T. Clark, 2005.

———. *Teaching the Bible: The Discourses and Politics of Biblical Pedagogy*. Maryknoll, NY: Orbis, 1998.

Bibliography

Segura, Harold. "Liberation Theology's Spiritual Legacy for the Latin American Church." In *The Oxford Handbook of Latin American Christianity*, edited by David Thomas Orique, Susan Fitzpatrick-Behrens, and Virginia Garrard, 377–92. Oxford: Oxford University Press, 2020.

Sison, Antonio D. *The Art of Indigenous Inculturation: Grace on the Edge of Genius*. Maryknoll, NY: Orbis, 2021.

Smith, Calvin L., ed. *Pentecostal Power: Expressions, Impact and Faith of Latin American Pentecostalism*. Leiden: Brill, 2011.

Soliván, Samuel. "The Holy Spirit—Personalization and the Affirmation of Diversity: A Pentecostal Hispanic Perspective." In *Teología en Conjunto: A Collaborative Hispanic Protestant Theology*, edited by José David Rodríguez and Loida Martell-Otero, 50–65. Louisville: Westminster John Knox, 1997.

———. *The Spirit, Pathos and Liberation: Toward an Hispanic Pentecostal Theology*. Sheffield, UK: Sheffield Academic, 1998.

Starr, Kevin. *Continental Ambitions: Roman Catholics in North America; The Colonial Experience*. San Francisco: Ignatius, 2016.

Stevens-Arroyo, Anthony, and Ana María Díaz-Stevens, eds. *An Enduring Flame: Studies on Latino Popular Religiosity*. New York: Bildner Center for Western Hemisphere Studies, 1994.

Takaki, Ronald. *A Different Mirror: A History of Multicultural America*. Boston: Little, Brown, 1993.

———. *A Larger Memory: A History of Our Diversity, with Voices*. Boston: Little, Brown, 1998.

Tamez, Elsa. *Las mujeres en el movimiento de Jesús, el Cristo*. Quito, Ecuador: Consejo Latinoamericano de Iglesias, 2003.

———. *Philippians, Colossians, Philemon*. Collegeville, MN: Liturgical, 2017.

———. *Struggles for Power in Early Christianity: A Study of the First Letter to Timothy*. Translated by Gloria Kinsler. Maryknoll, NY: Orbis, 2007.

———, ed. *Through Her Eyes: Women's Theology from Latin America*. 1989. Reprint, Eugene, OR: Wipf & Stock, 2006.

Tarango, Yolanda, Consuelo Covarrubias, Arturo Pérez, and Edward Foley, eds. *Así Es: Stories of Hispanic Spirituality*. Translated by Sarah Pruett and Elena Sánchez Mora. Collegeville, MN: Liturgical, 1994.

Tarango, Yolanda, and Kenneth Davis, eds. *Bridging Boundaries: The Pastoral Care of U.S. Hispanics*. Scranton, PA: University of Scranton Press, 2000.

Theuring, Ashley. *Fragile Resurrection: Practicing Hope after Domestic Violence*. Eugene, OR: Cascade, 2021.

Torres, Theresa. "What My Abuelita Taught Me about Prayer and Memory." In *Voices from the Ancestors: Xicanx and Latinx Spiritual Expressions and Healing Practices*, edited by Lara Medina and Martha R. Gonzales, 142–43. Tucson: University of Arizona Press, 2019.

Torres, Theresa L. "A Latina *Testimonio*: Challenges as an Academic, Issues of Difference, and a Call for Solidarity with White Female Academics." In *Unlikely Allies in the Academy: Women of Color and White Women in Conversation*, edited by Karen L. Dace, 65–75. London: Routledge, 2012.

Tulud Cruz, Gemma. *An Intercultural Theology of Migration Pilgrims in the Wilderness*. Leiden: Brill, 2010.

Bibliography

Uenuma, Francine. "During the Mexican-American War, Irish-Americans Fought for Mexico in the 'Saint Patrick's Battalion.'" *Smithsonian* magazine, March 15, 2019. https://www.smithsonianmag.com/history/mexican-american-war-irish-immigrants-deserted-us-army-fight-against-america-180971713.

Vaca, Nicolas. *The Presumed Alliance: The Unspoken Conflict between Latinos and Blacks and What It Means for America*. New York: HarperCollins, 2004.

Valentín, Benjamín, ed. *In Our Own Voices: Latino/a Renditions of Theology*. Maryknoll, NY: Orbis, 2010.

———. *Looking Forward with Hope: Reflections on the Present State and Future of Theological Education*. Eugene, OR: Cascade, 2019.

———. *Mapping Public Theology: Beyond Culture, Identity and Difference*. Harrisburg, PA: Trinity, 2002.

———, ed. *New Horizons in Hispanic/Latino(a) Theology*. Cleveland, OH: Pilgrim, 2003.

Valentin, Elieser. *Sermons from the Latino/a Pulpit*. Eugene, OR: Wipf and Stock, 2017.

Vega, Sujey. *Latino Heartland: Of Borders and Belonging in the Midwest*. New York: New York University Press, 2015.

Villafañe, Eldin. *Beyond Cheap Grace: A Call to Radical Discipleship, Incarnation and Justice*. Grand Rapids: Eerdmans, 2006.

———. "An Evangelical Call to a Social Spirituality: Confronting Evil in Urban Society." In *Mestizo Christianity: Theology from the Latino Perspective*, edited by Arturo Bañuelos, 209–23. 1995. Reprint, Eugene, OR: Wipf & Stock, 2004.

———. *The Liberating Spirit: Toward an Hispanic American Pentecostal Social Ethic*. Lanham, MD: University Press of America, 1992.

———. *Manda Fuego, Señor: Introducción al Pentecostalismo*. Nashville: Abingdon, 2012.

———. *Transforming the City: Reframing Education for Urban Ministry*. Grand Rapids: Eerdmans, 2002.

Watkins, Jordan T. *Slavery and Sacred Texts: The Bible, the Constitution, and Historical Consciousness in Antebellum America*. Cambridge: Cambridge University Press, 2021.

Weber, David. *The Spanish Frontier in North America*. New Haven, CT: Yale University Press, 2009.

Woodworth, Steven E. *Manifest Destinies: America's Westward Expansion and the Road to the Civil War*. New York: Knopf, 2010.

Young, Robert J. C. *The Idea of English Ethnicity*. Malden, MA: Wiley-Blackwell, 2007.

Zamora, Omaris Zunilda. "Let the Waters Flow: (Trans)locating Afro-Latina Feminist Thought." PhD thesis, University of Texas, 2013.

Name/Subject Index

abuelita theology, 87, 89, 93, 96, 108–10, 113–15, 156, 175
accent, xix–xx, 55–56, 148–49
acompañamiento, 123
African American, 7–8, 13–14, 18, 25–28, 69, 114, 126–27, 143, 150, 163, 166, 169, 171–72
African, 6–7, 25, 27, 30, 36, 49, 54, 61, 134, 158, 165
Afro-Latino/a/x, 6, 7, 35
Agosto, Efraín, 79, 155
Alanís, Javier, 53–54, 64
Alcántara, Jared, 81, 90, 155
Alfaro, Sammy, 64, 69, 117–18, 155, 169
Althaus-Reid, Marcella, 155
Anzaldúa, Gloria, 91, 156, 170, 172
Aponte, Edwin David, xiii, 4, 9, 11–12, 17, 33, 44–47, 64, 72–73, 86, 130, 137–39, 156–57, 164
Aquino, Jorge, 23, 35–36, 41, 156
Aquino, María Pilar, 1, 14, 22, 24, 91–92, 100, 102–5, 111, 115, 157, 167
Armas, Kat, 109, 115, 156
Asian American, 7, 69, 126–27, 169
Avalos, Hector, 30–31, 156

Bañuelas, Arturo, 9–10, 12, 22, 35, 66, 157, 161, 163
Bedford, Nancy Elizabeth, 104–5, 127, 157
belong/belonging, xvii, 2, 23, 28, 30, 55, 67, 89, 109, 125, 132, 164, 170

Bible, xviii, 38, 66–83, 87, 89–90, 106, 129, 130, 135, 144, 155, 158–60, 164, 166–68, 173–74, 176
bilingual, 6, 17, 29, 79, 113, 129, 147
borders/borderlands, xvii, xx, xxiv, 5, 11, 13, 15, 24–27, 68–69, 73–75, 80–83, 89, 102, 111, 123, 125–30, 133, 136, 144–45, 155–59, 161, 163, 165, 167–68, 170, 174, 176

Carmona, Victor, 131–32, 145, 158
Carroll R., Daniel M., 74–75, 79, 89, 129, 144, 158, 166
chicano/a/x, 14, 41, 71, 103, 127–28, 160
Christ/Christology, 8, 22, 32, 43–44, 50–59, 62, 64, 72, 81, 95, 116, 119–20, 123–24, 128, 133, 135, 140–41, 155, 158–61, 163, 166, 168, 172
collaboration, ix, xi, xiv, xx, 2, 9–17, 44, 66, 75, 83, 116, 148
colonialism, 16, 20, 37, 43, 51, 85, 91, 101, 147
complexity, 7, 15, 19–41, 46, 66, 74, 81–86, 103, 107, 126, 135, 138, 148–49
comunidad/community, x–xv, xvii. xix–xxi, 2–5, 8–11, 13, 15, 24–25, 28, 31, 33, 35–36, 38–44, 47, 50, 53–55, 57–70, 77–80, 86–9, 93–95, 97–99, 102, 104, 106, 110–16, 119–28, 139–45, 150, 152, 155–56, 159, 161–62, 166–68, 172

177

Name/Subject Index

Conde-Frazier, Elizabeth, ix–xiii, 4, 13, 46, 66–67, 69–70, 77, 79, 81–82, 85, 89, 92, 105–6, 111, 115, 120, 122, 124, 136, 145, 152, 158–59, 168

context, xi–xii, xvii–xx, 2–11, 15–17, 23, 39, 44–47, 55, 57–59, 61, 66–69, 76–77, 79, 81–88, 97, 101–3, 113, 118–19, 123, 131, 133, 137–41, 147–53, 155–56, 159, 165, 167–68

conquest, 19–21, 32, 43, 48–54, 100–101, 169, 172

conquistadores, 48, 53

coritos, 53–54, 60, 71, 72, 106

Costas, Orlando E., 14, 75, 116, 120, 159, 166

cotidiano, lo, xii, xxi, 38, 42–64, 65, 73, 91–92, 97, 116–17, 121, 123, 152, 170

convivencia, 47, 141, 160

culture, x, xxi–xxii, 1, 5, 6–7, 10–16, 18, 20–23, 26–27, 30–33, 39–42, 48–49, 58, 61–63, 65, 74, 78, 83, 85, 87–88

cultural memory, 31–34, 173, 175

Dávila, María Teresa, 73, 80, 125, 131, 141, 158, 159

De Anda, Neomi, xiii, 47, 55, 64, 92, 93, 101, 112, 115, 118, 122, 160

De La Torre, Miguel A., 3, 4, 7, 9, 11–12, 17, 34, 36, 43, 44–47, 53, 56, 58, 59, 64, 72–73, 78, 85, 86, 136–39, 145, 156–57, 160, 164, 169

diaspora, xxii, xxiv, 30, 78, 117, 125–31, 133, 137, 140, 145, 158, 170

Díaz, Miguel H., 41, 58, 112, 160–61, 169, 170, 174

dominant culture, xxii, 3, 7, 13, 16, 21, 24, 26–28, 31–32, 37, 40, 43, 49, 52–53, 58, 68, 74, 83, 88, 93, 97–98, 102–3, 114, 138, 146, 148–51

dominant narratives, 2–4, 7, 20, 22–23, 30, 83, 151

dominant theology, xxii, 2, 9, 12, 21, 23, 29, 43, 54, 77, 88–89, 133, 139

ecclesiology, 41, 44, 107, 162, 163

ecumenism, 13, 18, 29, 35, 44–46, 77, 102, 108, 117, 136, 155–56, 160–61, 169, 173

Elizondo, Virgilio, 22, 41, 55, 128, 161, 168

empire, xx, 7, 24, 26–27, 50–51, 135, 163, 169, 172

encomienda system, 49

enslaved peoples, 7, 135, 156, 176

eschatology, 4, 44, 107

Espín, Orlando O., xiii, xx, 3, 4–7, 9–11, 18, 22, 41, 45, 46, 48, 50–51, 53–54, 64, 79, 90, 112, 115, 121–22, 125, 137–38, 145, 153, 155–56, 158, 160–63, 165, 167, 169, 170–72, 174

ethics/ethical, xi, 6, 23, 25, 34–35, 37, 41–42, 47, 59, 72–75, 81, 87–88, 104, 118–21, 124, 131–39, 145, 156–58, 160, 162, 169, 176

eurocentric, 3–4, 24, 31, 59, 145, 160

evangélica, latina, 4, 15, 46, 56, 60, 66, 67, 69, 70–71, 83, 89, 93, 95, 105–8, 111, 115, 120, 122–25, 145, 168

exile, xxii, 55, 73–75, 78, 85, 117, 125–31, 137, 140, 145, 166, 170

faith, ix, x–xii, xviii–xxii, 6, 9–10, 15, 23, 28, 31–32, 37–38, 40–42, 50–54, 57–63, 75, 77, 79, 80–82, 87, 91, 95–97, 102, 106, 108–9, 112–15, 116, 118, 120–21, 125, 141, 145, 146, 152

familia, 46, 71, 98–99, 107, 139

feminista theology/Latina feminism, 1, 13–14, 22, 24, 84, 91–115, 140, 156, 157, 160, 162, 167, 171–72, 176

fiesta, 71, 99

First Peoples of the Americas, 4, 7, 82–83, 107, 127, 132, 161, 168

frontera, xxii, 117, 125–31, 137, 140, 142, 152, 156

Name/Subject Index

gender, 8, 38, 41, 63, 72–73, 79, 82, 101, 138–40, 147
García, Sixto, 50, 162
García-Johnson, Oscar, xiii, 3, 41, 117, 119, 120, 123, 124–25, 129, 140, 145, 162
García-Rivera, Alejandro, 33, 162–63
globalization, 133, 156, 158, 163
God/god, ix–x, xii, xiv, xxi, 2, 4, 6, 8–9, 12, 14–17, 30–32, 37–38, 42–66, 69, 71, 73–75, 77–82, 85, 87–88, 92, 95–97, 99, 101–12, 116–25, 132, 135, 137, 140–41, 144–45, 149–52, 158–62, 164, 167, 170, 172–73
Goizueta, Roberto S., 1–2, 22, 53, 55, 57, 58, 64, 120, 123, 127–29, 163, 171
González, Catherine G., 76, 164
Gonzalez, Juan, 24, 27, 163
González, Justo L., 2, 3, 14, 41, 48, 49, 66, 75–81, 85, 129–30, 164–66, 168, 171
González-Justiniano, Yara, 121–22
Gonzalez Maldonado, Michelle A., 5, 7, 25, 29–30, 36, 41, 92–103, 108, 109–11, 115, 164
Guadalupe, Our Lady of, 31–33, 40, 58, 71, 146, 158, 169, 170, 173

Henderson-Espinoza, R., 139, 140, 165
hermeneutics, xvii, 11, 57, 66–70, 72, 76, 78, 79, 82, 85, 87, 90, 100, 106, 128–29, 131, 135, 155, 159, 167, 173–74
histories, xii, xix, xxi, 3–10, 15–16, 19–42, 45–64, 67–68, 77, 84, 97–98, 102–3, 111–12, 116, 125–26, 128, 131–34, 137, 148–49, 152
Hidalgo, Jacqueline M., 82–83, 89, 155, 165
hispanic, 2–14, 22, 26–27, 29, 47, 57–58, 64, 66, 70, 75–77, 78–79, 81, 89, 92, 94, 96, 99, 105, 117, 118, 119–20, 125, 143–44, 145, 155–76
Holy Spirit, xxi, 4, 16, 46, 58, 60, 63–64, 80, 105, 107–8, 112, 116–25, 127, 137–38, 140–41, 144–45, 152, 156–57, 162, 169, 170, 175–76
homiletics, 76–77, 85–90, 155
hope, x, xii, xxii, 22–23, 26, 32–33, 53–54, 58, 72, 78–79, 91, 96, 99, 106, 112, 113–14, 116, 121–23, 134, 136–37, 140, 156, 160–61, 164, 166, 172, 175–76

identity, x, xii, xix–xxi, xxiv, 3, 4, 7, 15, 17, 19–42, 44–45, 55, 61, 65, 67, 78, 80, 81–82, 85–87, 89, 93, 97–98, 100, 110, 114, 116, 118–20, 124–26, 129, 133, 138–40, 143, 145–46
immigration, 16, 26, 70, 73–74, 78, 89, 92, 114, 117, 121, 125, 129–34, 136–37, 142–45, 155, 157–61, 164
indigenous, 4, 21, 23, 25, 27, 30–32, 35–36, 49, 54, 60–61, 71, 119, 128, 148, 160, 162, 165, 166, 171, 175
injustice, x–xi, xxi, 2, 23–24, 31–32, 47, 52, 78, 80, 98, 107, 111, 121, 123–24, 128, 133, 135, 141–42, 146, 153, 165, 171
intercultural, 1, 14, 17, 39, 44, 47, 80, 90, 93, 95, 100–105, 115, 136, 141, 155–57, 175
interdisciplinary, 7, 24, 47, 79–80, 83, 118, 141, 174
interreligious, 44
Isasi-Díaz, Ada María, 2, 12–13, 22, 35, 43, 64, 70, 86, 91, 92, 94–99, 112, 115, 119, 129–30, 166, 173

Jesús/Jesus. *See* Christ, Christology.
Jiménez, Pablo, 66, 77–81, 164
justicia, xxi, 70, 112, 116–41

kingdom of God, xviii, 17, 55, 59, 62, 64, 116, 121, 124, 135, 144,
kin-dom of God, 119

language, xix–xx, 4, 12–13, 17, 25, 31, 33, 39–40, 58–59, 73–74, 78, 86, 99, 108, 111, 113–15, 125, 143–44, 167, 170, 174
Latin American, xix, xxiv, 13, 18, 21, 23, 25–27, 35, 39, 48–49, 61–62,

Name/Subject Index

78, 103–5, 111, 117, 122, 125, 131, 134, 144, 147, 156–59, 161, 162–75
latinamente, xxi, 60, 65–90, 92, 117, 151
latino threat narrative, 8, 85, 133–34, 136–37, 155, 158
LGBTQI+, 83, 138, 144, 150
liberation, xxiv, 12, 33, 53, 64–65, 70, 76, 83, 87, 91–92, 97, 106, 109, 111, 117, 138, 139–41, 167
liberation theologies, xxiv, 1, 12, 13, 25, 60, 73, 95, 101–3, 121–22, 127, 155, 157–58, 160, 162–66, 169, 173, 175
liturgy, 109, 113, 163, 167
lived experience, 12, 15, 23, 29, 37, 42, 54, 55–56, 70–71, 81, 96, 100–101, 106, 120
locus theologicus, 12, 42, 45–46, 48, 64, 97, 116, 127, 170
Lozada, Francisco, Jr., 11, 65–68, 75, 82, 83–85, 89, 90
lucha, xxi, 13, 22, 43, 64, 91–115, 117, 149, 166
Lugones, María, 94–95, 161–62, 167

Machado, Daisy, 5, 24, 26–27, 30, 100, 102, 106, 111, 115, 125, 156, 167
machismo, 99, 113, 115, 139, 157, 167
Madrazo, Tito, 81, 89, 167
Maldonado, David, 6, 27–29, 55, 69, 157, 168
Maldonado Pérez, Zaida, 4, 46, 66–67, 89, 105, 115, 120, 122–23, 125, 145, 168
mañana, 3, 66, 140, 163
manifest destiny, 26, 88, 168, 176
margins/marginalization/marginalized/marginality, ix, 5, 9, 11, 20, 22, 24, 26–27, 31–33, 36–37, 45, 47, 50, 56, 58–61, 66–68, 72–73, 75–79, 83–85, 89, 93–97, 107, 109–10, 115, 119–20, 122–23, 126–27, 133–37, 140, 145, 146, 151–52, 156, 158–60, 162, 167–68, 172, 174

Martell, Loida I., xiii, 1–2, 4, 18, 22, 46, 54, 56–57, 59–60, 64, 66–67, 70–72, 75, 85, 89, 92–93, 95, 105–8, 111, 115, 120, 145, 168, 173, 175
master narrative, 83–84
Medina, Néstor, 20–21, 23–24, 34, 35–38, 41, 47, 79, 94, 109–10, 117–19, 121–23, 128, 141, 145–46, 160
mestizo, mestizaje, xxi, 9–14, 19–41, 49–50, 55, 65–66, 82, 85, 97, 116, 118, 123–24, 128, 132, 140, 146, 148, 156–57, 160–63, 169, 176
migration, migrant, xix, xxii, 1, 16, 34, 55–56, 73–74, 79, 81–83, 89, 117, 123, 125–31, 133–35, 137, 140, 142, 145, 155, 158, 167, 171–73, 175,
minoritization, minoritized, minority, xxiii, 3, 5, 67–68, 73, 76–77, 83, 95, 97, 105, 107, 140, 157, 167–68, 170, 174
mujerista/mujerista theology, 13, 43, 64, 70, 86, 91–103, 111–13, 115, 119, 129, 140, 160, 166, 172
mulato, mulatez, 27, 29, 34–35, 97, 132
muslim, 6, 76, 170, 173

name/naming, xvii–xviii, 21, 24, 29, 40, 50, 54, 57, 71, 87, 91–93, 96–97, 109, 111, 113, 125–26, 136, 146, 149
Nanko-Fernández, Carmen, xiii, 18, 29, 42, 45–47, 58–59, 64, 80, 86, 122, 127–31, 140
Native American, Native populations. *See* First Peoples of the Americas

oppression, xxi, 22, 31, 43–45, 48, 50, 56, 58–59, 85, 91, 93–100, 102–3, 115, 117, 121, 138–41, 153, 167, 171
Ortega, Ofelia, 94, 103, 171–72

patriarchy/patriarchal, 73, 75, 88, 123
Pedraja, Luis, 3, 10, 58–59, 171

Name/Subject Index

pentecostalism, 28, 64, 69, 77, 79–80, 83, 117–19, 120, 124, 145, 155–57, 159, 162–63, 169, 172–76

Pérez-Bullard, Altagracia, xiii, xxii, 146–47, 152–53, 171

Pineda-Madrid, Nancy, 13, 43, 92–94, 100–103, 111, 115, 129, 172

Pinn, Anthony, 1, 13, 18, 162, 172

pneumatology, 44, 119, 120–24, 141, 145, 158, 162, 169

politics, xvii, xxiii, 8, 11–12, 15, 19, 21, 25–26, 31, 34, 36, 49, 51, 53, 55, 56, 58–59, 64, 67, 76, 78, 82, 92, 100, 102–5, 112, 115, 118–19, 120, 122, 124–25, 128, 131, 134, 141, 145, 155, 160–62, 165, 170, 172–74

popular religion, 22, 33, 58, 64, 99, 158, 161, 168, 172

postcolonial, 34, 46, 74, 78, 84–85, 101, 107, 128, 173–74

power(s), 3, 11, 19–20, 22–27, 29–32, 34, 36–37, 48, 50, 52–59, 62, 68, 83–86, 92, 94, 97–98, 100, 104, 108, 111, 116–26, 135, 137, 145, 147, 156–57, 165–68, 175

preaching, 50, 60, 75–81, 84–85, 88–89

Puerto Rico, 6, 14–16, 32, 49, 56, 80, 102, 106, 118, 130, 142, 144, 164–65

queer theologies, xxii, 46, 117, 137–41, 162, 165

racism, 8–9, 36–38, 41, 50, 55, 78, 94, 100, 126–27, 134, 162, 173

Recinos, Harold, ix, 8–9, 11, 37, 58, 64, 125, 141, 161, 168, 172

Rivera, Mayra Rivera, 101, 102, 173

Rivera-Pagán, Luis N., 49, 118, 133–36, 145, 172

Rodríguez, Jeanette, 31–34, 53, 95, 100, 103, 156, 167

Roland Gúzman, Carla, xiii, 153, 173

Romero, Robert Chao, xiii, 27, 30, 145

Rosado-Nunes, Maria José, 1, 14, 103–5, 115, 156–57

Rosario Rodríguez, Rubén, 36, 41, 115, 160, 162, 173

Ruiz, Jean-Pierre, 68–76, 79, 81, 90, 128–31, 174

sacrament/sacramental, 44, 61, 135, 161

salvation, 4, 13, 32–33, 44, 60, 64, 107, 110–11, 115, 120–21, 129, 163, 168, 172

Sánchez, David A., xiv, xvii, xx, xxiii, xxiv, 68, 71, 82, 174

Sánchez Walsh, Arlene, 120, 174

Sauceda, Teresa Chavez, 105

self-awareness, 47, 77, 95, 100

scripture, x, xviii, xxi, 4, 8, 13, 15–16, 37, 44, 54, 60, 65–90, 92, 96, 102, 106–7, 113, 117, 130–31, 134–35, 155, 168

Segovia, Fernando F., xiii, xxii, xxiii, 2, 11, 47, 66–69, 75, 78, 82–83, 85, 90, 97, 129, 155, 157, 162, 166–68, 173–74,

sexism, 9, 78, 91, 94, 103

social location, xx, 22, 43, 45, 46, 57, 71, 77, 86, 88, 97

Soliván, Samuel, 120–21, 130, 175

Spanglish/*Espanglish*, 18, 29, 58–59, 86, 170

suffering, 13, 23, 33, 43, 53, 56–58, 60, 69, 70, 78, 85, 87–88, 92, 96, 99, 107, 111, 115, 121, 123–24, 129, 132, 134, 136, 172

Takaki, Ronald, 19–20, 25, 175

Tarango, Yolanda, 12–13, 92, 94, 96, 160, 166, 175

teología en conjunto, x, xii, xx–xxi, 1–18, 21, 37–38, 42, 50, 65–66, 69, 76, 79, 92, 96, 105, 108, 116, 136, 148, 152–53, 171, 173, 175

testimonios, 60, 71

Torres, Theresa, 103, 109–10, 175

transgender, 138–39

trinity, 4, 46, 59, 107, 110, 120, 161

Valentin, Eliesar, 13, 79–80, 90, 176

Name/Subject Index

Valentín, Benjamín, 1, 8, 13, 18, 118, 145, 159, 163, 164, 172, 176

Villafañe, Eldin, 3, 78, 118–20, 145, 171, 176

violence, xx, xxiii, 7, 22, 25, 32–35, 48–50, 53, 59, 82–83, 91, 95, 98–99, 106, 111, 118, 128–29, 135–38, 141, 147, 162, 172–73, 175

Virgin Mary, the 57, 102, 122, 160, 170

voice/voiceless, x–xii, xxi–xxii, 3, 8–9, 12–14, 20, 22, 25, 30, 33, 35, 40, 42–43, 54, 64, 68, 70, 72–73, 76, 79, 81, 87–92, 94–96, 98–99, 102–3, 105–15, 135–38, 143–44, 148–51, 163–64, 166, 168–69, 172–76

white/whiteness, 3–4, 8, 10–11, 15, 19, 20, 27, 36–39, 43, 49–50, 76, 85, 88, 95, 100–103, 113, 128, 140, 143, 148, 151–52, 159–60, 165, 173, 175

wisdom, xi, xii, 89, 91–92, 96, 100, 105, 107–15, 124, 156

women, xviii, xx–xxi, 6–7, 12–13, 22, 35, 40, 62–64, 69–72, 77, 83, 86–87, 91–115, 117, 122–23, 129, 135, 148, 152–53, 156–57, 159, 163, 166, 168, 170–75

xenophilia, 133–36
xenophobia, 133–36

Scripture Index

OLD TESTAMENT

Genesis

1	74
1:1—2:4	78
12	74
12:10–20	74, 75
18	74
21:1–2	77

Deuteronomy

10:17–19	80

Ruth

1:16–17	74, 174

2 Kings

4:8–10	74

Nehemiah

13	74

Job

31:32	74

Psalms

23	15, 16
146:9	80

Isaiah

6:1–2	80
58:6–7	74

Jeremiah

31:15	79

Ezekiel

20	74

APOCRYPHA

Wisdom of Solomon

19:13–14	80

NEW TESTAMENT

Matthew

2:18	79
9:20–22	136
10	77
16:21–28	56
19:19	119
20	74
20:1–16	74
23:34–40	80
25	75
25:35	79

Scripture Index

Mark

1:29–39	79
5	69
7:24–30	
8	79

Luke

1:57–66	77
3:21–22	77
4	80
4:16–21	80
7:36–50	72
7:44–47, 10	72
12	75
17	77
22:39–44	80
	56

John

1:1	59
1:5	xxiii
4	62, 68, 174
4:4–42	71
10:10	72

Acts

2	80, 121

I Corinthians

11–21	78
16:5–12	75

Galatians

4:13–14	75
5:25	120

2 Timothy

1:3–5	109
1:5	109

Hebrews

11	77

James

2:1–8	121

Revelation

12	71

www.ingramcontent.com/pod-product-compliance
Lightning Source LLC
Chambersburg PA
CBHW031426150426
43191CB00006B/421